The Bible's Many Voices

University of Nebraska Press
Lincoln

THE BIBLE'S MANY VOICES

Michael Carasik

The Jewish Publication Society
Philadelphia

© 2014 by Michael Carasik
All rights reserved. Published by the University of Nebraska Press
as a Jewish Publication Society book.
Manufactured in the United States of America.

Library of Congress Cataloging-in-Publication Data
Carasik, Michael.
The Bible's many voices / Michael Carasik.
pages cm
Includes bibliographical references and index.
ISBN 978-0-8276-0935-8 (cloth: alk. paper) — ISBN 978-0-8276-1161-0 (epub) —
ISBN 978-0-8276-1162-7 (mobi) — ISBN 978-0-8276-1134-4 (pdf)
1. Bible—Old Testament—Criticism, interpretation, etc. I. Title.
BS1178.H4C37 2014
220.6—dc23   2013033689

Set in Adobe Caslon by Laura Wellington.
Designed by J. Vadnais.

*This book is dedicated
to my sister Karen
and to my friend Edbird,
even if neither of them remembers asking me to write it.*

Contents

Acknowledgments	ix
Read Me First	xi
Whose Bible Is It?	1
1. The Sound of the Biblical Voices	23
2. Historical Voices	62
3. Theological Voices	98
4. Legal Voices	133
5. Prophetic Voices	174
6. Women's Voices	208
7. Voices of the Wise	238
8. Foreign Voices	275
9. Voices of Song and Legend	301
10. Echoes and Reverberations	329
Jewish and Christian Biblical Order	351
Index	353

Acknowledgments

It is impossible for me to thank everyone who has contributed indirectly to this book. But I must thank my friends Ben Sommer, who provided a sounding board at an early stage, and Johanna Markind, who helped me with the Pennsylvania Consolidated Statutes.

By rights I should list here the names of all the teachers, colleagues, students, and friends who have helped me learn Bible over the years. But I will limit myself to recording the names of three teachers whom I recall with fondness from the days when I was engaged in the study of Bible strictly for love of learning, at what was then called Spertus College of Judaica in Chicago: Mayer Gruber, Rachel Dulin, and Shalom Paul. Professor Paul ended every semester by telling us, "Don't stop learning"—and I never have.

Finally, and as always in the place of honor, I offer profound thanks to my wife, Yaffa, whose love over the years has made it possible for me to follow my path as a writer and teacher of Bible.

Read Me First

On this page you'll find some basic explanations that apply throughout the book.

Dates

The secular calendar in use all over the world today is actually a Christian one, whose count of years begins in the year that Jesus was (theoretically) born, AD 1. (Scholars now think he was born in 4 BC or perhaps a year or two before.) And both of the century identifiers are statements of Christian belief. "AD" stands for *anno domini*, "in the year of the Lord," where "Lord" refers to Jesus as Lord; "BC" stands for "before Christ," and "Christ" is not Jesus's family name but a Greek equivalent of the title "Messiah." **This book uses the secular equivalents, "CE" ("Common Era") for "AD" and "BCE" ("Before the Common Era") for "BC." The year numbers themselves are exactly the same.** But the terms that assert Christian doctrines are replaced by terms that anyone, Christian or not, can use.

The Name of God

God is referred to in different ways in the Bible, including a Hebrew word that is the equivalent of the English "god." In English, "god" with a small *g* can refer to any being who is given that designation ("the baseball gods," "Mars, the god of war"). But "God" with a capital *G* always refers to the one God worshiped by adherents of the three monotheistic religions of Judaism, Christianity, and Islam, as well as by others. In the Bible, this God has a name, which is rarely seen in translation. The name is spelled with four Hebrew letters, the equivalents of Y, H, W, and H again, and is therefore referred to as "the Tetragrammaton," Greek for "four letters." According to Jewish tradition, this name is no longer pronounced. Instead, it is replaced (when reading aloud) by the Hebrew word *Adonai*, "my Lord," and it is usually indicated in translation by "LORD" (in all caps) or "Lord" (in small caps).* But part of my effort in this book is to help you see the Bible with fresh eyes as well as listening to it with fresh ears. **In this book, I "translate" the Tetragrammaton by transliterating it as YHWH.** Whenever you see these letters, you should understand that God is being referred to by his personal name.

Chapter and Verse Citations

For ease of reference, biblical books are divided into chapters, and each chapter is divided not into sentences but into "verses." I use the following to indicate where in the Bible you'll find the word, phrase, or passage that is being quoted or discussed:

Gen. 1:1—the book of Genesis, chapter 1, verse 1

1a—the first half of v. 1

1b—the second half of v. 1

v. or vv.—a verse or verses in the chapter or passage being discussed

---

* If the name is preceded by the actual word "Lord," it is replaced by "GOD" or "God" instead.

Translations

Throughout the book, we will look at biblical words and passages in English translation. **Unidentified translations from the Hebrew or Aramaic parts of the Bible are by me.** Unidentified translations from the New Testament are from the King James Version (KJV). You will occasionally find translations that I identify as being from the NRSV (New Revised Standard Version), the NJPS (the "New" Jewish Publication Society translation, as opposed to the "Old" JPS translation from a century ago), and the NEB (New English Bible).

The Bible's Many Voices

Whose Bible Is It?

The Bible belongs to everyone, of course. But I want to start this book by telling you about *my* Bible—one of 'em, at least. Not the one that's being held together with strips of blue electrical tape; not the four-dollar paperback I acquired as a college student in Florida (no sales tax on Bibles in Florida, at least not in those days); not the souvenir bedside Hebrew Bible I persuaded the Dan Pearl Hotel in Jerusalem to give me. (I could go on.) No, the Bible I want to tell you about is a King James Bible. Like most books from the shelves of a book lover, it comes with a story.

It's leather bound, with a black ribbon and gold trim, beautifully printed by Oxford University Press, but just three inches wide by five inches tall—small enough to fit into a side pocket of the big yellow backpack I used to own. That's the same backpack U.S. customs agents nearly tore apart one afternoon many years ago looking for the drugs they were sure long-haired, college-age me must be carrying. Three gray-haired ladies who were kind enough to share a cab with me between the train station in Windsor, Ontario, and the one in Detroit waited patiently while the officers ripped away at my things—until suddenly one of them discovered the Bible. They pretended halfheartedly to keep searching for a couple of minutes and then waved me through.

I wasn't carrying drugs, and if I had been, I wasn't clever enough to have thought of using the Bible as a decoy. It was there because I'd brought it with me on a trip to Israel. It seemed like a reasonable thing to take, as a guide to the geography and history of the country. But the truth is that I had barely opened it the whole time I was there. Somehow I knew that I ought to have a Bible—but I had no idea what I was supposed to do with it. Rashi, the great French Jewish medieval commentator on the Bible (if only I had known about him in those days) had the answer, in a few words near the beginning of his long comment on Gen. 1:1, where he has the verse itself speak up and demand, "Explain me!"

Without Rashi, it took me another dozen or fifteen years to figure out the task that was waiting for me: to understand and explain what the ancient writers of the Bible meant by what they wrote. The Bible is—for many of us—a sacred book. Yet it is simultaneously a human book. I'm not a rabbi, priest, or minister, and I don't have anything to say about God or religion in this book except what the Bible itself tries to say. The purpose of the book is to begin showing you the answers that biblical scholars have found by reading the words of a biblical verse, passage, or chapter and asking, "What does this mean?"

The Bible's Many Voices

Paradoxically, the English translations in which most of us read the Bible most of the time make it sound as if the Bible was written in a single, somewhat archaic voice. In fact, the Bible is made up of many separate books, composed by different writers, in a wide range of voices. One of the first things you do when you begin to study the Bible as a human book is to begin to learn how to distinguish between those different biblical voices.

The purpose of this book is not to prove or disprove any particular theory about when the books of the Bible were written, or by whom (though I won't be afraid to express my own opinions). Instead, what I want to do is help you recognize the voices of some of the most important biblical writers and hear the differences between them. They were trying hard to communicate things of utmost importance, and my job, both as a biblical scholar and as a translator, is to help them transmit their messages across the many centuries intervening between them and us.

The different parts of the Bible were written at different times, in different styles, by different people with differing perspectives. Some were written as works of history, others as poetry. Some were political and others theological. Some were written after long, careful consideration; others were as spontaneous as blog posts. It is only when you start to distinguish these different voices that you can begin to get a clearer picture of the world out of which the Bible grew. That world, like our own, was one in which people disagreed, often loudly, about politics and about religion. These disagreements, along with other compositions that can sometimes be very personal, are all found today lumped together in what we call "the Bible." But . . . what *is* the Bible?

What Is the Bible?

That's not an existential question, but a very down-to-earth one. Before I can begin to talk about the Bible in a serious way, I have to explain what I mean by the word "Bible." Despite the way we experience it today, in houses of worship and on our bookshelves, the "Good Book" is not really a single book at all.

If you buy a copy of *Huckleberry Finn* or *Don Quixote* or *David Copperfield*, you know what's going to be inside the cover. More to the point, you also know what you're getting when you pick up a Qur'an or a Book of Mormon. But "the Bible" means different things to different people. Leaving aside the many variations that reflect different translation styles, three different books are all called "the Bible" by different groups: the Bibles of the Jews, the Protestants, and the Catholics. (The Bibles used by Eastern Orthodox Christians are somewhat different from those used by Catholics, but fall into the same overall category.)

Let's look at them in that order. It is not chronological but rather runs from the shortest, least inclusive Bible to the longest, most inclusive one. Though it sounds paradoxical, the Bible that includes the most books is also the most *ex*clusive—it is accepted only by Catholics. The Bible that includes the fewest books, the Jewish Bible, contains only the books that everyone, Christians and Jews alike, accepts as biblical.

The Jewish Bible

The books in the Jewish Bible are the oldest. The writings here date from the twelfth century to the second century BCE. All of them were originally written in Hebrew, with the exception of two chapters in Ezra and six chapters in Daniel, which are written in Aramaic, a cousin language to Hebrew. (Some scholars have suggested that a few of the other books were originally written in Aramaic as well, but we'll leave these technical discussions aside for now.) All the books in the Jewish Bible are found in all the Christian Bibles as well, though Christians arrange them in a different order than Jews do. With just three exceptions, which we will meet in chapter 7, all these books are more or less concerned with the (often rocky) love affair between God and the Jewish people.

The Protestant Bible

The Protestant Bible has all the books of the Jewish Bible plus a separate section of books dating from the mid-first to mid-second centuries CE and written originally in Greek. (A few scholars believe that one or two of these may have originally been written in Hebrew or Aramaic or based on earlier documents written in these languages.) These books are the "New Testament," focused on the life of Jesus and the early history of the religion that developed into the Christianity we know today. In all Christian Bibles, therefore, the books of the Jewish Bible are grouped into a collection called the "Old Testament," contrasting with the New Testament.

The Catholic Bible

The Catholic Bible is more inclusive than the Protestant Bible. But instead of adding yet newer books to the Old and New Testaments of the Protestant Bible, it fills the chronological gap between them with the books that Jews and Protestants call "the Apocrypha." This is Jewish literature of the "intertestamental" period—the second and first centuries BCE. Most of it was written in Hebrew or Aramaic, but some of the books were written in Greek. These books were left—or pushed—outside the canon of the Hebrew Bible, but they were preserved in the Greek translations of the Bible used by Egyptian Jews and by many early Christians.

However, when Jerome prepared a new Latin version of the Bible, he made a translation directly from the Hebrew text—which did not contain these extra books. They were nonetheless accepted as part of the Christian Bible, but they fall into a different category than the "Old Testament"; they are considered "deuterocanonical," belonging to a second ("deutero-") grouping of the books that predated Jesus. Martin Luther moved them to the end of his Old Testament translation and labeled them Apocrypha; this prompted Catholics to officially declare them part of the Christian Bible.

This means that both Jews and Catholics—the groups whose perspectives on the Bible rely largely on a later group of sacred writings (Rabbinic literature for Jews, Patristic literature for Catholics)—have a Bible that maintains historical continuity from beginning to end. The Catholic Bible does not have the same linguistic continuity that the Jewish Bible has, but the Apocrypha do bridge the chronological gap that separates the two parts of the Protestant Bible with books from the period when Jewish literature was expanding from Hebrew into Greek. (The Dead Sea Scrolls date from this same period.) So Jews and Catholics both have Bibles that tell a more or less continuous story. Protestants, whose *sola scriptura* ("Bible-only") perspective was a major cause of the break with Catholicism, have a Bible in two sections that are separated from each other both in time and in language.

The bottom line is that the Bible is a unique book. You may open someone else's copy of it and discover that books you expected to find are missing or that books you don't consider to be part of the Bible are there. So when someone says "The Bible," you always have to ask which Bible he is talking about. In this book—though we will hear some voices from the Apocrypha and New Testament in chapter 10—the voices we will be listening to are those of the books that are in *everyone's* Bible. For Christians, these are the books of the Old Testament.

The "Old Testament"

You may be wondering why I said that "the books that are in everyone's Bible" are the Old Testament—for Christians. Isn't the Old Testament the part of the Bible that everyone accepts, Jews and Christians alike? In fact, it's common for Jews and Christians alike to refer to the Jewish Bible as the "Old Testament." But that is a misconception.

It's true, of course, that none of the books of the New Testament or Apocrypha are part of the Jewish Bible. But that doesn't mean that what is left is the Old Testament. Here's why:

First, of course, "Old" Testament implies the existence of a "New" Testament, which Jews don't in fact accept. "Testament" in this sense really means "covenant" (as it does in Latin, where English got it from). In Jer. 31:31, God announces that he intends to make "a new covenant with the House of Israel and the House of Judah"; the letter to the Hebrews, in the New Testament, announces that Jesus is the mediator of a "better covenant" (Heb. 8:6) which therefore makes the original covenant "old"—in the words of the NRSV, "In speaking of 'a new covenant,' he has made the first one obsolete" (Heb. 8:13). That is why Christians who are sensitive to Jewish feelings sometimes refer to this part of their Bible not as the "Old Testament" but as the "Primary Testament" or (awkwardly) the "Hebrew Bible/Old Testament." The bottom line, in any case, is that "Old Testament" is a Christian term and not a neutral one.

Differing Perspectives

But there's a much more important reason not to call the Jewish Bible the "Old Testament." It's not just a matter of perspective; the contents of the two books are arranged in a different order. This means that a

Christian looking through a Jewish Bible, or a Jew looking through a Christian one, may sometimes get lost. Some books of the Bible will just not be where you expect to find them. But the difference means something much more important: the two different arrangements of these books tell two different stories.

The Old Testament starts (of course) with Genesis, and it carries the historical story all the way through the book of Esther. Then there's a short grouping of (mostly) poetic books, followed by the prophets, ending with Malachi.

The Jewish Bible begins the same way as the Old Testament, and (with one slight change) follows the same order as far as the end of the book of Kings. But the Jewish Bible is not divided into history, poetry, and prophecy, but into Torah, Prophets, and Writings. (They're capitalized because these three parts of the Bible are conceptually distinct. Each plays a different liturgical role in Judaism.) So the first five books, from Genesis to Deuteronomy, constitute a section on their own. Then come the books of the "Prophets," arranged in two sections, one historical section and one prophetic. Finally, the catchall "Writings," ending with Chronicles. A careful reader will notice that both the first chapter of the Prophets section, Joshua 1 (see v. 8), and the first chapter of the Writings section, Psalm 1 (see v. 2), say that one should be absorbed in the first section, the Torah, day and night.

Both the arrangements of these books, Christian and Jewish, begin with the creation of the world. It is how they end that makes the difference. Here (in the King James translation) is how the Old Testament ends:

> MAL. 4:4 Remember ye the law of Moses My servant, which I commanded unto him in Horeb for all Israel, with the statutes and judgments. ⁵ Behold, I will send you Elijah the prophet before the coming of the great and dreadful day of the LORD: ⁶ And he shall turn the heart of the fathers to the children, and the heart of the children to their fathers, lest I come and smite the earth with a curse.

Then you turn the page, and (in a Protestant Bible, at least) the New Testament begins:

> MATT. 1:1 The book of the generation of Jesus Christ, the son of David, the son of Abraham.

As promised in Mal. 4:5, "Elijah" shows up in Matthew 3, in the person of John the Baptist, and the Old Testament prophecies ending with Malachi begin to be fulfilled.

As you may imagine, nothing like this occurs in the Jewish Bible. To begin with, the end of Malachi is a bit different:

> MAL. 3:22 Remember the Instruction of My servant Moses, which I commanded him at Horeb for all Israel—laws and rulings. 23 Now, I am sending you Elijah the prophet before the coming of the great and fearful day of YHWH. 24 He will turn the hearts of parents to their children, and the hearts of children to their parents, lest I come and smite the earth with destruction. Now, I am sending you Elijah the prophet before the coming of the great and fearful day of YHWH.

The first thing you will notice is that I have made my own new translation of these verses from the Hebrew. This is not the place for a long discussion of the Malachi passage, but it is worth remembering two things: (1) anything you read in English is not the Bible itself, but a translation of it; and (2) Bible translations differ depending on who writes them and when they are written.

The next thing to notice is the extra line at the end, in smaller type. It is not that there are more words in this version of the Bible. Look again and you will see that the second sentence of the paragraph is simply repeated at the end. Rather than end a biblical book with "destruction" or, as the KJV translation has it, "a curse," Jewish Bibles go back and add the second-to-last verse of the book once more, thus ending it instead with "YHWH," the name of God. (There are three other books in the Bible where this happens. Can you find them? We will encounter another of them in chapter 7, where I will name all four.)

Torah, First and Last

Finally, these verses are numbered differently in the Christian and Jewish Bibles. It is not that something has been added or is missing; it is just that the Christian Bible ends Malachi 3 after v. 18 and starts a new chapter. It's a reasonable guess that the purpose of this is to emphasize that the last six verses are in fact an introduction to the Old Testament's "sequel," the New Testament. The Jewish Bible did not need to do this because in it Malachi is very much a conclusion. The Prophets section ends, and a different section, the Writings, begins, not connected in any literary way to the previous one. Instead, as we've seen, both the Prophets and the Writings are explicitly connected back to the *first* section, the Torah.

The story line of the New Testament—that the prophecy of Malachi is fulfilled by John the Baptist and Jesus—is completely missing here. Instead, by its differing arrangement of the books, the Jewish Bible tells a very different story. It is a book not of fulfillment but of potential. God redeems the Jewish people ("the people of Israel," as the Bible calls them) from slavery in Egypt, and they build a Temple for him in Jerusalem. But they fail to live up to his high hopes for them, and he permits the Babylonians to destroy the Temple and exile the Jews from their homeland to Babylonia. At last the Babylonians, in their turn, receive their comeuppance and are conquered by the Persians. Here is how the Jewish Bible ends:

2 CHR. 36:22 In the first year of King Cyrus of Persia, to complete the word of YHWH spoken through Jeremiah, YHWH awakened the spirit of King Cyrus of Persia. He had the following announcement proclaimed throughout his kingdom, aloud and in writing: 23 "Thus said King Cyrus of Persia: All the kingdoms of the earth have been given to me by YHWH, the God of Heaven. He has assigned me to build Him a House in Jerusalem, which

is in Judah. Anyone among you who are of His people—may YHWH his God be with him, and let him go up."

The historical story told in the Bible actually continues in Ezra and Nehemiah, the books that *precede* Chronicles. In fact, you will find that these verses at the end of Chronicles are the same as Ezra 1:1–3, with one important difference: Chronicles stops in the *middle* of a sentence!

> 2 CHR. 36:23 "Thus said King Cyrus of Persia: All the kingdoms of the earth have been given to me by YHWH, the God of Heaven. He has assigned me to build Him a House in Jerusalem, which is in Judah. Anyone among you who are of His people—may YHWH his God be with him, and let him go up—"

The end of the Jewish Bible is the beginning of the return from exile. In this version, the Bible itself ends as the Torah, its first and (for Jews) most important part ends—with the Jews on the point of returning to their homeland.

The bottom line is that the Old Testament is arranged to introduce the New Testament, while the Jewish Bible is arranged to introduce the Jews to ongoing life in their homeland. Implicitly, the Temple will be rebuilt, and they will live happily ever after. So even though the (Christian) Old Testament and the (Jewish) Bible contain exactly the same material, they tell a very different story.

Why Is There a Bible?

One thing Jews, Protestants, and Catholics all agree on is that the Bible's story is a story that must be told. But—why? It can be difficult for us to remember, but the religious world of biblical times is different from every period afterward in one dramatic way: In the biblical period, there was no Bible. Abraham never read the book of Deuteronomy, any more than Jesus read the letters that Paul did not write until after his death, when there were Christians to write them to.

The reason the New Testament exists is more understandable. If a prophet has proclaimed that there will one day be a new covenant, and you think you are living in the era when that new covenant has come into being, it makes sense that the old story needs to be supplemented to take account of the new situation. But why did the story begin to be told in the first place?

Many people today think that the Bible originated when God gave Moses the Torah—by which they mean the books of Genesis, Exodus, Leviticus, Numbers, and Deuteronomy—at Mount Sinai. But the Bible itself does not say this. What the Torah itself says is merely that God told Moses to say various things to the Israelites. Exod. 34:28 tells us that the two tablets of the covenant had "the Ten Commandments" written on them, but even these, as we will see in chapter 4, are given in a *different* version when Moses repeats them in Deuteronomy 5. Exodus 24:4 suggests that the words of Exodus 21–23 were also written down, and Numbers 33 and Deuteronomy 32 are also identified as written texts—but not the Pentateuch as a whole.

If we take a historical perspective, it is not hard to understand why the various biblical books were written. As we saw in the case of the Apocrypha, religious books of various kinds were always being written. But why is there a *Bible*? How did these books begin to come together into a collection that was taken to convey a divine message? We will never know for sure, but here is the story as I perceive it.

How (Perhaps) the Bible Came to Be

In the year 701 BCE, the tiny kingdom of Judah faced a crisis greater than any it had seen since the kingdom of Israel split in two after the death of Solomon, late in the tenth century. Just two decades before, in 722 BCE, the mighty Assyrian army had conquered the northern part of the country and transferred its inhabitants north and west to parts unknown. Now Jerusalem was under siege by that same invincible army.

At the height of the siege, a voice spoke out. The prophet Isaiah announced to King Hezekiah, "Thus said YHWH: Do not be afraid of the blasphemies you have heard the underlings of the king of Assyria utter against Me. I am going to put a spirit in him, and he will hear a rumor that will make him return to his own land" (2 Kgs. 19:6–7). And this assurance came true!

What actually happened is not completely clear. The Bible itself tells the story in different ways (see 2 Kgs. 18–19), and the Assyrians give us yet another version of the story. (We know their version from the cuneiform Annals of Sennacherib, which is preserved in three copies; you can see them at a local museum if you live in Chicago, London, or Jerusalem.) All these versions differ in the details, but the bottom line is the same: The Assyrians did not conquer Jerusalem. Events proved Isaiah's confident assertion correct.

I have to think it is not coincidence that our oldest prophetic texts date from just these last few decades of the eighth century BCE—when the Assyrians threatened the northern kingdom, conquered it, then threatened Jerusalem but *failed* to conquer it. David had a prophet named Nathan, but there is no Book of Nathan; Ahab was challenged by a prophet named Elijah, but there is no Book of Elijah. We know about them only from the stories about them that continued to be told. But the words of Amos, who prophesied "in the days of King Uzziah of Judah and King Jeroboam son of Joash of Israel, two years before the earthquake" (Amos 1:1)—shortly before the middle of the eighth century—were preserved, as were those of Hosea and the prophets who came along in the succeeding decades.

What prompted the Israelites to begin collecting prophecies and saving them? I believe it was the success of Isaiah's unlikely prediction that Jerusalem would withstand the Assyrians. In his day, the words of prophets from a much earlier time were no longer in living memory. But those of more recent prophets whose pronouncements had been fulfilled—Amos, Hosea, and others—were still available. Now they began to be preserved.

As yet, however, these did not constitute anything that could be called a Bible. It was another attack on Jerusalem—a successful one—

that proved to be the grain of sand around which the pearl of our Bible could begin to coalesce. A century after Isaiah, in the early sixth century BCE, it was Jeremiah who stood in his place. This time, Jeremiah proclaimed, what God intended for Jerusalem was not triumph but tribulation: "How dare you steal, murder, commit adultery, swear to lies, make offerings to Baal, and follow other gods whom you do not know, and then come and stand before Me in this Temple called by My name and say, 'We are saved!'" (Jer. 7:9–10). This threat came true just as Isaiah's promise had. The Temple was destroyed, Jerusalem was burnt, and the priests and other leaders of the people were deported to Babylonia.

It was there, I believe, that the idea of a "Bible" took shape. The details of the historical events that had brought Israel out of Egyptian slavery and ultimately back into Babylonian captivity began to crystallize, in story form, along with the prophetic pronouncements that explained them. The Bible had begun to be born.

Who Wrote the Bible?

But isn't everything in the Bible the word of God? It may surprise you to learn that, according to the Bible itself, the answer to this question is "No." Much of the Bible, of course, consists of the quoted words of its human characters, some of them quite ungodly. That may strike you as a trick answer to the question. Weren't the biblical books, at least, all composed (if not actually written) by God? There are religious traditions that say so, but the Bible itself rarely asserts this. The one part of the Bible that can lay some claim to having been written by God is the Ten Commandments. They are introduced in Exod. 20:1 by the words "God spoke all these things." But even the Ten Commandments are found, as we shall see, in several variations.

It's true that some of the prophets are said to have received the "word" of God. An example is Jer. 1:4, "The word of YHWH came to me." Let's stop for a moment to consider the meaning of that word "word," as used in Jer. 1:4. It does not mean a single "word" of a language, the kind of word you might look up in a dictionary. Rather, it is a communication, a message. Before the message begins to be transmitted, it is identified this way:

JER. 1:1 The words of Jeremiah son of Hilkiah, one of the priests in Anathoth, in the territory of Benjamin.

And when it concludes, it is labeled like this:

JER. 51:64 Up to this point, the words of Jeremiah.

The divine communication is referred to by these phrases as "the words of Jeremiah." And what about the opening and concluding phrases? These words are part of Scripture too, but who wrote them?

It turns out that, in the case of Jeremiah, we do know who wrote them. It was a man by the name of Baruch son of Neriah. (He has a book of his own in the Apocrypha.) He is mentioned twenty-three times in the book of Jeremiah, and his role is presented most clearly in a verse later in the book that mentions both the "word" of God and the words of Jeremiah: "The word that Jeremiah the prophet spoke to Baruch son of Neriah, while he wrote these words in a document, at Jeremiah's dictation, in the fourth year of Jehoiakim son of Josiah, king of Judah" (Jer. 45:1). Baruch is clearly described here as being what today we would call the prophet's secretary. The words that begin the book, then, "the words of Jeremiah son of Hilkiah" (and so forth), would seem to have been written not by God, but by a human being, Baruch.

You may consider this, too, a somewhat trivial example. The prophet received God's "word" and repeated it in his own voice so that other human beings could have access to it, after which his assistant wrote the words down. (In Jer. 45:1, unless Baruch is speaking of himself in the third person, still another writer is giving us this information.) But it was probably not so simple.

One of the great religious thinkers in history, Moses Maimonides, said in his *Guide for the Perplexed*, "Know that every prophet has a kind of speech peculiar to him, which is, as it were, the language of that individual, which the prophetic revelation peculiar to him causes him to speak to those who understand him."* Maimonides goes on to describe certain expressions that are very common in the words of the prophet Isaiah, though they are rare elsewhere. The implication is that the prophet receives God's word not as a transcription, but in a moment of revelation, perhaps akin to the intellectual experience that we have when we suddenly "realize" something. Afterward, the prophet transmits the contents of his experience to others *in his own (human) words*.

For another example, let's turn to the book of Leviticus, where we are told over and over again, "YHWH spoke to Moses" (e.g., Lev. 4:1), frequently followed by the words "Speak to the Israelites as follows." This in turn is followed by words that are therefore presented as a direct quotation from God. But who is telling us this? If our narrator—the one who wrote "God said to Moses"—were God himself, we would expect him to have written, "I said to Moses." If it were Moses, we would expect him to have written, "God said to me." Instead, although we are presented with words that purport to be God's own, we have them from the pen of a writer whose own identity is carefully concealed.

The Word of God

Some years ago, a (deservedly) popular book posed the question "Who wrote the Bible?" and answered it by describing the historical and social circumstances in which the *human beings* who composed the Bible lived. This book will proceed from a similar perspective. If so, is there anything here for readers who take the Bible to be God's word from beginning to end?

I believe there is. Let me explain. Most of those who insist that the Bible is God's word would also agree (for example) that Solomon

---

* Moses Maimonides, *The Guide of the Perplexed*, 2:29, trans. Shlomo Pines (Chicago: University of Chicago Press, 1963), 337.

wrote the book of Ecclesiastes. There is, of course, no contradiction between these two beliefs. Solomon was not listening to dictation, but was "inspired" to write as he did by "the Holy Spirit." Yet he was writing in his own voice.

Many of the different "voices" that will be presented in this book (like that of Ecclesiastes) are so distinct, and so distinctive, that any good reader of the Bible will be able to hear them clearly once they are pointed out. If all these writings are simultaneously the word of God, this variety of voices suggests, I believe, something that many traditional Bible readers have not thought about. It is obvious that God, conveying his word in Hebrew, a bit of Aramaic, and (for Christians) Greek, must be operating under a self-imposed limitation, deciding to reveal his message in human language in order to communicate with the more limited human intellect. But he must also have decided to convey "God's word" not merely in these three particular languages, but also in *differing* human voices within each language. For that is what we find in the Bible. *The Bible's Many Voices* is meant to improve your ability to distinguish these different voices in the Bible.

Another way of putting it is simply to say that you will gain a better understanding of what the Bible really says. When Samuel tells Saul, the first king of Israel, that God has rejected him as king, he tells Saul that it will do him no good to repent. God "does not lie and does not change His mind—for He is not a human being, that He should change His mind" (1 Sam. 15:29). But in v. 11 of the same chapter, sending Samuel to tell this to Saul, God explicitly says, "I have changed My mind." Once you have seen this apparent contradiction (and even to see it, you must read a version that translates the Hebrew verb with the same English word in both verses), you must then ask: Did Samuel misunderstand God? Is he lying to Saul? If so, why? Does God indeed change his mind, or does he simply prefer not to give Samuel a more complicated explanation? (We'll look at this passage again in chapter 3.)

Why Read the Bible?

Another possibility—by no means a certain one—is that v. 11, where God says that he has changed his mind, and v. 29, where Samuel denies it, were written by two different people. The great philosopher-theologians of the Middle Ages understood God in just the way that 1 Sam. 15:29 presents him: a being who does not change. Changeability is a characteristic of matter, but God is immaterial and does not share this characteristic. If these words were indeed put in Samuel's mouth to deny the possibility that God might change, we have "cut the Gordian knot"—there are two different voices here. But that turns the conflicting statements in these two verses from a contradiction into an argument.

Suddenly an already dramatic story about a decisive moment in early Israelite history has been ramped up by an order of magnitude. It now is framed within an argument about the *nature* of God and (implicitly) of the world we live in. Is the course of events inevitable, or can it change? Is it predetermined, or is it random? Do our actions change the future, or do they not? Whether or not they do, are we responsible for them?

A story that asks these questions, even a story about real characters in real history, is no longer merely reporting facts, but asking readers to think about them. A simplistic attitude toward the Bible—an insistence that it is "without error," and that therefore nothing about it can be questioned—ignores the many places like this one where the Bible seems to *demand* that it be questioned. Much more is at stake here than whether or not God was going with Plan B when he told Samuel to replace Saul with David as king of Israel. That, even with all its future implications, might simply be of historical interest. After all, by now it is a done deal.

But questions about the nature of God and of the world we live in have existential implications. Such questions, it seems, will never be answered definitively. Yet thinking people have pondered them since the dawn of time. We must therefore consider a third possibility for 1

Samuel 15—that both verses, with their contradictory statements about whether God does or does not change his mind, were indeed written by a single author, but an author with a small "a," a human author telling the story of a pivotal transition in Israelite history with goals that are not (merely) political and historical, but also philosophical, theological, and literary.

From my perspective, it doesn't make much difference whether you want to capitalize the "A" of "Author" or not. The distinction between those who view every word in the Bible as divine and those who view every word in the Bible as human is not that one group is clear sighted and the other misguided, but that they have chosen opposite sides on a question whose solution rests at bottom not on rational thought and observation, but on belief. In either case, the Bible remains what it has always been: the one thousand-year slice of civilization that has shaped the culture we live in today.

As you might expect, one thousand years of writing could not possibly be in a monotone. My obligation (and my joy) as a scholar, my challenge (and my pleasure) as a writer, are to introduce you to as many of the biblical authors as I can within the space of this small book. Jewish tradition says that when we recite the words spoken or written by the dead, their lips move in the grave. I have spent many happy hours listening to the voices of the biblical writers and of their later interpreters. The purpose of this book is to make them come alive for you as they have for me.

What's Coming Up?

Admittedly, this book will be something of a whirlwind tour. And we will not be moving through the Bible straight from beginning to end (according to anyone's version). Instead, each chapter will look at biblical voices of a different kind. So, before we begin, let me give you an overview of where we will go from here.

Chapter 1, "The Sound of the Biblical Voices," begins with the most basic fact about the Bible, and the easiest to forget: It was not written in English. When you read it, as most of us do, in English, you are reading a translation. The fact that there are so many different Bible translations tells you right away that there is more to the Bible than any single translation can convey. In this chapter we will look at the many things that Bible translations hide, and we'll take our first steps in distinguishing the different voices that can be heard in the original text.

Chapter 2, "Historical Voices," will give us an opportunity to begin looking deeper into some of the Bible stories most of us learned as kids. We'll see that many of them were originally written, like books of history in our own era, to explain the history that mattered directly to contemporary readers—in this case, the Israelites. Moreover, though "Bible stories" almost always tell things just one way, the Bible contains *competing* explanations of many historical events. Focusing on the differences between the way history is told in Samuel and Kings (the "Deuteronomistic History") versus the version we read in Chronicles (more attuned to priestly concerns), this chapter will begin to show us some of those differences, and why the competing versions made it into the Bible.

Chapter 3, "Theological Voices," traces the religious voices we discovered in the historical sources back into the Pentateuch. Many people are familiar with the phrase "the Documentary Hypothesis," the first suggestion that the Five Books of Moses were not a single text written by Moses. But few people realize that the different voices in the Pentateuch represent very different views on the nature of God and God's relationship with humanity. This chapter will lay out those differences and show how and why they shaped later books in the Bible as well.

Chapter 4, "Legal Voices," will broaden our perspective on the Pentateuch by looking at the laws that are woven into its fabric—including at least *two* (count 'em, two) different sets of the famous Ten Commandments. We'll see how the word *torah* ("instructions") turned into the capital-T name of a sacred book and how one of the pentateuchal sources managed to integrate the Deuteronomic and priestly viewpoints into a single perspective that shaped later Judaism and Christianity.

Chapter 5, "Prophetic Voices," takes us further back into history, when God's word was understood to be transmitted not in written form but through "His servants the prophets" (2 Kgs. 17:23). Despite what we often think, predicting the future was the least of their tasks. Instead, we will find the prophets too at the intersection of history, theology, and law.

Chapter 6, "Women's Voices," will take us further into the realm of the individual voices we'll have begun to encounter in chapter 5. These are not ideological voices, but those of specific people—real women who lived during the biblical period, whether or not we know their names—who left their mark on the biblical text and, as I will argue, wrote two of the books of the Bible.

In chapter 7, "Voices of the Wise," we will take an extended look at two of the most creative and thoughtful individual voices in the Bible, the voices of the books of Ecclesiastes and Job. But to understand them, we must first look once more at the voices of an anonymous group, the sages who shaped the book of Proverbs. These are not the voices of priests or prophets, but of people with no claim to heavenly knowledge thinking their way through the problems of human existence.

Thinkers in other cultures faced those same problems, of course. In chapter 8, "Foreign Voices," we will see that not only the sages of Israel but also the lawgivers and poets were influenced by the surrounding cultures. In a more indirect way, foreign influences shaped the lives of everyone during the biblical period.

Chapter 9, "Voices of Song and Legend," will demonstrate that the myths of surrounding cultures actually shaped the Bible's perspective on how the Israelite nation and even the world itself came into being. As we'll see, the creation of the world and the exodus from Egypt are not merely two of the most important Israelite legends; they are inextricably linked with each other. Only knowing what the ancient Israelites knew—how the Egyptians, Mesopotamians, and Canaanites looked at the world—can give us the fully three-dimensional picture that the Bible is trying to present.

In chapter 10, "Echoes and Reverberations," we'll take the briefest possible look at the afterlife of the Bible. The biblical voices continue to echo and reverberate down to our own day. As this chapter will show, the voices of the biblical writers were not simply "voices crying in the wilderness." But the voices, and how we hear them, have changed (sometimes immeasurably) since they were first heard. Once you've read this book, you'll have an understanding of what the original voices were trying to say, and you'll begin to hear how the way we read the Bible nowadays may harmonize with the original voices or obscure them.

Each of these chapters—historical voices here, theological ones there—could be a book of its own, perhaps even a library of books. The few biblical texts we'll be able to look at here—like the last paragraph of Chronicles, which we glanced at a moment ago—are all interesting in their own right, but their main purpose is to let you hear the biblical voices in their native habitat. A reminder: These texts *are* the Bible. Alongside the role that each of them plays in illustrating the ideas presented in this book, they are intended to demonstrate that the biblical voices demand and repay careful listening.

Once your ear is tuned to these biblical voices, I know you will want to argue with some of them and make friends with others. There are still others we will not have time to meet; I don't think Zephaniah is going to make the cut. But you can find him later—the Bible isn't going anywhere. We will have more than enough to do to begin listening to the many, many voices of that Bible that we *will* encounter in the following pages. I am excited to introduce you to them.

I
The Sound of the Biblical Voices

What is the very first thing that the Bible says, the first words that the Bible "speaks" to us? Even in an era when familiarity with the Bible is no longer taken for granted, most people still have an answer for this question: "In the beginning, God created the heaven and the earth." But the Bible doesn't say that at all. What the Bible says is this:

בראשית ברא אלוהים את השמים ואת הארץ

b'reishit bara elohim et ha-shamayim ve-et ha-aretz

It's Hebrew, not English. It may sound foolish to emphasize that the Bible says something in Hebrew rather than those English words that we all know. But it's not just a trivial point. Translations are never able to give you everything that you'd get from the original text. And translations of the Bible, as we'll see, hide some things that the translator of a modern novel or poem doesn't have to deal with. We'll meet some of those features shortly. But before we begin to discuss the many voices in the Bible itself, let's look for a moment at some of the different *English* voices in which we hear the Bible today.

Beyond "The Heaven and the Earth"

As a translator, I can tell you that translators are always making choices. Anyone who translates the Bible is faced with two major choices in the first verse of the Bible, and another in v. 2. There's a lot on our plate, so let's get started.

The traditional translation of Gen. 1:1 tells us that God created "the heaven and the earth," but "the heaven and the earth" doesn't mean the same thing as *et ha-shamayim ve-et ha-aretz*. For one thing, the Hebrew *shamayim* is a plural word—"heavens," not "heaven." More importantly, the phrase is part of a linguistic phenomenon that is much more important in Biblical Hebrew than it is in English: using words in pairs. In high-flown language, certain words automatically call for their own regular pair word. For example, when Joseph accuses his brothers of stealing the silver cup he has planted in their baggage, they reply, "The extra silver which we found in the mouths of our sacks we brought back to you all the way from Canaan—how could we steal silver or gold from your lordship's house?" (Gen. 44:8). They have not been accused of stealing gold, but they add the word for rhetorical emphasis. Using the word pair "silver" and "gold" makes their denial more impressive.

"Heavens" and "earth" make up one of the most common word pairs in Biblical Hebrew. They appear together dozens of times. For example, "Give ear, O heavens, and let me speak; O earth, hear the sayings of my mouth" (Deut. 32:1). Now "heavens" and "earth" are not the same kind of pair as "hear" and "give ear," which are poetic terms for the same thing, or even as "gold" and "silver," which are terms for the same *kind* of thing, one more valuable than the next. "Heavens" and "earth" are opposites. As a pair, they form a particular literary device that the Hebrew Bible often uses, called a "merism" (from a Greek word meaning "division"). When opposites are paired, they mean not just the two items themselves, but everything in between. Though the New Testament is written in Greek, the same phenomenon is found there—as when Jesus says of himself, "I am the alpha and the omega" (Rev. 22:13), the first and last letters of the Greek alphabet. This doesn't mean that Jesus is the alpha and then some other people are beta, gamma, delta, and so on, until omega comes around and it's Jesus again. It is an assertion that Jesus is "everything," from first to last, beginning to end. In its context, in the last chapter of the Christian Bible, it also asserts that even what Christians call the "Old Testament" is in some sense "about" Jesus.

Similarly, "heavens" and "earth" in Biblical Hebrew are a merism—meaning the heavens, the earth, and everything else that is in, on, or between them. Thus when the Bible says that God created *et ha-shamayim ve-et ha-aretz*, it doesn't merely mean that he created the heavens and that he also created the earth. It also means that he created what we would call "the universe." So when people tell you what the Bible says, and they tell you something in English, the first lesson is to make sure that they are not missing something that's in the Hebrew.

To Replicate or to Rewrite?

Because the Bible is a sacred book, many translations of it aim to stick as closely as possible to a word-for-word translation of the Hebrew. The most famous of these is the King James Bible, from which our "In the beginning" translation comes. When the King James translators had to add a word that isn't directly found in the Hebrew, a different typeface was used to show that there was no matching word in the original. For example, Biblical Hebrew often omits the verb "to be" where English requires it, as in the second verse of the Bible: "And the earth was without form, and void; and darkness *was* upon the face of the deep" (Gen. 1:2, KJV). The Hebrew text has no equivalent of the second "was," which is needed to make the sentence good English. (You can still find some editions of the KJV that print these "extra" words in italics.)

In Gen. 1:1, this careful method of translation, to be as literally accurate as possible, simply translates each word separately: *ha-shamayim* is "the heaven" and *ha-aretz* is "the earth." Perhaps this kind of care is what makes some people think that (as a contemporary bumper sticker claims) the King James translation is "the Bible God uses."

We must also take into account the built-in imperfection of all translation of any kind. "The translator is a traitor," says the famous Italian proverb—or rather, *traduttore traditore* (whatever that really means). In our Genesis example, someone who chooses to translate *et ha-shamayim ve-et ha-aretz* as "the heaven and the earth" is depriving the reader of the knowledge that the verse is talking about the creation of the universe. But someone who translates it as "the universe" (as the "Good News Bible" does) is depriving the reader of a number of things, too. First of all, someone who reads "the universe" won't know, any more than someone who reads "the heaven and the earth," that Biblical Hebrew uses a merism to indicate that concept. A translator who writes "the heaven and the earth" gives you the merism, but without the tools to understand it; one who writes "the universe" gives you the meaning, but the merism itself—the way the Israelites thought about what we call "the universe"—has vanished. Secondly, a reader who sees "the universe" will have no clue that the first word of the next verse, *ve-ha-aretz* ("and the earth") has already been mentioned in v. 1. Thirdly, the Bible is not a brand-new book. Almost everyone who speaks English knows the sentence "In the beginning God created the heaven and the earth," and if we were to read "the universe" instead, alarm bells would go off. All of this can be made clear with footnotes and commentary, but that is explanation, not translation.

Finally, a simple point, but one that is often forgotten. Languages change, not least of them our own. So a translation that was right for one age may not be right for another. "Universe" in something like today's sense first occurs in English at the end of the sixteenth century, just a few years before the publication of the King James Bible in 1611. Did it sound, as to some it still does today, too contemporary for the Bible? Everyone knows that the Bible is an ancient book, and sometimes it is translated in slightly archaic language to suggest its antiquity. Even the King James Bible did this to some extent. To complicate things even more, the Hebrew of the Bible is itself not uniform, but contains elements that may have already sounded archaic when they were first written down in Biblical Hebrew. All of this adds an extra level of difficulty to Bible translation.

Breaking through the Translation Barrier

How can the ordinary reader, who doesn't know Hebrew and must simply trust a translator, get behind the veil of the translation to the real thing? The best way to do this is to have two different translations handy. One of them should be a translation that tries to be very literal, like the King James. This is worth having anyway; the King James Bible should be on the shelf in every English-speaking home simply for the beauty of its language. It is no accident that Shakespeare and the King James Bible, the two foundations of modern English literature, were contemporaries. The other translation ought to be one that tries to write in English that is as contemporary as possible, such as the NJPS version or the NRSV. Again, a contemporary translation is worth having just for its own sake. If you want to sit down and read through an entire biblical book to see what happens, even a short book like Ruth or Esther is tedious to read in archaic English; but it is surprisingly easy to read even the longer historical books when they are written in the kind of English we are used to reading.

Together, the literal translation and the contemporary one provide a key to the Hebrew original, even for readers who wouldn't recognize an *aleph* (the first letter of the Hebrew alphabet) if it bit them on the nose. Follow along with both translations simultaneously until you find a place where they differ. The literal translation will give you something pretty close to what the original Hebrew "says"—in our example, "the heavens and the earth"—while the contemporary translation will give you something pretty close to what it "means"—in our example, "the universe."

There is another way that this method is useful for people who must read the Bible in a language other than Hebrew. Though translations, by their nature, are always written to be comprehensible, not every word in the Bible is perfectly understood. The double translation system will help you know when there is general agreement on the meaning of a biblical word or phrase, and when the meaning is not certain. Adding a second, different contemporary translation will help in this even more. (Three translations may sound like a lot, but it isn't. I can reach five different English translations without moving from where I sit, and click on still more. Fortunately, despite the high cost of books these days, unless you want a fancy binding, most Bibles aren't that expensive—no author's royalties.) The difference between "the heaven and the earth" and "the universe" is simply a matter of the translator being forced to choose between two alternative ways of expressing a single Hebrew phrase in English. But sometimes biblical scholars and translators do not know for sure what a particular Hebrew phrase means. Or two different scholars, or groups of scholars, may both know "for sure" what a particular phrase means, but the two may disagree.

If we continue reading Gen. 1:2 from where we left off, we will find a prominent example of this. Contrast these translations:

And the Spirit of God moved upon the face of the waters (KJV).

. . . and a wind from God sweeping over the water" (NJPS).

. . . and a mighty wind that swept over the surface of the waters (NEB).

Before we turn to the difficult beginning of this phrase, let's look at the end of the verse, the simple part, to compare the methods of these three translations. As we would expect, the King James is the most literal, "upon the face of the waters" ("waters" because the Hebrew word for "water" is grammatically plural; I don't know why they did not translate "heavens" in v. 1). The New English Bible explains the idiom: the "face" of the water is its surface. The NJPS version treats this common Hebrew expression simply as a preposition: "over." The tone of these three translation voices is different, but the meaning presented in each case is the same.

This is not so for the beginning of the phrase, however. Here, the very meaning of the Hebrew words *ruaḥ elohim* is in dispute. The word *ruaḥ* has a much wider range of meaning than does any single English word; it can certainly mean either "spirit" or "wind." How then is the translator to choose? The King James rendering "Spirit of God" was probably prompted by the Christian doctrine of the Trinity, aided by the fact that God says, in Gen. 1:26, "let *us* make." The NEB "mighty wind" may have been prompted by our contemporary scientific picture of the primordial earth. (Most scholars think that *elohim*, usually "God" or "god," can also be used in Biblical Hebrew as an intensifier: "a godalmighty wind." When the King James translation calls Nineveh "an exceedingly great city" in Jon. 3:3, it is translating "a great city to *elohim*." But in Gen. 1:1, they gave *elohim* its more usual meaning.) Finally, the NJPS "wind from God" tries its best to hint at both meanings. "Wind" is meteorological, but a wind "from God" may be something more than mere weather.

A Further Complication

Before we leave these first verses in the Bible, we must look at an additional level of complexity. We might think that the essential problem here is simply one of our own ignorance. Perhaps when this text was new, the meaning of the words (one way or the other) was simply obvious in a way that it no longer is to us today. But there is another possibility—that the Hebrew phrase is *deliberately* ambiguous, as if written in stereo, leaving the two images unresolved and both possible. In such a case, the poor translator, forced to choose one or the other English word, must indeed become an unwilling traitor to the original biblical text, which has somehow managed to speak a single word in two different voices simultaneously.

The truth is that difficulties and differences in translation actually begin with the very first word in the Hebrew Bible: *b'reishit*. The equivalent of this in the English translation that we all know is "in the beginning." But most likely that is not what *b'reishit* means. As Rashi, the great medieval Jewish biblical commentator, explains, the standard way to say "in the beginning" in Biblical Hebrew is *ba-rishonah*. The expression the Bible actually uses here, *b'reishit*, everywhere else means "at the beginning of . . .". Thus the verse does not say, "In the beginning God created," but "at the beginning of God's creating." Here is a case where the King James translation—the most familiar words of the English Bible—changes the original meaning. (We will eventually see why, but not until chapter 10.) And the difference in meaning between the two translations is considerable. Compare Gen. 1:1–3 in these two translations:

> ¹ In the beginning God created the heaven and the earth. ² And the earth was without form, and void; and darkness was upon the face of the deep. And the Spirit of God moved upon the face of the waters. ³ And God said, Let there be light: and there was light. (KJV)

> ¹ When God began to create heaven and earth— ² the earth being unformed and void, with darkness over the surface of the deep and a wind from God sweeping over the water— ³ God said, "Let there be light"; and there was light. (NJPS)

The translation difference here makes a complete difference in meaning. According to the King James translation, God's first creative act was to create the heaven and the earth. Apparently he created them out of nothing (*ex nihilo*, in the Latin phrase favored by philosophers), but the text doesn't tell us how. According to the NJPS version, some sort of formless world, covered with water, already existed. God's first creative act was to say the words "Let there be light."

The Ancient Translations

The first group of multiple voices in which the Bible speaks to modern readers, then, is that of the many English translations in use today. But Bible translation is not a new phenomenon. The oldest biblical translations we know of, the Aramaic and Greek translations, go back more than two thousand years. Naturally, these translations share some of the difficulties that modern English translations continue to have with the biblical text. Their importance for us, however, is that they add an extra dimension to our study of the Bible's many voices. For they take us back to a time before the Bible existed as a single, unified book. In some cases, they even allow us to watch the Bible in formation.

Three major examples will begin to show you what I mean. They are taken from the Septuagint, the ancient Greek translation that takes its name from the seventy (Latin *septuaginta*) translators who, according to one version of the legend, created it for King Ptolemy. It turns out that we can use the Septuagint to begin to understand how the Bible came together.

Our first piece of evidence is the book of Proverbs. As you can easily see in an English translation, some of the verses in this book are headings that divide the book into separate sections:

"The proverbs of Solomon, son of David, king of Israel" (Prov. 1:1).

"The proverbs of Solomon" (Prov. 10:1).

"These, too, are attributed to the sages" (Prov. 24:23).

"These, too, are proverbs of Solomon, which were transmitted by the men of King Hezekiah of Judah" (Prov. 25:1).

"The words of Agur son of Jakeh" (Prov. 30:1).

"The words of Lemuel" (Prov. 31:1).

The likelihood is that many of these sections existed as separate works long before there was such a thing as the book of Proverbs that we have in our Bibles today. The Greek translation of Proverbs gives us a tantalizing look at the prehistory of the Bible, for it contains all of the same sections, but not in the same order. For example, the Hezekiah collection, Proverbs 25–29, comes in the Septuagint just before the poem about the "Woman of Valor" that begins in our Bibles at Prov. 31:10. That means the Greek translation skips directly from Proverbs 24 of our Bibles to Proverbs 30:15. (The first half of Proverbs 30 occurs even earlier.) Thus it seems that Proverbs took shape in at least two different ways during the Bible's formative period, assembling the separate sections in different ways. One of those editions entered our standard Bibles. A different edition is preserved in the Septuagint.

The second example is the book of Esther. Here is a case where the Greek translation actually has large sections that are not in the Hebrew Bible at all, 107 verses all told. For example, let us look at Esther, chapter 4. Mordecai tells Queen Esther that the king has called for a massacre of the Jews and begs her to intercede. She replies that she cannot, for she has not been called to the king's presence for a month and anyone who enters the king's presence without being called faces death. We pick up the story in v. 13:

> ESTH. 4:13 Mordecai said in reply to Esther, "Do not imagine that you, in the king's house, will escape, of all the Jews. ¹⁴ For if you do keep silent at this time, relief and rescue will arise for the Jews from another place; but you and your father's house shall perish. And who knows whether it was not for just such a time that you attained majesty?" ¹⁵ Esther said in reply to Mordecai, ¹⁶ "Go gather all the Jews in Shushan and fast for me. Do not eat or drink for three days, day and night. I and my maids will fast the same way. Under those circumstances, I will come before the king in defiance of custom; and if I perish, I perish." ¹⁷ So Mordecai went and did all that Esther had commanded him.
>
> 5:1 On the third day, Esther dressed herself in majesty, and stood in the inner courtyard of the palace, opposite the throne room.

But the Greek version fills the time before "the third day" (the beginning of Esther 5 in our Bibles) with the text of two long prayers, one recited by Mordecai and the other by Esther. In this case, we might guess that the Greek translator added his own voice to the original Hebrew and created scenes that "ought" to have been in the story. The Greek translation of Esther has a total of six scenes that are "missing" from the Hebrew original. (Along with them, there are over fifty references to God, who does not appear at all in the Hebrew version.) Creative writers of our own day, like the Septuagint translators, may still be inspired to add scenes that the Bible seems to be lacking—for instance, in Gen. 4:8, just what *did* Cain say to Abel? But such creative writing does not get added to the text of the Bible. In the case of the Greek "additions" to Esther and similar additions to the book of Daniel, however, it did.

Our third example comes from the book of Jeremiah. The Greek and Hebrew texts of this book are more radically different than those of any other book in the Bible. Here, for example, is how the fifty-two chapters of the Hebrew text are rearranged in the Greek version: 1–24, half of 25, part of 49, 46, 50, 51, the rest of 49, 48, the end of 25, 26–45, 52. It looks like a game of 52 Pick-up! Moreover, so much of the Hebrew text is missing from the Greek version—in chunks ranging in length from a single word to thirteen verses—that the Greek text has almost 15 percent fewer words than the Hebrew one does. If the Gideon Bible in your hotel room had been translated from Greek instead of Hebrew, Jeremiah would have been ten pages shorter. On the other hand, the Septuagint also has two "additions" to Jeremiah. But in this case, they are printed as separate books called "Baruch" (as you remember, he was Jeremiah's secretary) and "The Epistle of Jeremiah."

Because the differences between the Hebrew and Greek versions of Jeremiah present us with the most complicated picture of the development of the biblical text that we have, that picture is probably also the most realistic. Notice that, despite the wildly mixed-up order of the chapters, two large chunks of more than twenty chapters each are the same in both versions: 1–25 and 25–45. It is a single, smaller section of the Hebrew text, chapters 46–51, oracles against foreign nations, that the Greek version places in a different order, in the middle of chapter 25 of the Hebrew version. Our window into the past is once again showing us a late stage in the development of the Bible. Long after the prophet himself lived, the Greek and Hebrew texts present two very different "editions" of Jeremiah. Unlike the case of the additions to Esther, however, it is hard to imagine a translator so blithely rearranging his material and then cutting 15 percent of it to boot. Could the Greek Jeremiah have been translated from a Hebrew original different from the one we have today?

A Different Original Bible—Among the Dead Sea Scrolls

One of the first pieces of evidence suggesting that differences in the Greek Bible might go back to a different Hebrew version came from a tiny scrap of leather, no more than an inch or two on a side, from a manuscript scholars call 4QExod^b. "4Q" means that it was found in Cave 4 of the famous site of Qumran, overlooking the Dead Sea. Like 4QExod^b, many of the famous Dead Sea Scrolls are not writings that were previously unknown, but copies of various parts of the Bible. The fragment we are interested in has just twelve words on it, but it can clearly be identified as Exod. 1:5, "All the souls who came from Jacob's loins amounted to seventy souls"—with one minor difference. On the fragment, Jacob's descendants are seventy-*five* souls, not seventy. This same number is found in the Greek translation! So this tiny scrap of leather found at Qumran tells us that the biblical collections of the last two centuries before the Common Era had two different Hebrew versions of Exodus, one that said "seventy" and one that said "seventy-five." Far from being a mistake, or a deliberate alteration, the Greek version was translating a Hebrew word that is no longer found in our standard Bibles.

If this were all—seventy or seventy-five—it would be a fairly trivial matter. But, though most of the biblical texts from Qumran match the text of the standard Hebrew Bible, a great many of the variations in the Greek translation have now turned up among the Dead Sea Scrolls in Hebrew. And that's not all. One of the most remarkable of the biblical texts found at Qumran has a paragraph that was known to us not even from the Greek translation of the Bible but from a

Greek-language history written at the end of the first century CE, Josephus's *Antiquities of the Jews*. This paragraph tells how Nahash, king of the Ammonites, gouged out the right eye of every Israelite who lived on the east bank of the Jordan, except for seven thousand of them who escaped to a town called Jabesh-Gilead. This story would have made a perfect introduction to 1 Samuel 11, and in a Dead Sea Scroll text called 4QSam[a], that is exactly where we find it. Since Josephus's history follows the book of Samuel closely, we must assume that the version of Samuel he knew resembled 4QSam[a] rather than the one in our standard Bibles. Somehow the section about Nahash, a whole paragraph of narration, vanished from the Bible for two thousand years—apparently by accident—until it was recovered half a century ago in Qumran Cave 4. Like its cousins in the Septuagint, it is a witness that many voices that were originally biblical did not make it into the Bibles we use today.

"Parallel" Texts in the Bible

The finds at Qumran, then, show us what the Greek translation hints at. Twenty-one hundred years ago, some of the texts that are now in our Bibles were circulating in more than one version. In fact, sometimes two of these variant texts were both included in our Bibles, for many biblical texts are repeated elsewhere in the Bible at greater or lesser length—but with small variations.

Sometimes the variations are extremely minor. For instance, Psalm 108 is made up entirely from pieces of two other psalms, Ps. 57:8–12 (vv. 7–12 in Christian Bibles) plus Ps. 60:7–14 (vv. 5–12 in Christian Bibles), with a few slight changes. Psalms 60:12/10 and 108:12/11 both say, "You have spurned us, O God," but the Hebrew wording is slightly different: "you" is written out in Psalm 60, while in Psalm 108 it is merely part of the verb form. Other such differences, though small, can be more interesting. For example, Psalms 14 and 53 are essentially identical, but there is one difference between them that hints at a significant and presumably deliberate change. Wherever Psalm 14 uses "YHWH," the personal name of the Israelite God (four times in seven verses), Psalm 53 uses "God" instead. This may seem like a simple stylistic change, but there are two reasons to think that something more is going on. First, Psalm 53 is part of a group of psalms, 42–83, in which "God" is used far more frequently than "YHWH." In the rest of the psalms, the reverse is true. The difference is so striking that we assume the change must have been purposeful.

Second, we know from the Bible itself that some of the biblical writers considered the distinction between the various names of God to be extremely significant. In Exodus 6, we hear that the distinction was originally made by God himself:

> EXOD. 6:2 God spoke to Moses and said to him, "I am YHWH. ³ I appeared to Abraham, Isaac, and Jacob under the name El Shaddai [sometimes translated as "God Almighty"], but I was not known to them by My name YHWH."

Since this announcement of God's name takes place at the crucial historical moment when Moses is summoned to free the Israelites from slavery, we know that at least one biblical writer considered the revelation of God's personal name to Moses—"YHWH" rather than the generic "God"—to be of paramount importance. We don't know quite how, but the two different voices in Psalms 14 and 53 must also reflect a theological difference.

Which Bible Verse to Believe?

Many of the parallel texts differ in minor literary features, and sometimes in minor factual details as well. There is not always a good way to resolve these. For example, the final chapter of Jeremiah, in both the Greek and the Hebrew versions, is a sort of historical appendix to the prophet's career, copied from 2 Kings 25 (and the last three verses of 2 Kings 24). It describes the fall of Jerusalem in 586 BCE and the destruction of the Temple by the Babylonians. There are a number of numerical discrepancies between the two accounts. 2 Kings 25:8–9 explains that the Temple was burned on the seventh day of the month, while Jer. 52:12–13, otherwise almost an exact copy, gives the date as the tenth of the month. It is hard to know for certain which of these is correct. Still a third date, the ninth, is given in some versions of the Greek and Syriac translations, but here it is easier to guess what happened. The Second Temple, burnt by the Romans in 70 CE, was destroyed at just this time of year, and Jewish tradition fixed upon the ninth day of the month for both destructions. (The Jews were expelled from Spain in 1492 on the same date, too.)

Though our Bibles preserve statements to the contrary, no doubt some of the ancient translators felt justified in correcting these to conform to what everyone "knew" was true. (You will find similar discrepancies in the figures in 2 Kgs. 25:17 and 27 vs. Jer. 52:22 and 31.)

There are many, many examples of texts that are almost, but not quite, exactly repeated in two or more places in the Bible. I have a book in front of me that has two hundred pages of them, printed in side-by-side columns—far too many to discuss here. By far the largest number of these fall in the book of Chronicles, which seems to have used Samuel and Kings as its source books for a retelling of Israelite history. As we will see in the next chapter, when we turn to our study of the Bible's historical voices, the Chronicler often corrected things in his sources that he "knew" must be mistaken. That is the great advantage of parallel texts for learning about the biblical past. The differences between them can show what people at different times or in different groups "knew," that is, what basic assumptions they made about their world.

Biblical Writers Who Read the Bible

Another thing the differences between parallel texts may tell us—at least when, as with Kings and Chronicles, we can establish which came first—is which of the biblical texts were already being read when. For this purpose, we don't need the kind of exact parallel texts we have been discussing up until now; much looser parallels also have a lot to teach us. For example, the law code of Deuteronomy includes this provision: "Parents shall not be put to death on account of their children, and children shall not be put to death on account of their parents; a person shall only be put to death for his own crime" (Deut. 24:16). This is a principle of law intended for application in human courts. But Ezekiel has taken this guideline and turned it into a principle of *divine* justice: "The soul which sins, *it* shall die; a child shall not suffer for a parent's iniquity, and a parent shall not suffer for a child's iniquity" (Ezek. 18:20). Ezekiel has turned the legal language of Deuteronomy into religious language. We know he is quoting Deuteronomy because, following the custom of the ancient Hebrew writers, he reversed the original order of the clauses to indicate that he was citing another verse.

One of my favorite examples of these looser parallels is based on the famous creation story of Genesis 1, with which our chapter began. This, of course, describes in organized, almost scientific fashion the creation of the sun, moon, and stars; of the firmament in the heavens that divides the waters above from the waters below; of the earth; of the monsters in the ocean depths; of the animals, the creeping and flying things; and of people. Another text, Psalm 148, clearly follows the story of creation as told in Genesis 1, but transforms it from an objective, third-person account of the technical details of the job into a lyrical hymn of praise for the God of creation:

1 Hallelujah.
Praise YHWH in the heavens, praise Him from the heights.
2 Praise Him, all His angels, praise Him all His hosts.
3 Praise Him, sun and moon, praise Him, all bright stars.
4 Praise Him, the highest of heavens, and the waters above the heavens.
5 Let them praise the name of YHWH, for He commanded and they came into being.
6 He set them in place forever and ever, fixed a rule that shall never pass away.
7 Praise YHWH from the earth, sea-monsters and all Deeps.
8 Fire and hail, snow and smoke, stormwind that does His word,

⁹ The mountains and all the hills, fruit trees and all the cedars,
¹⁰ Animal and beast, creeper and bird on the wing,
¹¹ Kings of earth and all nations, princes and captains of the earth,
¹² Youths and maidens, old and young,
¹³ Let them praise the name YHWH, for His name alone is exalted, His majesty over earth and heavens.
¹⁴ He exalts the horn of his people, in praise to all His loyal ones, to the Israelites, the people close to Him. Hallelujah!

We can't say for sure that the author of Psalm 148 was "reading" exactly the same version of Genesis 1 that we have today, but he is certainly using the plot of that version. (As we will see in chapter 9, ancient Israel had other ways than this one of telling about the world's beginning.) Still, the psalm injects the creation story with an emotional intensity that contrasts vividly with the ordered, almost sterile calm of Genesis 1.

Double Readings in the Biblical Text

There is one more important set of "parallel" voices in the Bible, but this is one that translations most often conceal. We have seen that when a biblical text is repeated in a different place, there usually are slight differences between the two texts—a missing pronoun here or a spelling variation there. The standard Hebrew Bible text in use today, which was established about a thousand years ago by the Masoretes (the scholars who invented the vowel and punctuation markings), sometimes actually preserves variations like this in a single spot. That is, a word will be written one way in the body of the text and a variation of the word will be written somewhere on the margin of the page. These variants are technically called by the ancient Aramaic terms explaining how they are used, the Ketiv (that which is supposed to be "written") and the Qere (that which you are supposed to "read"—though not all such variants occur in texts that are read aloud as part of the synagogue ritual).

As I noted in the "Read Me First" section, the unpronounceable written name YHWH is always replaced in reading by something else, almost always the word *adonai*, "my Lord." This is a "Qere perpetuum," a word that is written one way but always, automatically, pronounced another way. Because this example occurs so frequently, the text expects readers to know it without being told about it in a marginal notation. (It is a strange blend of these two forms that gave rise to our English word "Jehovah," a word that never existed in Hebrew.) But a wide variety of other Ketiv/Qere, or written and reading variations, are found in the Bible. For example, in Gen. 36:5, in a list of the sons of Esau, the name of one of his sons is spelled "Jeish," but a marginal note says that when the text is read aloud the name is supposed to be pronounced "Jeush," with a *u* instead of an *i* vowel. (In handwritten Hebrew manuscripts, the two letters look extremely similar.) The same name appears in v. 14, again with the same reading variation, but in v. 18, the written text has "Jeush" with no variation!

One obvious explanation for such variants presents itself immediately. Most likely, the correct name was "Jeush," just as it is written in v. 18 (and in 1 Chr. 1:35), but in two places a scribe who was copying the text without much thought wrote the name as "Jeish" instead. What difference does it make anyway? Do we really care about this minor difference in the name of one of Esau's sons? Perhaps not. But even this first tiny example—and there are hundreds in the Bible—shows that a thousand years after the last books of the Bible were written, those who wished to preserve the text of the Bible most carefully often gave it *two* simultaneous voices.

Many of the variations, even ones that may originally have arisen simply as a scribe's mistake, actually make a difference in the meaning of the text. For example, a difference of only one letter, and almost no difference in pronunciation, creates two quite different meanings in Ps. 100:3. Compare them:

> Know ye that the Lord he is God: it is he that hath made us, and not we ourselves (KJV, translating the written variation).

Know that the LORD is God! It is He that made us, and we are His . . . (NJPS, translating the reading variation).

This variation between "not" and "His"—two variants of the Hebrew syllable *lo*—is quite common. Another common variation is to see two letters switched, as in Prov. 23:26:

My son, give me thine heart, and let thine eyes observe my ways (KJV, reading variation).

My son, mark my words, and accept my guidance with a will (NRSV, written variation).

Don't let the differences between the ancient and contemporary translation styles here confuse you. The King James is translating *titzorna*, "observe," while the NRSV is translating *tirtzena*, "be willing." In both of these cases, and many others like them, the Hebrew Bible preserves two possibilities where a translation can only give you one.

Although the meanings are different in the two cases we have just looked at, they are not contradictory. Each fits into its context and conveys the same *general* idea. But what about 2 Sam. 12:24, where the alternation of a single letter in a verb prefix changes which character in the story is acting? The situation is this. King David has committed adultery with Bathsheba, the wife of Uriah the Hittite. He sends orders to Joab, his military commander, to make sure to arrange the fighting so that Uriah is killed, and he takes Bathsheba as his wife. But the son whom they had conceived in adultery dies as an infant. "Then David comforted his wife Bathsheba. He came to her, lay with her, and she bore a son whom s/he called 'Solomon.'" I use "s/he" to indicate the two different readings the Bible gives us. The written variation says that David named the child, and the reading variation says that Bathsheba did.

You must realize that this whole story is written with great care. For example, Bathsheba is called David's wife here, but when she is described in v. 15 as giving birth to the first child, she is called Uriah's wife, though Uriah was already dead by then, to remind the reader that the first child was conceived in adultery. Now, when David and Bathsheba's second child—the future king of Israel—is given the name Solomon (from the Hebrew *shalom*, suggesting peace and reconciliation), is it David or Bathsheba who gives him this name? Again, the translations must pick one or the other, but the Hebrew Bible actually preserves both possibilities. As in the English "s/he," in this case one Hebrew letter makes the difference.

Some of these variants are not changes of a single letter, of the kind that might have originally been copying mistakes, but deliberate changes. For example, the double readings include a number of cases where euphemisms are supposed to be read out loud for cruder words that are preserved in the written text. Thus in 2 Kgs. 18:27, the Assyrian emissary to besieged Jerusalem warns the king's men that, if the siege continues, the inhabitants of the city will be forced "to eat their own excrement and drink their own urine." Apparently the words in the written text were considered too coarse to read aloud, so a later copyist wrote more presentable words in the margin.

In the variants that we've just looked at, the details may differ, but the overall meaning of the text remains mostly the same. But in Job 13:15, the "not" and "his" variants are diametrically opposed:

> Though he slay me, yet will I trust in him (KJV, translating the reading variation).

> He may well slay me; I may have no hope (NJPS, translating the written variation).

Which of these is what the Bible "really" says? Like it or not, the Bible is saying *both* of them!

Different Kinds of Language in the Bible

Our final example of the double voices that are sometimes preserved in a single word of the Hebrew version comes from 2 Kgs. 4:3. Here, as in the case of Esau's son in Gen. 36:5, the difference in spelling is again just a single vowel, and the difference in meaning is nil. Since the word with the variation is not a proper noun, no translation will ever bother to show you the difference. In this case, the variation is probably intended to give the word a different *accent*, one that characterizes a different Hebrew dialect. The story here involves Elisha the prophet telling a widow who has asked him for help to borrow empty jars from her neighbors. She will miraculously be able to fill as many of them as she can borrow by pouring out the oil from the one small cruse she still possesses. The reading text here says *sh'khenayikh*, which is standard Hebrew for "your neighbors," but the written text says *sh'khenaykhi*, adding a tiny, extra vowel at the end.

Since Elisha is a prophet of the Northern Kingdom, it is most likely that the original text of this story had the characters speaking in the Israelite dialect of Hebrew, not the Judean dialect of Jerusalem and the Southern Kingdom that ultimately became the standard language. We know that the two dialects were slightly different from inscriptions that have been dug up by archaeologists in both parts of the country. Most likely, the written variation, and the others like it in this story, were altered at some later stage—either because they were thought to be mistakes, or because a scribe wanted to make them sound more contemporary, as we change the spelling and punctuation of English-language texts from the seventeenth and eighteenth centuries for readability, to conform with our current standards. But the written text still preserves the way this character originally spoke.

Different Dialects, Different Languages

We actually find a number of cases in the Bible where the different voices speak in different accents and even different languages. You don't have to know much more than the story of the Tower of Babel to realize that not all the characters in the Bible speak Hebrew. Some of them are even bilingual. For example, when the Assyrian envoy made his challenging speech to the people during the siege of Jerusalem, telling them that if they did not surrender they would find themselves eating excrement and drinking urine, the king's counselors replied to him this way: "Please, speak to your servants in Aramaic, for we understand it; do not speak to us in Judean in the hearing of the people on the wall" (2 Kgs. 18:26).

The envoy, of course, was speaking Hebrew (in the "Judean" dialect of Jerusalem) deliberately, in order to demoralize the inhabitants. But ordinarily communications between Judea and Assyria would have gone on in the *lingua franca* of that time, Aramaic. With each other, the Assyrians would have spoken still a third Semitic language, Akkadian (albeit with an Assyrian accent). We know this because the Assyrian historical description of the siege, discovered by archaeologists in the ruins of Nineveh, is written in that language.

Even among Hebrew speakers, there were different accents. Most of us who remember the name of the Babylonian king who conquered Jerusalem think of him as "Nebuchadnezzar," for this is what he is called some fifty-eight times in the Bible, and that is how we usually refer to him in English. But elsewhere in the Bible, another thirty-three times (mostly in the book of Jeremiah), he is called "Nebuchadrezzar," with an *r* instead of the second *n*. The two letters, *n* and *r*, both represent phonetically "liquid" sounds, which are sometimes exchanged. Since Nebuchadnezzar was a Babylonian, both Hebrew forms are attempts to represent the way his real, Akkadian, name, "Nabukudurri-utzur," sounded to different people. As you can see, the *r* variation, not the one we use in English, is the more accurate of the two.

Biblical Hebrew in Different Times and Places

Some differences in the Hebrew of parallel texts represent changes in the language over time. Thus, the parallel texts in Kings (mostly written around 600 BCE) and Chronicles (written at least two centuries later) show us many differences between the earlier form of the language—often called Standard Biblical Hebrew—and the later—often called Late Biblical Hebrew. There are changes in vocabulary, grammar, even pronunciation. For example, the famous city of Damascus was called *Dammések* in Standard Biblical Hebrew; in Late Biblical Hebrew, it must have begun to be pronounced *Darmések*, with an *r*, for this spelling is found four times in Chronicles. Many of the differences in Late Biblical Hebrew were influenced by Hebrew's kindred language, Aramaic, which the exiled Judeans heard around them in Babylonia in the sixth century BCE.

But of course some of the differences in accent were not chronological, but regional. We have already discussed how people from the northern part of Israel spoke differently than those in the south. In fact, even within the north, there were differences in accent between the people of "Ephraim" (the west bank of the Jordan) and of "Gilead" (the east bank). Sometimes such differences in accent could be quite dangerous, as in this wartime episode from Judges 12 when some Ephraimites were trying to flee to Gilead:

> ⁵ The Gileadites captured the fords of the Jordan to the land of Ephraim. When the Ephraimite fugitives would say, "Let me cross," the Gileadites would ask him, "Are you an Ephraimite?"; if he said "No," ⁶ they would tell him, "Say *shibboleth*"; but he would say "*sibboleth*," for he could not pronounce it that way. So they would seize him and slay him at the fords of the Jordan. Forty-two thousand Ephraimites fell at that time.

A *shibboleth* can be an ear of grain or a stream; in English, from this story, it has come to mean a way of speaking or a catchword that distinguishes a particular group. In the story from Judges 12, the Bible again is allowing us to hear some of the variant voices of ancient Israel.

Multiple Voices in a Single Text

Not all the variant voices in the Bible belong to texts written in different times or places. Mark Twain wrote the following explanatory note to readers of *Huckleberry Finn*:

> In this book a number of dialects are used, to wit: the Missouri negro dialect; the extremest form of the backwoods Southwestern

dialect; the ordinary "Pike County" dialect; and four modified varieties of this last. The shadings have not been done in a haphazard fashion, or by guesswork; but painstakingly, and with the trustworthy guidance and support of personal familiarity with these several forms of speech.

I make this explanation for the reason that without it many readers would suppose that all these characters were trying to talk alike and not succeeding.

The biblical writers too sometimes put different voices in the mouths of different characters. We have seen this with accents in the shibboleth story, but sometimes more subtle literary techniques give different voices to the characters. For example, listen to this exchange from 1 Samuel 9, when the future King Saul (young, handsome, and a head taller than anyone else in Israel) goes looking for some asses belonging to his father Kish that had wandered off. On the way into town, he and his servant run into some girls coming out to fetch water and ask, laconically, "Is the seer in town?" "Yes!" the girls reply:

> 1 SAM. 9:12 Here he is right up ahead of you—hurry—because he came to town today because the people have a sacrifice at the shrine today— **13** right when you come into town, that's where you'll find him before he goes up to the shrine to eat because the people will not eat until he comes because he'll bless the sacrifice—then the guests will eat—go on up, because he—because today—you'll find him!

The contrast between the question (only three words in Hebrew) and the answer (forty-four words) is clear. "Yes!" would have been enough to answer the question, but something else is going on here. The author has deliberately shown them speaking in a way that conveys their excitement at seeing Saul and that also gives the reader the feeling of a whole group of them talking at once. Saul's character too comes through in the words he uses, few and to the point. We can well imagine that the young David, devil-may-care and a bit of a rogue, would have spoken to the girls quite differently.

The Narrator Intrudes

These literary effects are fairly rare, it's true, though it is likely that Israelite readers or hearers of the Bible, with their native understanding of the language, recognized more of them than we do. But while we are reading with an ear to literary technique, we must not forget two more voices in the story of Saul that we just looked at.

The first is that of the narrator. When this voice is restricted to stage directions like "he went" and "he said," it is easy to forget about; but in fact this is the disguised voice of the author who is artfully shaping the story. In this story, there is a more noticeable narrative voice, which deliberately calls attention to itself before Saul asks whether "the seer" is in town, as it explains, "Previously in Israel, this is what a man would say when he went to inquire of God: 'Let's go to the seer.' For the 'prophet' of today used to be called a 'seer'" (1 Sam. 9:9).

Was the original story written back in the days when "seer" was the normal term, and the explanation of the unusual word added by someone later? Or was the story written later by an author who used an archaic word and added the explanation himself? In either case, the usually invisible narrator suddenly intrudes on the story, calling attention to a chronological change in the Hebrew language.

A far more striking example of such an "intrusive" narrator occurs in Deuteronomy 2. Here Moses is standing with the Israelites on the east bank of the Jordan, the river that they are about to cross but he is not. He is recounting the history of their travels and travails, when suddenly he is interrupted by what almost amounts to a scholarly footnote:

> DEUT. 2:8 We then moved on, away from our kinsmen, the descendants of Esau, who live in Seir, away from the road of the Arabah, away from Elath and Ezion-geber; and we marched on in the direction of the wilderness of Moab. 9 And the LORD said to me: Do not harass the Moabites or provoke them to war. For I

will not give you any of their land as a possession; I have assigned Ar as a possession to the descendants of Lot.—
¹⁰ It was formerly inhabited by the Emim, a people great and numerous, and as tall as the Anakites. ¹¹ Like the Anakites, they are counted as Rephaim; but the Moabites call them Emim. ¹² Similarly, Seir was formerly inhabited by the Horites; but the descendants of Esau dispossessed them, wiping them out and settling in their place, just as Israel did in the land they were to possess, which the LORD had given to them.—
¹³ Up now! Cross the wadi Zered!
So we crossed the wadi Zered.

It is worth noting a couple of things about this passage. First, though some English versions set off the "footnote" typographically, as does the NJPS version above, the ancient writers did not. The text of this chapter in a Hebrew Bible or a synagogue Torah scroll, as in the most ancient biblical manuscripts, has no brackets or parentheses, no asterisk, no dashes, no indentation. All there is to guide the reader is the change in "voice." But this change, though it would be complicated to describe, is easy to spot.

To prove it to yourself, continue reading Deuteronomy 2, and find the other "footnote" inserted here. This time, I will remove the typographical clues:

DEUT. 2:16 When all the warriors among the people had died off, ¹⁷ the LORD spoke to me, saying: ¹⁸ You are now passing through the territory of Moab, through Ar. ¹⁹ You will then be close to the Ammonites; do not harass them or start a fight with them. For I will not give any part of the land of the Ammonites to you as a possession; I have assigned it as a possession to the descendants of Lot. ²⁰ It, too, is counted as Rephaim country. It was formerly inhabited by Rephaim, whom the Ammonites call Zamzummim, ²¹ a people great and numerous and as tall as the Anakites. The LORD wiped them out, so that [the Ammonites] dispossessed them and settled in their place, [22] as He did for the descendants of Esau who live in Seir, when He wiped out the Horites before them, so that they dispossessed them and settled in their place, as is still the case. [23] So, too, with the Avvim who dwelt in villages in the vicinity of Gaza: the Caphtorim, who came from Crete, wiped them out and settled in their place. [24] Up! Set out across the wadi Arnon! See, I give into your power Sihon the Amorite, king of Heshbon, and his land. Begin the occupation: engage him in battle. [25] This day I begin to put the dread and fear of you upon the peoples everywhere under heaven, so that they shall tremble and quake because of you whenever they hear you mentioned.

(Did you spot the "footnote"? It is vv. 20–23.)

The other thing to note is the *number* of voices that are being deployed here:

(1) a scholar, adding an encyclopedia-style footnote within a speech of

(2) God, whose earlier speech is being quoted by

(3) Moses, whose extensive farewell address is introduced by

(4) a narrator, whose voice was created by

(5) an author, whom we call "the Deuteronomist."

Even if, as is possible, the "footnotes" were added by a different writer altogether at a later time, at least the middle three voices were all created by a single writer. So even without the complications introduced by the thousand-year timespan between the earliest and the latest writings in the Bible, we must always be careful to ask not just what the Bible is saying, but in what voice it is speaking.

Deliberate Double Readings

Let me add one final dimension to our discussion. Some biblical texts, written by a single author and in a single voice, are nevertheless *delib-*

erately ambiguous. That is, the words are clear and easy to understand, but they could possibly carry two different meanings, and the author deliberately used them to make the reader hear both meanings at once. We have already raised this possibility in connection with Gen. 1:2.

For a more complex example, let us turn to 2 Samuel 16. Here is the situation. Absalom, the son of King David, has seized power from his father. In the previous chapter, David, fleeing for his life, has told his adviser Hushai the Archite to remain in Jerusalem under cover. Ostensibly, he will shift his allegiance from David to Absalom, but secretly he will remain loyal to David and be David's "plant" in Absalom's court. Here is what happens:

> 2 SAM. 16:16 When Hushai the Archite, David's friend, came to Absalom, Hushai said to Absalom, "Long live the king! Long live the king!" 17 Absalom said to Hushai, "Is this your loyalty to your friend? Why did you not go with your friend?" 18 Hushai said to Absalom, "No! For the one whom YHWH has chosen, and this people and every man of Israel, I shall be for him, and with him I shall dwell. 19 And secondly, whom shall I serve if not his son? As I served before your father, so shall I before you."

Absalom is completely taken in by Hushai's apparent switch of loyalties. (In fact, as you will see if you continue reading the story, God so arranges it that Absalom follows Hushai's advice and is killed, letting David ultimately regain his throne.) But the reader, who is in on the plan, hears Hushai's words differently than Absalom does. When Hushai says, "Long live the king!" Absalom assumes "the king" is himself, Absalom, and is even somewhat offended on his father's behalf. We readers can guess that Hushai is thinking, "I mean the real king— David." When Hushai says he follows "the one whom YHWH has chosen," again we, unlike Absalom, know that this means David. Finally, when Hushai promises to serve before Absalom just as he served before David, we readers know that he means it literally: now, just as before, with *David's* best interests in mind. Interestingly, v. 18

also includes a Ketiv/Qere double reading. Though the text to be read, translated above, says "I shall be for him," the written text says "I shall *not* be." Is this a copyist's mistake, or a deliberate double reading to hint at the deliberately double-voiced nature of Hushai's reply to Absalom?

Multiple Sides of a Question

Of course, the premise of this book is not just that the Bible was written with great skill and subtlety, but that there are multiple voices within the original text of the Bible itself that express different, sometimes conflicting opinions on the same subject. This is no secret, and never has been, for some of the voices are quite obvious to anyone who opens the Bible. Take, for example, the following verses from chapter 26 of the book of Proverbs:

⁴ Do not answer a dullard in accord with his folly,
Lest you bring yourself down to his level.
⁵ Answer a dullard in accord with his folly,
Lest he be wise in his own eyes.

Well, which is it? Which of these two explicit biblical instructions, right next to each other and giving exactly opposite advice, are we supposed to follow?

You recognize, of course, that I'm deliberately asking a foolish question here. (Did you answer me or didn't you?) Part of reading the Bible involves knowing what kind of material you are reading in order to interpret it correctly. We know that most of Proverbs, including chapter 26, is a collection of one-liners that give good advice in small packages: sound bites of the sages, if you will. What is more, these two contradictory maxims are not even necessarily spoken in different voices. It's possible that one sage insisted that the smartest thing to do was to show the dullard what a fool he was, and that some other sage claimed that it would be foolish to descend to that level, but it is just as likely that one person could give both pieces of advice. "Look before you leap" and "he who hesitates is lost" do not make up an irrational combination; they are simply appropriate for different occasions. So if Prov. 26:4 and 5 sound like different voices, they may simply be the same person speaking at, or for, different times.

But sometimes people do have different points of view. Occasionally, the Bible lets these people speak for themselves, and we hear two different voices that provide both sides of an argument. One example of this comes in Jeremiah 26, where Jeremiah has just prophesied the destruction of Jerusalem. Not only that, but he has done so in the very Temple itself. The story goes on to let us hear both the voices of his enemies and those of his supporters:

> JER. 26:11 The priests and prophets said to the officials and to all the people, "This man deserves the death penalty, for he has prophesied against this city, as you have just heard with your own ears."

At this point, Jeremiah defends himself, explaining that he was sent with a message from God, and that if they kill him, they will be guilty of shedding innocent blood.

> ¹⁶ Then the officials and all the people said to the priests and the prophets, "This man does not deserve the death penalty, because he has spoken to us in the name of our God YHWH."

Then some of the elders remind the people that Micah had made similar prophecies during the reign of King Hezekiah. The elders ask:

> ¹⁹ Did King Hezekiah of Judah, and all of Judah, put *him* to death? Didn't he fear YHWH and beseech YHWH, so that YHWH changed His mind about the evil things He had intended to do to them? We are about to do a great evil to ourselves!

The prophet Uriah, who came with a similar message, was in fact killed, according to vv. 20–23; but one of the court officials, Ahikam the son of Shaphan, protected Jeremiah, "so that he was not handed over to the people for execution" (v. 24). Here we have a raging political argument, at a time of crisis for the nation. Rather than recounting dispassionate history, this biblical text preserves for us the living voices of those who knew Jeremiah as their contemporary and lived through the tumultuous years that led to the destruction of the First Temple. We hear both the voices of those who wished to heed Jeremiah and the voices of those who wished to silence him. (We will look at this event in more detail in chapter 5.)

In this controversy, the inclusion of the argument within the book of Jeremiah implies a value judgment. Those who wished to prevent Jeremiah's death, and to heed his message, were right, and those who wished to put Jeremiah to death were wrong. But on many important issues, different parts of the Bible preserve voices that may differ or even contradict each other. Yet they are presented in their separate places without counterarguments. For example, compare these two quite different pronouncements on the nature of mankind:

PS. 8:4 What is Man that You are mindful of him,
The son of Adam, that You pay him any mind?
5 Yet You have made him little less than God,
Crowned him with glory and honor.*

ECCL. 3:19 For the fate of humans is the fate of the beast; they have a single fate. As this one dies, so dies that one; all have the same spirit. A human is in no way superior to a beast; for all this is illusion. 20 All go to one place; all came from dust and all return to dust.

Which of these opposite pronouncements is "what the Bible says" about humanity? Clearly, both are biblical. Yet clearly, too, they are both contradictory—and both complementary. We *are* animals, as Ecclesiastes says; yet the Psalmist is correct to feel astonishment at

---

* Ps. 8:3–4 in Christian Bibles.

how far we transcend our animal nature. Both views together give a richness to the Bible's picture of humanity.

The "New Heart"—Two Prophets Disagree

It is worth remembering that each biblical voice is, originally, the voice of a single individual, and each is colored by an individual's upbringing, intellect, and temperament. We can see an example of this in the motif of the "new heart," which is common to both of the two major prophets of the period just before and just after the destruction of the First Temple, Jeremiah and Ezekiel. Both prophets believed that sin was the cause of Israel's problems, and both believed that sin was a result of the nature of the heart—that is, the mind and the will, for which "heart" is the biblical image. Yet the solution to the problem, the change necessary to make the "hearts" of Israel amenable to God's will, seemed different to each. For Jeremiah, the heart's ability to follow its own counsel is at the root of the problem. Once God's commandments are imprinted directly into the mind, obedience to them will be a matter of instinct, not a matter of choice:

> JER. 31:33 For this is the covenant which I shall cut with the House of Israel after those days—says YHWH—I shall put My Teaching inside them and write it on their hearts, and I shall be their God and they shall be My people. 34 No longer will anyone teach his friend or his brother, "Know YHWH," for they all shall know Me, from the smallest of them to the greatest—says YHWH—for I will forgive their iniquity and no longer remember their sin.

For Ezekiel, the problem is the opposite. You may be familiar with the story of the exodus, when Pharaoh's heart is "hardened." This does not mean that he becomes cruel, but that his anger has made him so stubborn that he cannot think clearly enough to save himself and his people. For Ezekiel, too, a mind that is currently fixed in its obstinacy must be made flexible enough to be able to respond to the logic of God's commandments:

EZEK. 11:19 For I shall give them one heart, and put a new spirit inside you. I shall remove the heart of stone from their flesh and give them a heart of flesh, 20 so that they may follow My laws, and keep My statutes, and do them. They shall be My people and I shall be their God.

Thus, for Ezekiel, it is the old heart that is hard as stone, and the new one that is soft. For Jeremiah the too-flexible heart must be replaced by an inflexible one; for Ezekiel, the problem is the opposite. Yet both men were not only contemporaries, but envisioned their respective "new hearts" as the basis for a renewed covenant between God and Israel, signified by the same solemn phrase, "They shall be My people and I shall be their God."

Why Was the Temple Destroyed?

To conclude this wide-ranging survey of the many different kinds of voices in the Bible, let us look at one of the most crucial moments in the history of biblical times: the destruction of the Temple in Jerusalem in 586 BCE. As we noted in the introduction, this event was in some ways the spark that began the process which ultimately led to the creation of the Bible. How does the Bible itself explain this pivotal historical moment?

2 Kings 25 gives a straightforward political and military background to the event. After Jerusalem was captured by Nebuchadnezzar in 597, Judah essentially became a Babylonian satellite. So King Zedekiah's feeble attempt at independence demanded to be ruthlessly put down:

2 KGS. 24:20 Zedekiah rebelled against the king of Babylon. 25:1 In the 9th year of his reign, on the 10th day of the 10th month, King Nebuchadnezzar of Babylon and his whole army reached Jerusalem, camped there, and built a siege ramp against it all around. 2 The city went on being in a state of siege until the 11th year of King Zedekiah. . . . 8 On the 7th day of the 5th month—that is, in the 19th year of King Nebuchadnezzar of Babylon—an un-

derling of the king of Babylon, Nebuzaradan, the chief of the guards, arrived in Jerusalem. ⁹ He burned down the Temple of YHWH, the king's palace, and all the houses of Jerusalem.

Notice, by the way, the subtle care of the narrator, to date the beginning of the rebellion according to the year of Zedekiah's reign, just as has been done all the way through the book of Kings, and then, on the eve of Jerusalem's destruction and the end of Davidic kingship, to register the date by using the reign of the king of Babylon. The switch in calendars marks a new historical era. Still, in this description, the destruction of the Temple is simply an event in political history.

2 Kings 17, the chapter that describes the fall of the Northern Kingdom in 722 BCE, presents a comparable reason for its destruction:

⁴ The king of Assyria caught Hoshea [king of Israel] conspiring against him, for he had been in communication with King So of Egypt and had stopped paying the annual tribute to the king of Assyria. The king of Assyria arrested him and threw him into prison. ⁵ Then the king of Assyria marched against the whole land, including Samaria [the capital of the northern kingdom], which he besieged for three years. ⁶ In the 9th year of Hoshea, the king of Assyria captured Samaria. He deported the Israelites to Assyria and settled them in Halah, on the Habor River (the Gozan), and in the cities of Media.

But this chapter goes on to reveal an underlying religious cause for the political defeat:

⁷ This was because the Israelites had sinned against their God YHWH, who had brought them up from the land of Egypt, from under the control of Pharaoh king of Egypt. Yet they worshiped other gods ⁸ and followed the laws of the nations whom YHWH had dispossessed on behalf of the Israelites, which the kings of Israel had reintroduced.

Since Kings (as we will see in our next chapter) was written from a Judean perspective, what happened to the Northern Kingdom is presented as a warning of what might (and eventually did) happen to the Southern Kingdom as well:

> [13] YHWH warned Israel *and Judah* through each of his prophets and seers: "Turn back from your wicked ways, and keep My commandments and My laws, following the whole Teaching that I commanded your ancestors, which I sent you through My servants the prophets." [14] But they did not obey.... [18] YHWH grew tremendously angry at Israel, and He removed them from His presence. Only the tribe of Judah alone remained.
> [19] But not even Judah kept the commandments of YHWH their God; they followed the laws that Israel had introduced.

So now we have a second explanation. The ostensible background of power politics that led to the destruction of Jerusalem was actually manipulated by God, behind the scenes, as punishment for idolatry. Israel had "worshiped other gods."

Jeremiah, who was dragged to Egypt with a group of those fleeing the reprisals expected after the assassination of Gedaliah, the Babylonian-installed ruler of occupied Judah, confirmed this religious explanation of the disaster (in Jeremiah 44) but emphasized God's emotional involvement:

> JER. 44:2 Thus says YHWH of Hosts, the God of Israel: You have seen all the evil that I brought on Jerusalem and on all the other cities of Judah. They lie in ruins to this very day, and no one inhabits them, [3] as a result of the evil things they did to irritate Me—going to offer sacrifices and worship other gods whom they had not known—"they" being you and your ancestors.... [6] so My hot anger was poured out against the towns of Judah and the streets of Jerusalem and burnt them. They became a desolate ruin, as they are to this day.

It was indeed God who was responsible for the destruction of Jerusalem, but not as a matter of calmly responsive punishment. No, Jerusalem was destroyed because God lost his temper. (See Ezekiel 8–11 for a much more detailed, and somewhat different, account of God's anger.)

If it was idolatry that brought down God's wrath on the city, then why are the escapees still sacrificing to other gods? It's because their own explanation is the opposite of Jeremiah's. The Bible gives us their reply to him:

> JER. 44:16 What you told us "in the name of YHWH"? We're not going to listen to you! **17** No! We're going to do everything we promised about making offerings to the Queen of Heaven and pouring libations to her, just as we and our ancestors used to do—and our kings and officials, too—"in the towns of Judah and the streets of Jerusalem." We had plenty to eat; we lived well, and never saw misfortune. **18** But ever since we stopped making offerings to the Queen of Heaven and pouring libations to her, we have lacked everything, and war and famine have practically finished us off.

The play of voices is actually very subtle here, for the exiles are throwing Jeremiah's own words back at him. When they mention "the towns of Judah and the streets of Jerusalem," they are making bitter fun of Jeremiah's own prophecies, which regularly use this phrase (see v. 6 above, and also Jer. 7:17, 11:6, and 33:10). Nor was Jeremiah deaf to the allusion:

> JER. 44:21 Yes, those offerings you and your ancestors presented "in the towns of Judah and the streets of Jerusalem"—your kings, your officials, and all the people of the land—YHWH noticed them and kept them in mind. **22** When YHWH could no longer stand the wickedness of the abominations you practiced, your land became a desolate, uninhabited ruin, and a curse, as it is to this day.

Again, we hear both sides to an argument. Everyone agrees that the people were sacrificing to the Queen of Heaven. The dispute is whether destruction came because they were doing so, or because King Josiah forced them to *stop* doing so.

Why Was the Temple Destroyed? (*The Next Generation*)

Jeremiah (and Ezekiel) had to deal with the immediate aftermath of the destruction. Seventy years later, with the exiles now returned, the rebuilding of the Temple began. The prophets' explanation was now accepted and standard among the group of returnees. But the times called for a softened presentation of it, focusing instead on the task at hand. A Persian commission of inquiry, worried that the new construction was actually fortifications to be used as the base for a revolt against the government, sent back this explanation in its report to King Darius, quoted in Ezra 5:

> 11 Here is how they answered us: "We, the servants of the God of heaven and earth, are rebuilding the Temple that was originally built these many years ago. A great king of Israel completed the building of it. 12 But because our ancestors angered the God of Heaven, He handed them over to King Nebuchadnezzar of Babylon, the Chaldean, who demolished that Temple and deported the people to Babylonia. 13 But in the first year of King Cyrus of Babylon, King Cyrus issued an order to rebuild that Temple of God."

Since this was a response to a Persian government inquiry, the role of Cyrus, the Persian conqueror of Babylon, was recounted straightforwardly. But we know that others believed that not only Cyrus's permission to rebuild the Temple, but even his ascension to power, was a direct result of God's intervention. Here (in the NJPS translation but for God's name) is the majestic pronouncement of Isaiah 45:

> 1 Thus said YHWH to Cyrus, His anointed one—
> Whose right hand He has grasped,

Treading down nations before him,
Ungirding the loins of kings,
Opening doors before him
And letting no gate stay shut:
² I will march before you
And level the hills that loom up;
I will shatter doors of bronze
And cut down iron bars.
³ I will give you treasures concealed in the dark
And secret hoards—
So that you may know that it is I, YHWH,
The God of Israel, who call you by name.
⁴ For the sake of My servant Jacob,
Israel My chosen one,
I call you by name,
I hail you by title, though you have not known Me.

In the report to the Persians, the reference to God was made in a "secular" voice. "The God of heaven and earth" was a universal God, and one whom the Persians could understand, for "the God of heaven" was a Persian term as well. But here, in the prophecy to the Judeans who would return from exile, God is referred to by his personal, Israelite name, YHWH.

Finally, 2 Chronicles 36—the very end of the Jewish edition of the Bible—rounds up all these explanations together and adds a final nuance of its own. The political, military, religious, and theological explanations are all there, along with the hope that lay in rebuilding. But the Chronicler weaves into this harmony an additional theme. All the things he tells about happened "in fulfillment of the word of YHWH spoken by Jeremiah" (2 Chr. 36:21). What Jeremiah had said was this: "This country shall become a destroyed wasteland, and these peoples shall serve the king of Babylon for seventy years" (Jer. 25:1). In truth, Babylonian domination lasted fifty years, not seventy; but it was a full seventy years before the Temple was rebuilt—perhaps under the impact of this prophecy.

We have seen in our discussion of the Greek translation that the book of Jeremiah, as a book, was still in the process of formation several centuries after Chronicles was finished. We cannot say what form it had in the Chronicler's day. We saw, too, that in Jeremiah's own time the worth of his prophecies was a matter of hot dispute. Yet the Chronicler accepted them as "the word of YHWH." The conclusion is clear. The final voice in the Bible is a voice that is already reading Scripture.

Beyond "In the Beginning"

Everyone knows intuitively that a translation is not the same as the original. It's obvious, too, that there's no such thing as a perfect translation. If there were, we would certainly have one by now for the Bible. Instead, we're stuck with a mix-and-match, catch-as-catch-can approach that means no single translation can be the right one for every purpose.

In this chapter, we've seen that the sameness of the voice in any particular English translation of the Bible is actually concealing *two* things: (1) a wide range of opinions about what any particular text in the Bible means; and (2) a tremendous clamor of different voices in the original Hebrew text of the Bible, all competing—some of them with each other—for our attention. In the next chapter, we'll turn down the noise and listen to just one set of biblical voices, the historical voices. Surprising though it may seem, it can be much harder than you think to answer a simple question: What does the Bible tell us about what *happened* during biblical times?

2
Historical Voices

We have all heard the phrase "The Bible says . . . ." After reading the previous chapter, you know that this phrase is not as simple as it sounds; after all, most of the people who tell us what the Bible "says" tell it to us in a language that the Bible didn't originally "speak," or in just one of two or more versions of the same story. Moreover, the biblical writings contain many different characters, each with his or her own, often distinctive, voice. So even when the Bible is "speaking" directly to us, very often it is doing so in a multitude of voices.

But this is not what we usually mean when we say "the Bible says." When the Judeans in Egypt explain that Jerusalem was destroyed because they had stopped sacrificing to the Queen of Heaven, this is not "what the Bible says" about the subject. True enough, it is a biblical verse; but it is clearly presented as the opinion of some of the people living at the time, and not as the true explanation. The biblical writers clearly believe that Jerusalem was destroyed because the God of Israel, not the Queen of Heaven, decreed it. That is what "the Bible says" about the destruction of Jerusalem. Even here, the biblical voices are a rich harmony; but they are saying essentially the same thing.

Not everything "the Bible says," though, is so easy to figure out. The Queen of Heaven, for example. Is she, and are the other gods worshiped by the surrounding nations and by renegade Israelites, real or imaginary? Are there multiple gods, all of them subordinate to the God of Israel, or is that God the only God that exists? To use the technical terms, were the Israelites monotheists (believing in the existence of only one God) or henotheists (believing in the existence of many gods but worshiping only one of them)? Different biblical texts seem to suggest different answers to this question. Similarly, what does "the Bible say" about reward and punishment, or life after death? These are not easy questions to answer. They require a wide acquaintance with biblical literature and a great deal of interpretative skill. Moreover, different biblical texts seem to give opposite answers to the same question.

But these are theological and philosophical questions. No one can objectively prove the "answers" to them; they are just opinions. So let's start with something easier, something more objective; not a theological question that requires interpretation, but a simple matter of historical fact. What does "the Bible say" about . . . who killed Goliath?

Who Killed Goliath?

This is one of the most famous of all Bible stories, still regularly used as a metaphor (I saw a reference to it on this morning's op-ed page), so even today almost everyone knows the answer to this question: it was David, the brave young shepherd boy, who killed the mighty Philistine strongman Goliath with a stone from his slingshot. You will find the whole wonderful story told in great detail in 1 Samuel 17. The Philistine champion (vv. 4 and 23 identify him as Goliath), a giant of a man, scoffs at the puny Israelites and defies them to do their worst. David, bringing a care package from home to his big brothers who are serving in the front lines, hears about the challenge and volunteers to fight the giant. King Saul gives David the king's own suit of armor to wear (a telling detail for us readers, who know that David will succeed Saul as king of Israel), but when David puts it on, he finds that he can't walk! So he faces the giant with nothing but a slingshot and his trust in God:

> 1 SAM. 17:48 When the Philistine began to come toward David, David hurried up to the battle line to meet the Philistine. ⁴⁹ David

put his hand into the bag, he took out a stone and slung it, and hit the Philistine in the forehead. The stone sank into his forehead, and he fell on his face to the ground. ⁵⁰ David overpowered the Philistine with a sling and a stone; David struck the Philistine down and killed him, without a sword in his hand. ⁵¹ David ran up and stood over the Philistine, grasped his sword and pulled it from its sheath. He dispatched him and cut off his head with it.

This story is probably the most famous of all the stories about David, and it must have been so in ancient times as well as today, for it is alluded to several times again as the Bible continues to tell the story of David. In the following excerpt from 1 Samuel 21, for example, David has realized that Saul, in his mad rage, is determined to kill him. David decides to defect to the Philistines to save his life. He stops in the town of Nob, where he tricks the local priest, Ahimelech, into giving him arms and provisions by telling him that he is on a mission for the king:

> 1 SAM. 21:9 David said to Ahimelech, "Haven't you got a spear or sword here on hand? I didn't bring my sword or any of my other weapons with me, because the king's errand was so urgent." ¹⁰ The priest said, "The sword of Goliath the Philistine, whom you killed in the valley of Elah, is right over there, wrapped in a piece of cloth, behind the ephod [part of the religious furniture of the shrine]. If you want to take that one, take it, for there is no other here but that one." David replied, "There is no other like it! Give it to me."

Again, there is more to this than just a colorful detail; the sword that David used to behead his first enemy is now back in his hands. What is more, Goliath's is no ordinary sword, but a giant one. In chapter 17, we are told how large and heavy Goliath's armaments were; the iron head of his spear weighed six hundred shekels (somewhere around fifteen pounds) all by itself, and the shaft of the spear was the size of a weaver's beam (v. 7). When David, too small to wear armor, picked it up after felling the giant, we could picture him with a massive sword as tall as himself, wielding it with two hands to cut off Goliath's head. Now, in chapter 21, he has grown into the role. He straps it on without a second thought and makes tracks for Gath.

There is a third, more subtle reference to the Goliath story. Still later, when David is living in the hills as the chief of an outlaw band, he comes down (in chapter 25) to Carmel to collect protection money from a wealthy rancher named Nabal, who is shearing his sheep there. Nabal indignantly refuses, but his wife Abigail—who will later marry David—knows David's worth and his reputation:

1 SAM. 25:29 If someone should rise to pursue you and seek your life, the life of my lord [David] will be bound up in the bundle of life with YHWH your God; He will sling away your enemies' lives in the hollow of a sling.

Abigail knows that David is no ordinary criminal, but is running for his life because God has chosen him to succeed Saul as king of Israel. She assures him—using the same Hebrew words as were used in the Goliath story—that God will fling away his enemies just as easily as David flung the fatal stone at Goliath.

It's Not That Simple After All

So the famous story of David and Goliath was not merely as well known in ancient Israel as it is to us today, it is in some ways the linchpin of the rest of 1 Samuel, the biblical story of how David became Israel's king. But even with historical facts, things are not so simple. As we will see in this chapter, the historical statements in the Bible— "what really happened," in the words of one historian—are shaped, and sometimes even bent out of shape, by the different voices that recount the history to us.

Even with something so simple as the name of the man who killed Goliath, there is still one more biblical voice to be heard. The story of

David's own reign takes up most of the book. of 2 Samuel, but the last four chapters are not part of the continuous story; they form a sort of appendix of various tales, poems, and lists that have to do with David—as if to fill in the historical record. (The last days of David are recorded immediately following, in the first two chapters of the book of Kings.) In one of the anecdotes in the appendix, in 2 Samuel 21, we read the following:

> ¹⁹ There was more fighting with the Philistines at Gob; and Elhanan son of Jaare-oregim the Bethlehemite killed Goliath the Gittite, whose spear had a shaft like a weaver's beam.

We all "know" the Bible says that David killed Goliath, and indeed it does. In fact, we were able to trace echoes of David's famous youthful deed all through the biblical story of how he rose from shepherding his father's flock to shepherding God's flock as king of Israel. Here, however, we have one tiny voice—but a biblical voice—telling us, in the plainest possible Hebrew, with no elaboration, that Goliath was killed by a man named Elhanan. It would be stretching credulity to imagine that there were two different Goliaths, and indeed all the identifying details point to the fact that the Goliath killed by Elhanan was the famous Goliath of legend. He was a giant (we know this because the story is part of a little collection of tales about Israelite heroes who killed giants); he is a Gittite, and we know the legendary Goliath came from Gath (1 Sam. 17:4); clearest of all is the identifying detail of the giant spear with "a shaft like a weaver's beam," exactly what we were told of Goliath in 1 Sam. 17:7. But this version of the story—not from a legend or an ancient tablet, but in the Bible itself—tells us something unexpected: that Elhanan, not David, killed the giant. What to do?

One reason not everyone knows about this apparent contradiction is because not every English version tells the story this way. Here, for example, is the same verse, 2 Sam. 21:19, as found in the King James Bible:

And there was again a battle in Gob with the Philistines, where Elhanan the son of Jaare-oregim, a Bethlehemite, slew *the brother of* Goliath the Gittite, the staff of whose spear *was* like a weaver's beam.

According to this translation, Elhanan didn't kill Goliath at all! The man Elhanan killed was Goliath's brother (thus accounting for the family resemblance). But this is not what the original Hebrew text says. Careful King James readers would know this, because (if your edition of the KJV continues this practice) the crucial words *the brother of* are in italics. As I mentioned in chapter 1, this indicates that a translator has added something that was not in the Hebrew text. Similarly, at the end of the verse, the King James translators wrote that the staff of the spear "*was* like a weaver's beam," because good Biblical Hebrew leaves out the Hebrew equivalent of "was" in a sentence like this. In order to make the English sentence grammatically correct, let alone idiomatic, they had to add the word "was," and the addition is marked by italicizing it.

But there was no linguistic reason for adding the words *the brother of.* The English sentence would have made perfect sense without this addition. In fact, adding these words (unlike adding *was*) actually changes the meaning of the original Hebrew words of the Bible. How could the translators possibly dare to do this?

As far as I know, the team that translated 2 Samuel for the King James Version left no record of how they reached their decision on this particular translation, but their logic is fairly easy to follow in this case. First of all, they knew, as we have just seen, that it was not a question of one verse saying, "David killed Goliath," versus a second verse saying, "Elhanan killed Goliath." There is just one verse saying that Elhanan killed him, but a very detailed story says that David killed him, and it is referred to over and over again in the story of David's life. Secondly, and more important, the King James translators knew that the biblical history told in Samuel and Kings is mostly retold, sometimes even repeated word for word, in the books of Chronicles.

Sure enough, this statement about Elhanan is almost exactly repeated in Chronicles—*almost* exactly. Let's put the two of them side by side so we can compare them conveniently.

2 SAM. 21:19	1 CHR. 20:5
Again there was fighting with the Philistines at Gob; and Elhanan son of Jaare-oregim the Bethlehemite killed Goliath the Gittite, whose spear had a shaft like a weaver's beam.	Again there was fighting with the Philistines, and Elhanan son of Jair killed Lahmi, the brother of Goliath the Gittite; his spear had a shaft like a weaver's beam.

We can see at once where the King James translators got the idea that Elhanan had killed not Goliath, but his brother. It is written right in the text of Chronicles. If the version of Samuel from which the Chronicler copied originally had *the brother of*, the slightest slip of the pen could have changed it into what we read in Samuel today: אחי ("the brother of") > את (a grammatical marker). So the King James committee must have reasoned as follows: *The statement in Samuel contradicts everything we know from the rest of the story; the statement in Chronicles resolves the difficulty. The Chronicles version must be correct, while the Samuel version is misleading.* They added the words *the brother of* in italics—not, this time, to have the verse make grammatical sense, but to have it make historical sense.

We too might assume that Chronicles is correct, and that the similar appearance of the two Hebrew words means that the Samuel version is the result of a copyist's error. But that may not be the only possible explanation for why the Samuel verse and the Chronicles verse say that Elhanan killed different people. After all, there are a few other differences between the two verses. We know that the Chronicler wrote centuries later and used a version of Samuel as one of his sources. He made a number of changes in this verse to correct things that didn't seem to fit. Perhaps he arbitrarily invented "Lahmi" as a brother for Goliath here because the Samuel verse made no historical sense to *him*. But his decision might have been wrong.

Two Views of David

If this were the only difference between Samuel and Chronicles, we wouldn't have that much to talk about. To err is human, the Samuel verse might actually be a scribal mistake, David really did kill Goliath—end of story. But this is not the only difference. Chronicles tells the story of David quite differently than do Samuel and Kings. Let's look at one difference between Samuel and Chronicles, a subtle one, that will open up the larger subject for us.

1 Chronicles 11:11 begins with the words "This is the list of David's warriors," and vv. 11–25 relate a number of anecdotes about the great heroes who served in David's army. The longest of these stories, and probably the most famous, tells how once, when the Philistines were occupying David's home town of Bethlehem, he felt a craving for some water from the cistern by the main gate there. (Water from anywhere but your home town always tastes a little bit funny.) Three of his men sneaked through the Philistine lines to bring him some of the water. David was so moved by their courage and devotion that he refused to drink the water, but instead poured it out onto the ground as a libation to God in recognition that they had risked their lives to bring it to him. The larger part of the chapter, though, beginning at v. 26 and extending to the end of the chapter (v. 47), is just a list of names, identified as "the valiant warriors." Of the forty-five or fifty warriors whose names are listed here, most are people we know nothing else about. But one, the first name in v. 41, is of particular interest to us. It is the name "Uriah the Hittite."

David and Bathsheba—and Uriah

The story of David and Goliath is probably the most well known of all the stories about David, but the story of David and Bathsheba must surely run a close second. The story, which is told in 2 Samuel 11, takes place at a time in David's career when he no longer led the army but stayed in the royal palace at Jerusalem while his warriors went out to battle. One such day, David was strolling on the roof of the palace when he spied a beautiful woman bathing. He found out who she was—the wife of Uriah, a soldier who was then on active duty—but nevertheless had her brought to the palace, slept with her, and got her pregnant.

David had Uriah recalled, ostensibly to report on conditions at the front, and then sent him home to sleep with his wife before returning, presumably so that Uriah would think the child was his; but Uriah would not do it: "The Ark and Israel and Judah are living in shelters, and my master Joab and my master's servants are camping in the open field. And I should go home and eat and drink and sleep with my wife? As sure as you live, I swear by your life I will not do this!" (v. 11). Eventually, David sent Uriah back to the front with a sealed note addressed to Joab, the commander in the field: "Place Uriah in the front lines, where the fighting is fiercest; then retreat and let him be killed" (v. 15). Uriah, ever the good scout, carried the note back to Joab and went to his death, never knowing that it was due not to the chances of battle, but to betrayal.

In the list of heroes of 1 Chronicles 11, Uriah's name does not stand out. It is simply mentioned in a long list of others. But this section of Chronicles, like 1 Chr. 20:5, is copied (with some alterations) from the "appendices" at the end of Samuel, specifically 2 Sam. 23:8–39. (The story of the three heroes who brought David water from Bethlehem is told here too.) One of the changes made by the Chronicler was to introduce the long list of names (with no exploits given) as "the valiant warriors." In 2 Samuel 23, the men on this list are identified as being "among the thirty," for the chapter is structured this way: first come David's three greatest warriors; then a second group of three who did not quite make it to the top; and then the thirty heroes who did not make it into "the three" or the second "three." Chronicles' list has another dozen and a half names on it after Uriah's. But in 2 Samuel 23 the very last name—*thirty-first* in the list of thirty—is that of Uriah the Hittite. To make sure we get the point, the last words in the chapter (v. 39) are these: "thirty-seven in all."

It doesn't take a degree in the higher mathematics to realize that $31 \neq 30$, and that $3 + 3 + 30 = 36$, not 37. So what is going on here? The answer is surprisingly simple, and simply surprising: This innocent-seeming appendix to the story of David was constructed to make sure that the glory of David's rise from shepherd to shepherd-king does not blind the reader to the less savory parts of David's biography. Yes, David had thirty great heroes, but one of them . . . had to be replaced.

Unlike the verse about Elhanan, which might possibly be explained as the result of errors in copying the text, this arrangement of names and numbers has to have been deliberate. Anything that altered it would garble the message and obscure the fact that Uriah was the odd man out. In fact, this is exactly what has happened in Chronicles—and not by mistake.

In Chronicles, Uriah is still thirty-first in the list of names, but the list is fifty percent longer, so he is buried somewhere in the middle of it. "The thirty" are still mentioned in one of the exploits (see 1 Chr. 11:25), but the former list of thirty has simply become "the valiant warriors," and the final total of thirty-seven of 2 Samuel 23, like an irritating stone in one's shoe, is simply thrown away. Like the purloined letter, Uriah in 1 Chronicles 11 is hidden in plain sight. Once again, the appendix to the book of Samuel is subtly puncturing David's balloon, and Chronicles is just as quietly eliminating the problem.

Who Was the Chronicler?

Why would the Chronicler make this kind of change? In fact, why write his book at all? To answer that question—which means trying to understand the motivations behind this unique historical voice—we must take a broader look at some of the things that distinguish Chronicles from its major source, Samuel and Samuel's companion volume Kings. As part of this broader look, let's first set them into the context of general Israelite history. What was happening in Israel when these books were written?

I have been saying all along that Chronicles came after Samuel and Kings, and even used them as its source. This is not merely an unthinking reflex from the fact that Samuel and Kings precede Chronicles in our modern Bibles. In fact, though many of the stories in Samuel and Kings are certainly old, some perhaps as old as the time of David himself, the two were edited together into a comprehensive history of Israel sometime in the late seventh century BCE, that is, just before the year 600;* Chronicles cannot be dated this exactly, but as a very rough guess the early fourth century BCE, that is, just after the year 400, will do fine. The passing of two hundred years would naturally cause a change in historical attitudes, but those two intervening centuries encompass something more. In between the earlier version of Israel's history in Samuel-Kings and the later one in Chronicles, a major discontinuity affected the Israelites and their land: the destruction of the Temple, exile to Babylonia, and return.

We will have much more to say later about this crucial event of biblical history. But for now, let's just consider what difference this political upheaval would have made in people's attitudes toward David. When the original history was edited, before the exile, Judah was a small but independent country. Most importantly, four centuries after David, one of his descendants was still sitting on its throne—a remarkable record when you realize that the kingdom of Israel, in the northern part of the country, had been ruled by kings from nine different families, one of them for as short a reign as seven days. After the exile, however, the situation was completely different. True, the "Judeans" were now back in their own land, but it was no longer the kingdom of Judah but a Persian province called Yehud, ruled by a Persian-appointed governor. There was no descendant of David's family on the throne and, by the Chronicler's time, no prospect of one.

In a situation like this, it probably did not do to have a history that told . . . well, the truth about David: that he was a human being like

---

* It was slightly updated shortly after the fall of Jerusalem in 586 BCE; see the end of this chapter.

the rest of us, who took credit for some things he didn't do and found that his human appetites, for life, for power, and for sex, got him into trouble that he hadn't planned on being in. The Chronicler did not want to show David the way Cromwell demanded that his portrait be painted, "warts and all." He wanted David with a halo.

It is worth spending a little bit more time with Chronicles, this history book that's hidden away at the back of the Jewish Bible. For one thing, it will tell us something about the Jews who lived during the period of Persian rule, a time of which we know relatively little. For another, as you might expect from seeing Chronicles turn David from a flesh-and-blood human being into a saint, it will give us some insight into how the religion of the Israelites began to change into the Judaism that we know today. We have spent a little bit of time looking at how the Chronicler treated David; now let's see what he says about Solomon.

Solomon and Hiram

Again, let's start with a relatively small example. We all know that what Solomon was famous for—besides his wisdom and his love affair with the Queen of Sheba—was building the Temple. However, not everyone remembers something else that the Bible clearly tells us—that he built it with the assistance of King Hiram of Tyre, a Phoenician. (Tyre is on the Mediterranean coast; you will find it in the southern part of Lebanon on today's maps.) The Phoenicians were not only skilled builders, which the Israelites were not, but they had an ample supply of "the cedars of Lebanon," the beautiful, fragrant, and sturdy wood out of which Solomon intended to build what he hoped would be a magnificent Temple to God.

Naturally, the Phoenicians were not interested in contributing to Solomon's Temple on a charitable basis; good lumber doesn't come cheap. It was all very businesslike. And in fact we read in 1 Kgs. 9:10–11, after Solomon has built the Temple and (next to it) a palace for himself,

---

[10] At the end of the 20 years it took Solomon to build the two buildings, the Temple of YHWH and the king's palace— [11] once

King Hiram of Tyre had supplied Solomon with all the cedar, cypress, and gold he wanted—King Solomon gave Hiram twenty cities in the land of Galilee.

This is how kings like to be paid off. Solomon gave Hiram some of the territory under his control. Partly, of course, this presumes that this region of the Galilee was not considered part of the "heartland" of the country in those days. But the power of countries, and of kings, is reflected in the territories they control. The fact that Solomon gave some of his territory to Hiram suggests that Hiram was politically the more powerful of the two kings.

Now let's look at 2 Chr. 8:1–2, where this is retold:

¹ At the end of the 20 years it took Solomon to build the two buildings (the Temple of YHWH and his own palace)— ² Now, Solomon built the cities that Huram had given to Solomon and settled Israelites there.

Huram—this is one of the cases where the Chronicler uses a slightly different version of a name than does Kings—gave the cities to Solomon! This is just exactly the opposite of the earlier description. We can tell from v. 1 that the Chronicler was looking at what was said in Kings. If he was looking at a version anything like the one we have today, we have to assume that he did not like what he saw there. Solomon gave away part of the Land of Israel? There must be some mistake—it must be that Hiram gave the cities to Solomon, and not the reverse. The suspicious repetition in Kings of "twenty" years and "twenty" cities may have helped to persuade the Chronicler that the report about the twenty cities was a mistake. Notice that in his own report he left the number of cities out.

Two Views of Solomon

This reassessment of the report in Kings about Solomon giving up twenty cities is a very small example—two verses, and a political fact with no reported consequences. Now let's look at a much larger political issue, one that will give us more insight into the Chronicler's attitudes. How is it that Solomon became king in the first place?

He was not, after all, David's eldest son, and not even the first son of his mother, Bathsheba. David's first son by Bathsheba, as we saw in chapter 1, died within a week of his birth (a remarkable and touching story that is told in 2 Samuel 12), but David had already had a number of wives long before he became king, and so Solomon naturally had some older brothers. One of them, Amnon, raped his half sister Tamar and was eventually murdered for doing so by her full brother, Absalom. Later Absalom rebelled against his father and, after ruling briefly, was slain in battle by David's army commander, Joab, and his men, and David regained the throne. Even so, at the beginning of the book of Kings there is still at least one more brother older than Solomon, and this brother, Adonijah, fully assumes that he is to be king after his father.

As Kings opens, David is on his deathbed, so old that a beautiful young woman must sleep with him to keep him warm, and so weak and frail that, the text tells us, he did not have sex with her (1 Kgs. 1:1–4). Meanwhile, Adonijah, anticipating his father's imminent death, has taken the opportunity to stage what amounts to his own coronation. Bathsheba, Solomon's mother, confers with Nathan the prophet, on whom David had always relied for the transmission of God's word. Nathan thinks Adonijah's move has put Bathsheba and her son in mortal danger. He gives her the following advice (1 Kgs. 1:13–14):

> **13** Go in to King David and tell him, "My lord the king, did you not swear to your maidservant, 'Your son Solomon shall rule after me, and he will sit on my throne'? Why has Adonijah become king?" **14** While you are still in there speaking with the king, I will follow you in and confirm your words.

This is exactly what she does. The two of them convince the dying David that he indeed made this promise, and he fulfills it by declaring

Solomon to be the new king. There is a lovely literary touch at the very end of this episode, where Bathsheba, having ensured her safety after the king's imminent death, thanks him and parts from him with the phrase, "May my lord King David live forever!" (1 Kgs. 1:31).

The "Godfather"

This is not quite the end of David, however, nor of a biblical picture of him that is quite unlike the image most of us have of the handsome and beloved king. For in 1 Kings 2, David gives Solomon, who has by now become king, some final words of advice. David does, indeed, tell his son to follow God's ways and to keep the laws of Moses, but this is a mere prelude to some more practical details of David's own unfinished business. "You know what Joab did," he tells Solomon. (He had assassinated Abner and Amasa, two former enemies of David who subsequently became Joab's rivals for military power.) "Act according to your wisdom—do not let his gray hair go down to the grave in peace" (1 Kgs. 2:6).

Next, David makes sure that Solomon will always take care of the sons of Barzilai, who sheltered him when he fled for his life during Absalom's revolt, and then remembers another old enemy. It is Shimei son of Gera, a partisan and kinsman of Saul who cursed David and threw stones at him as he fled Absalom. When David returned in triumph as king after Absalom was slain and his revolt was defeated, Shimei begged David's pardon for his offense, and David swore to him, "You shall not die" (2 Sam. 19:24). Now, however, we learn that David has always considered Shimei a bit of unfinished business. He literally tells Solomon, "You know what to do to him" (1 Kgs. 2:9). This is not what we usually think of when we think of King David, but in the last glimpse that the book of Kings gives us of him, he is not as concerned with his God or his people as he is with settling old scores.

Needless to say, this makes David look more like the patriarch of a mob family than a saint. So, as by now you can imagine, Chronicles tells this story quite differently. First of all, rather than being told as the beginning of Solomon's story (as it is in 1 Kings 1–2), David's death is told as the end of his own story (1 Chronicles 29). Secondly, by contrast with the Kings account, most of which takes place in hidden rooms in the palace with only Solomon and his mother Bathsheba present, in Chronicles David is on stage for most of the chapter, giving a grandiloquent address to the people, of the kind one finds in Thucydides. Here is how 1 Chr. 29:23–24 describes Solomon's accession to the throne:

> 23 Solomon successfully assumed the throne of YHWH as king in place of his father David, and all Israel obeyed him. 24 All of the officials and all of the warriors and even all of King David's sons swore loyalty to Solomon the king.

For Chronicles, Adonijah's preemptive attempt to claim the crown simply never happened. (Kings, on the other hand, continues the story, telling how Adonijah was finally put to death, eliminating the last threat to Solomon's throne—at least from one of his own brothers.) Instead, the throne was passed to Solomon peacefully, publicly, and with the kind of pomp and circumstance befitting a great and powerful king.

The bare bones of the facts are the same—Solomon succeeds his father David as king of Israel—but the voice of the Chronicler tells quite a different story than does that of the author or editor of Kings. We know that the Chronicler used Kings as one of his historical sources, but the backroom arrangements that give Solomon the throne in Kings are simply omitted in the Chronicler's retelling of the story.

Solomon's Temple—or David's?

Let's look at a few more of the differences between these two historical sources, to see what Chronicles was really interested in and why the changes in the story mattered so much. We can focus on these by asking another historical question: Who built the Temple?

No tricks this time. This is not a question with a surprise answer, like the question "Who killed Goliath?" True, the building of the Temple was, both historically and practically, a more complicated event than the killing of Goliath. For example, the Temple in Jerusalem may well have been designed by a Phoenician architect; archaeologists have discovered other temples with similar designs from Syria and from pre-Israelite Canaan, both Phoenician-influenced places. The people who actually did the physical labor involved came both from Israel and from outside; see 1 Kings 5, which gives us a tantalizing glimpse at what must have been a major political and social transformation. But the Bible attributes the building of the Temple to a single man: Solomon. There is no biblical text that suggests anything different. Here, then, is a case where the Bible speaks with a unanimous voice: Solomon built the Temple. But again, Kings and Chronicles tell the story differently.

In 1 Kings 5, early in his reign, Solomon sends a message to Hiram to set up the subcontracting arrangements (vv. 17–19 in Jewish Bibles, 3–5 in Christian ones). He explains the building of the Temple to Hiram in this way:

> **17** You know that my father David could not build a house for the name of YHWH his God because of the fighting all around him, until YHWH put them under the soles of my/his* feet. **18** Now my God YHWH has given me respite all around, with no adversary and no adversity. **19** So I have decided to build a house for the name of YHWH my God, just as YHWH said to my father David: "Your son, whom I will put on your throne after you—he shall build the house for My name."

This, of course, is well after David's death in 1 Kings 2, and already a number of chapters into the story of Solomon. The Chronicles passage that matches it, however, comes in 1 Chr. 22:7–10, long before the story

---

* "His" is preserved in the written text, "my" in the reading instructions—an alteration between two almost identical letters.

of Solomon's reign has begun, when David is still alive, still king, and still in the midst of his vigor:

> ⁷ David said to Solomon, "Son, it has always been my dream to build a house for the name of YHWH my God. ⁸ But the word of YHWH came to me: 'You have spilled blood in excess and waged great wars; you shall not build a house for My name, for you have spilled much blood on the ground before Me. ⁹ Now, a son will be born to you, who will be a man of rest. I will give him respite from all the enemies around him, for Solomon [*shelomoh*] will be his name and I will grant Israel peace [*shalom*] and quiet in his days. ¹⁰ He shall build a house for My name. He will become My son, and I will become his father, and I will establish his royal throne over Israel forever.'"

This is slightly, but significantly, different from the way the story is told in Kings. According to the older story, David indeed wanted to build the Temple, but the pressure of war right until the end of his reign simply made it impossible to for him to devote the time, attention, energy, and money necessary for the task. Chronicles focuses on the mention of war in this passage and turns it from a practical to a moral explanation: God would not let David build the Temple because he had blood on his hands. This is not, to be sure, the blood of Uriah, for (as we have already seen) Chronicles has erased this crime from the historical record. We may be sure that, for the Chronicler, all the blood that David shed in wartime, defending Israel against its enemies, was shed legitimately. Nonetheless, the blood of killing was a stain that could not be allowed to come into contact with anything holy. This kind of man could not build the Temple.

What does this say about the Chronicler's attitude toward David and Solomon? Is this a change in Solomon's favor and at David's expense? Despite the way it might sound on first reading, this is another retelling that makes David look better. After all, if David never built the Temple because he had other things to do and never got around to it, this would not reflect well on him. If, despite his heroism and sacrifice, he was prevented by God from building the Temple, to keep the taint of war from contaminating this holy spot, his failure to build the Temple is legitimate and even praiseworthy. It almost puts him in the tragic position of Moses, who wanted to lead the Israelites into the land of Canaan that had been promised to their ancestors but was prevented by God from doing so. That task was left to his successor, Joshua, who for all his greatness never achieved the stature of Moses. Similarly, David wanted to build the Temple, but this supreme task of fulfillment was left to his son and successor, Solomon. Like Joshua, we may suspect, Solomon for all his achievements is intended to be a slightly lesser figure.

The Temple Project

A little bit of further attention to the way the building of the Temple is treated in both sources will give us some more evidence to guide our thinking on this question. Five chapters in Samuel and Kings discuss the Temple. In 2 Samuel 7, David tells Nathan that he wants to build a Temple for God, and God (in essence) replies, Who asked you? (This is the story to which David refers in the speech to Solomon we have just quoted.) Kings, in turn, has four chapters (1 Kings 5–8; in Christian Bibles, this section begins at 1 Kgs. 4:21) describing Solomon's initiation of the project and describing in detail the intricacies of the building, its actual construction, and its dedication.

Chronicles has essentially those same chapters about Solomon (divided differently to make six chapters, 2 Chronicles 2–7; beginning with 2 Chr. 2:2 in Christian Bibles); but to the one chapter about David (1 Chronicles 17), the Chronicler adds *eight* more chapters that concern David and the Temple (1 Chronicles 22–29). Even though he could not build the Temple himself, according to the Chronicler (and *only* according to him), David laid out all the instructions for what was to happen in the Temple after it was built: how, where, and when the various priests and Levites were to serve; the design of the building and its accoutrements; and so forth.

Without quoting Chronicles at inordinate length, we can still summarize this last point by taking a look at how the ceremonial beginning of the project—the groundbreaking—is described in both sources. First, 1 Kgs. 6:1, a solemn invocation of this historic juncture in Israelite history and Solomon's role in it:

¹ In the 480th year after the exodus of the Israelites from Egypt, in Solomon's fourth year over Israel, in the month of Ziv (that is, the second month), he built the House for YHWH.

And here is how 2 Chr. 3:1–2 reshapes this information:

¹ Solomon began to build the House of YHWH in Jerusalem, on Mount Moriah, at the place where [YHWH*] had appeared to David his father, which David had prepared at the threshing-floor of Ornan the Jebusite. [See 2 Samuel 24/1 Chronicles 21 for this story.] ² He began to build on the second day of the second month, in year four of his reign.

The reference to the exodus, which Kings uses to locate Solomon in the grand scheme of Israelite history, is gone, leaving the actual date for the beginning of construction—at some point a few years into Solomon's reign—somewhat anticlimactic.

There's a surprising reason for this. The Chronicler wants to emphasize a most important "fact": that the Israelites have inhabited the land continuously since the time of Jacob. According to 2 Chr. 36:20, even the exile to Babylonia applied only to the inhabitants of Jerusalem. For the Chronicler, Israelites were settled in the land even during the period of Egyptian slavery. (See, e.g., 1 Chr. 7:20–29, where Joseph's son Ephraim, instead of spending his entire life in Egypt, is settled in Canaan with children and grandchildren.) So removing the date of "the 480th year" is not a casual change; instead, it deliberately turns

---

* This word is missing in the Hebrew text, leaving it unclear; but the ancient Greek and Aramaic translations have it.

the spotlight away from the Israelite sojourn in Egypt. (We'll look at this surprising attitude of the Chronicler once more at the end of the chapter.)

Meanwhile, David is placed on center stage instead of Solomon. It was he who, by divine intervention, was shown where to put the Temple: on the very spot where Abraham, also at the instruction of God, had almost sacrificed his son Isaac. (In Gen. 22:2, Abraham is told to take Isaac to "one of the mountains" in "the land of Moriah.") The Kings text hints that the building of the Temple, for which Solomon is responsible, is in some way the culmination of Israelite history. But the Chronicler gives David himself an almost prophetic role in achieving this culmination. Solomon, it would appear, is just getting around (and in no hurry) to what is really, after all, David's own final achievement.

Sanitizing Solomon

There are some other indications of what the Chronicler thought about Solomon that have nothing to do with the Temple. One clue can be found by comparing the description of Solomon in 1 Kings 10 and 11 with that found in 2 Chronicles 9. First comes a description of Solomon's riches. 1 Kings 10:23 tells us, "King Solomon outdid all the other kings of the earth in wealth and in wisdom"; and the next two verses, 24 and 25, explain how the whole world sought him out because of his wisdom, bringing vast wealth into his coffers. Verses 26–29 go on to explain about Solomon's vast cavalry, suggesting not only riches but also military power. Then the Kings passage continues, in 1 Kgs. 11:1–8, with the words, "King Solomon loved many foreign women" (v. 1). The old song that went

> King Solomon, that wise old man
> He had a thousand wives
> He bought a lovely charabanc
> To take them all for drives

was no exaggeration, for Kings tells us, "He had seven hundred official wives and three hundred concubines" (1 Kgs. 11:3). The problem with these thousand women, however, in the eyes of 1 Kings 11, was not that they made Solomon's domestic life relatively complicated, but that they turned his heart away from God to the worship of foreign gods and idols:

> ⁴ In Solomon's old age, his wives turned his heart after other gods, and his heart was not wholly with YHWH his God as his father David's heart had been. ⁵ Solomon followed Ashtoreth, the god of the Sidonians, and Milcom, the abomination of the Ammonites. ⁶ Solomon did what was evil in YHWH's sight, and did not completely follow YHWH, like his father David.
> ⁷ Then Solomon built a high-place to Chemosh, the abomination of Moab, on the mount opposite Jerusalem, and to Molech, the abomination of the people of Ammon. ⁸ So he did for all his foreign wives who offered incense and sacrifices to their gods.

Most of the rest of chapter 11 describes, as a natural consequence of his apostasy, the various difficulties that plagued Solomon's rule, including both foreign wars and internal challenges to his power. Most significantly, this is where we encounter the story of Jeroboam and his unsuccessful rebellion against Solomon. After the failure of the revolt, Jeroboam fled to Egypt, but he was promised by the prophet Ahijah the Shilonite that God would rip the Northern Kingdom of Israel out of Solomon's grasp and give it to him. This is how the "United Monarchy" of David and Solomon was ultimately split into a Northern Kingdom called "Israel" and a Southern Kingdom called "Judah."

How does Chronicles treat this passage? If we begin with the "wealth" section of 1 Kgs. 10:23–25, we see that 2 Chr. 9:22–24 basically copies and repeats these three verses with only the most minor of changes. The "cavalry" section of 1 Kgs. 10:26–29 is also followed closely in 2 Chr. 9:25–28. (The differences are somewhat greater here, partly because Solomon's cavalry is also mentioned in two other places in the Bible, and Chronicles adds in some of that information.) But the section about the wives is completely missing from Chronicles, and so is the one about Jeroboam. In fact, Chronicles completely eliminates the first forty verses of 1 Kings 11, picking up the thread again only with v. 41:

> 1 KGS. 11:41 And the rest of Solomon's affairs, and all he did, and his wisdom—are they not written in the book of *The Chronicles of Solomon*?

> 2 CHR. 9:29 And the remainder of Solomon's affairs, both first and last, are they not written in *The Words of Nathan the Prophet*, *The Prophecy of Ahijah the Shilonite*, and *The Vision of Jedo the Seer about Jeroboam son of Nebat*?

Both stories then continue with the information that Solomon ruled for forty years and was buried in the grave of his father David.

The Rebellion against Solomon

The fact that Chronicles so closely matches the beginning and the ending of this section of Kings makes it obvious that, as we have often seen, the Chronicler had Kings in front of him when he wrote. The omissions, then, were deliberate, and tell us something about the Chronicler's attitude. First, the story of Jeroboam. Let's take a look at the core of what the Chronicler omitted (1 Kgs. 11:26–40):

> ²⁶ Jeroboam son of Nebat, an Ephraimite from Zeredah (his mother was Zeruah, a widow woman) was one of Solomon's officials; he rebelled against the king. ²⁷ This was the way in which he rebelled against the king: Solomon built the Millo [part of Jerusalem] and closed up the breach in the city of his father David. ²⁸ Jeroboam was an able fellow, and Solomon saw that the young man was someone who could get the job done. So Solomon assigned him to all the forced labor of the House of Joseph [the northern part of the kingdom].

²⁹ Just at that time, Jeroboam was going out of Jerusalem, and Ahijah the Shilonite encountered him on the way; he was wearing a new garment, and the two of them were alone in the countryside. ³⁰ Ahijah grabbed the new garment that was upon him, and tore it into twelve pieces. ³¹ He said to Jeroboam, "Take ten of these pieces, for thus says YHWH God of Israel: 'I hereby tear the kingdom from the hand of Solomon and give it to you—the ten tribes. ³² But the one tribe shall remain with him, for the sake of My servant David, and for the sake of Jerusalem, the city which I have chosen from all the tribes of Israel. ³³ For they have abandoned Me and prostrated themselves to Ashtoreth, goddess of the Sidonians, to Chemosh, god of Moab, and to Milcom, god of the Ammonites. They have not followed My ways, doing what I consider right, My laws and rules, like his father David. ³⁴ I will not take the whole kingdom from his hand, but will leave him as ruler all the days of his life for the sake of My servant David, whom I chose, who kept My commandments and My laws. ³⁵ But I will take the kingship from the hand of his son and I will give it to you—the ten tribes. ³⁶ To his son I will give a single tribe, so that there will remain a "lamp" for David forever before Me in Jerusalem, the city where I have chosen to place My name. ³⁷ You will I take, and you shall rule over all that your heart desires; you shall be king over Israel. ³⁸ If you heed all that I command you, follow My ways, and do what I think right, keeping My laws and commandments as did My servant David, then I shall be with you and build you a faithful house as I built for My servant David. I shall give Israel to you. ³⁹ And I shall humble the seed of David for this; but not forever.'"

⁴⁰ Solomon tried to have Jeroboam killed, so Jeroboam fled to Egypt, to King Shishak of Egypt, and he stayed in Egypt until the death of Solomon.

We have already seen that the Chronicler is happy to praise Solomon for his wealth and his military might, but quietly eliminates the section in Kings that describes the apostasy to which his foreign wives led him. Since Jeroboam's accession to the throne of Israel is presented as a direct consequence of Solomon's disloyalty to the God of Israel, it is only natural that the Chronicler should omit it, too. Solomon was not (in the Chronicler's eyes) the acme of holiness that his father David was, but he certainly was the one who built God's Temple. So anything negative is simply eliminated from his portrayal. He was rich, wise, and mighty—but not lascivious or sinful.

The Kingdom Splits in Two

There is still another reason for the elimination of the story of Jeroboam, however. To understand it, we must remember when the two different histories of Israel were put together. I have said that the older history, that told in Samuel and Kings, was put together roughly around the year 600 BCE, and Chronicles roughly around 400 BCE. In between, of course, was the exile to Babylon. But the Northern Kingdom—the ten tribes given by God to Jeroboam in 1 Kings 11—had been exiled long before, in 722 BCE, and these exiles had never returned. (They are the famous "Ten Lost Tribes," the "ten tribes" of 1 Kgs. 11:31 and 35.) This was close enough to the time when Kings was written that it required an explanation.

How could God have done this to his people? Most likely, the Southern Kingdom had been flooded with refugees from the Assyrian destruction of the north. So the history of the separate Northern Kingdom of Israel, its creation and its destruction, was still a live issue in the year 600. By the Chronicler's time, however, it seemed that the mainstream of Israelite history flowed through Jerusalem. The Northern Kingdom was a dead end, a branch that had gotten lopped off Israel's family tree. Not only this section about Jeroboam but all the sections about the north in the book of Kings—which gives a fairly complete history of the Northern Kingdom—are simply missing from the book of Chronicles, even though telling the history of Israel without mentioning the Northern Kingdom is like telling American history without mentioning the Civil War.

Kings and Deuteronomy

We have seen that part of the Chronicler's motivation was theological. He wanted to sanitize the history of David and Solomon. But there are theological considerations at work in the earlier Kings history as well, and the story of Jeroboam will help us see some of them. We have spoken until now of Chronicles and Kings as two distinct historical voices, but if you read the story of Jeroboam in 1 Kings 11, it is quite easy to hear two distinct voices even in that single text.

The first and last paragraphs of the story (vv. 26–28 and 40) are strictly political in nature. (The paragraphing is also part of the traditional biblical text, as passed down to us by the Masoretes.) They tell of a competent and charismatic underling—a David to Solomon's Saul, playing the same role in Solomon's kingship that David played in Saul's—who rebelled against the king, failed to overthrow him, and fled to Egypt to wait for the king's death. (Chapter 12 of 1 Kings will explain that finally, under Solomon's son Rehoboam, the rebellion was successful.) But the intervening paragraph, vv. 29–39, gives a *theological* explanation for Jeroboam's rebellion.

For the two hundred years of its existence, the Northern Kingdom of Israel was by far the larger, richer, and more important of the two kingdoms. Little Judah and Jerusalem, where David's descendants ruled, were a backwater by comparison. This is easy enough to explain politically, but from a religious perspective in which David is central, it was harder to understand. The relative quietness of the political voice in 1 Kings 11, and the relative loudness of the religious voice, show us that this version of the history, too, like Chronicles, was religiously motivated.

1 Kings 11 contains two clues that will lead us to the source of this religious motivation. The first clue is the expression that I have translated "laws and rules" in 1 Kgs. 11:33. This expression is characteristic of the book of Deuteronomy. Half of all the occurrences of this phrase in the entire Bible are concentrated in Deuteronomy, and (as we shall see in chapter 4) the only other place where its use is prominent is a section heavily influenced by Deuteronomy. The second clue to the

religious motivation of this history also comes from Deuteronomy, and again we are pointed to it by a double voice. We said earlier that the "cavalry" section of 1 Kgs. 10:26–29 is copied in 2 Chr. 9:25–28, but not as closely as was the "wealth" section. That is because 1 Kgs. 10:26–29, which specifies that Solomon has "1,400 chariots and 12,000 horses," is itself quoting from earlier in the book of Kings: "King Solomon had 40,000 stalls of horses for his chariots, and 12,000 horsemen" (1 Kgs. 5:6). This part of Kings too is copied more or less closely in Chronicles (2 Chr. 1:14); all four mentions of the cavalry have similar variations in the number of horses (forty thousand, four thousand, a thousand four hundred) and all mention the twelve thousand horsemen. We can understand why the Chronicler mentions the cavalry twice. He was copying large sections of his history from Kings, which had already mentioned it twice. But why does Kings do so?

All the King's Horses

The answer again takes us to Deuteronomy, this time to Deut. 17:14–20, a section known as "the law of the king." Deuteronomy, of course, is the final speech of Moses to the Israelites, just before he dies and they cross the Jordan to take possession of the land of Canaan. In this section, Moses tells the people he has led out of Egypt that, if they want to have a king once they enter the land, they may do so. But the king will have to follow certain rules. Let's look at three of them in particular:

> **16** But he must not keep many horses, and he must not bring the people back to Egypt to get more horses, for YHWH has already told you, "You shall never more go back this way again." **17** And he shall not have many wives, and his heart shall not turn away [from God], nor shall he have too much silver and gold.

The special restrictive rules on the king, then, as put forward in Deuteronomy, are these: not too many horses, not too many wives, not too much money.

Remind you of anyone? According to 1 Kings 10–11, Solomon had more money than anyone else in the entire world, with horses and wives to match. The version in Chronicles, which only tells us about his money and his horses, sounds very positive. Read innocently, these two sections in Kings also sound positive; then you turn the page and read that Solomon also had a lot of women, foreign women at that, who turned his thoughts away from God so that he began to worship their foreign gods. But the historical voice in Kings is expecting the reader to recognize the combination of money, horses, and women, and to realize that all three are things that, according to God's law, a king is not supposed to accumulate.

Just as the political voice telling about Jeroboam in 1 Kings 11 is interrupted by a Deuteronomy-accented voice with a theological explanation of the (ostensibly political) splitting of Solomon's kingdom into two separate countries, so too the boastful voice that tells about Solomon's chariotry in 1 Kings 5 is echoed in 1 Kings 10–11 by a Deuteronomy-accented voice telling us the same information in a way calculated to *undermine* Solomon's greatness. As with his father David, in the earlier version of Israelite history (unlike the later version in Chronicles), the grand triumphal melody of Solomon's life has some disturbing chords underlying it.

Passover and Two Kings

Let's look at one more aspect of Chronicles, for a final comparison with Kings that will again lead us back to Deuteronomy—this time, in a way that will show us the probable origin of the book of Kings. We begin with a section from the Chronicler's history of King Hezekiah (2 Chr. 29–32):

> 2 CHR. 30:1 Hezekiah sent to all Israel and Judah, and wrote letters also to Ephraim and Manasseh, to come to the House of YHWH in Jerusalem to observe a Passover to YHWH, God of Israel. . . .
> 21 The Israelites who were in Jerusalem observed the Feast of Unleavened Bread for seven days, with great joy. The Levites and

priests were praising YHWH, day by day, with loud music to YHWH. ²² Hezekiah spoke encouragingly to the Levites, who used their skill well for YHWH. They [the Israelites] ate the feast for seven days, sacrificing offerings of well-being and confessing to YHWH, the God of their ancestors.

²³ The whole assembly decided to observe seven more days, and they observed seven days of joy. ²⁴ For Hezekiah king of Judah had contributed 1,000 cattle and 7,000 sheep to the assembly; the officials had contributed 1,000 cattle and 10,000 sheep to the assembly; and many priests consecrated themselves. ²⁵ The whole assembly of Judah rejoiced, along with the priests, the Levites, and all who came from Israel, as well as the resident aliens who came from the land of Israel and were living in Judah. ²⁶ There was great joy in Jerusalem, for since the days of Solomon son of David, king of Israel, there had been nothing like this in Jerusalem.

Chronicles is telling us that late in the eighth century BCE, for the first time since the days of Solomon, there was a mass celebration of Passover in Jerusalem—an unforgettable experience.

If we look in the story of Hezekiah as told in Kings, we will not find any such celebration. So this is not a case where the Chronicler copied and subtly changed the version of the story told in the earlier history. Instead, he seems to have copied an *idea* from the earlier story—and moved it from one king to another. For we do find something comparable to this celebration in 2 Kgs. 23:22–23, in the story of the reign of Josiah, who lived a century *after* Hezekiah:

²² Nothing like this Passover had been observed in the days of the judges who ruled Israel, or all the days of the kings of Israel and the kings of Judah, ²³ until in the eighteenth year of King Josiah there was observed this Passover to YHWH in Jerusalem.

Not only had nothing of the kind happened during the reign of Hezekiah—David and Solomon didn't do it either, nor had the "judges" who had preceded them as rulers of Israel after Joshua's death. It was Moses, Joshua, and then . . . Josiah!

We are not told by the Chronicler what prompted Hezekiah's Passover. But Kings does tell us what prompted Josiah's: "The king commanded all the people, 'Observe a Passover to YHWH your God, as is written in this Book of the Covenant'" (2 Kgs. 23:21). The "Book of the Covenant" that prompted Josiah's Passover was a scroll (not literally a bound book as we have today) that had been found in the Temple. The Temple had fallen into disrepair and Josiah, as a good king, arranged for it to be rehabbed. But in the course of the job, the workmen found a scroll—a scroll described as a "book of the Torah" and authenticated as such by Huldah the prophetess. Naturally, this threw the kingdom into an uproar. You can read the entire remarkable story in 2 Kgs. 22–23. We will take another look at it in chapter 3.

We tend to assume, as the legends of later tradition recount, that Moses gave the Israelites the entire book that we now call "the Torah" or "the Pentateuch," that is, the first five books of our current Bibles, and that we have had them ever since. The Bible itself, though, as we saw in the introduction, does not say this. Here in the book of Kings, in fact, the Bible tells quite a different story. According to this story, something called "Torah" appeared, as if for the first time, in the reign of King Josiah. Again, as by now we might expect, there is a telltale clue leading us to Deuteronomy: "YHWH your God" is a phrase that is particularly characteristic of that book. Most scholars today believe that the document found in the Temple during Josiah's reign was some form of what today we call the book of Deuteronomy.

The Deuteronomistic History

It is quite reasonable, then, to take Josiah at his word (as reported in Kings) and to think that the discovery of this scroll is, indeed, what prompted him to lead the people in an observance of a Passover unlike any that had happened since the days of Moses and Joshua. It is also reasonable to suspect that it was the discovery of this scroll that prompted the theological voice that we heard explaining Jeroboam's revolt in 1 Kings 11. No doubt there were historical records, as well as legends and stories, that went back much earlier; but the kind of history that we have now in the books of Joshua, Judges, Samuel, and Kings—a history that focuses primarily on the *theological* ramifications of the political and military history of Israel—seems to have first been put together during the reign of King Josiah, and probably as a response to finding the book we now call Deuteronomy. Scholars therefore call these four books "the Deuteronomistic History" and their editor (and partial author) "the Deuteronomistic Historian."

What Makes a History "Deuteronomistic"?

Several factors in addition to the finding of the scroll in the Temple connect the history of Joshua–Kings with the book of Deuteronomy. First, Joshua–Kings makes heavy use of words and phrases that are particularly characteristic of Deuteronomy's quite distinctive style. We have already mentioned the phrase "YHWH your God." Although it sounds as if it might be found on any page of the Bible, it actually occurs in Deuteronomy far out of proportion to its use elsewhere (80 percent of all occurrences of the phrase anywhere in the Bible)—and that usage is continued in Joshua–Kings. Similarly, many more of Deuteronomy's characteristic phrases, like "as YHWH has spoken" and "to walk in the ways" of YHWH, are regularly used also in the Joshua–Kings history.

Second, every king is evaluated, when his reign is introduced, as to whether he properly supported worship of God in, and *only* in, the Jerusalem Temple. As we will see in chapter 3, this is a key element in the religious outlook of Deuteronomy. Exactly this is illustrated in Josiah's response to the finding of the scroll: "He brought in all the priests from the cities of Judah and profaned the high-places where the priests had burned sacrifices, from Geba to Beersheba" (2 Kgs. 23:8).

True, Josiah attacks idolatry (see vv. 4–7 and 10–14), but he also destroys *all* the shrines that are outside Jerusalem and relocates their priests to Jerusalem. Moreover, he is careful to destroy the rival Temple to YHWH that Jeroboam had built in Bethel with the express purpose—according to the Deuteronomistic History (see 1 Kgs. 12:26–29)—of wooing the Israelites away from Jerusalem and the Davidic dynasty: "The altar in Bethel, too, the high-place which Jeroboam son of Nebat had made with which he caused Israel to sin—that altar, too, and that high-place, [Josiah] pulled down" (2 Kgs. 23:15).

The Deuteronomistic Historian's View of History

We have seen that the Deuteronomistic Historian rated each Israelite and Judean king on the basis of loyalty to YHWH, Israel's God. Anything that affected the Temple, or that involved the relationship between the two kingdoms which (in the Deuteronomistic view) ought to have been united under Davidic rule, was important and deserved to be told in detail. Other details of history were of less importance and could be dismissed in a sentence or (for all we know) completely omitted. For example, 2 Kgs. 12:21 (v. 20 in Christian Bibles) tells us that King Jehoash of Judah was assassinated in a palace conspiracy. The next verse begins with the names of the two assassins, but that is absolutely all we are told about this event—momentous by the standards of political history. By contrast, vv. 5–17 (4–16 in Christian Bibles) earlier in the same chapter tell in great detail how repairs to the Temple were funded during Jehoash's reign.

Before the time of the kings, it is the Israelite people as a whole that is judged. And the Deuteronomistic Historian makes clear that it is loyalty to YHWH that determines the ups and downs of Israel's political history. The book of Judges, which describes Israelite history from the death of Joshua until shortly before the establishment of the kingship, follows this pattern over and over again. For example, Judges 3 tells the exciting story of how Ehud, a left-handed Israelite hero, assassinates the oppressive King Eglon of Moab and leads the Israelites in a successful battle for independence against the demoralized Moabite army. But the story is presented within a framework that demonstrates that YHWH is manipulating the historical situation as a response to Israel's behavior:

¹² Israel continued to do what was evil in YHWH's sight, and He strengthened King Eglon of Moab against them—for they had done what was evil in YHWH's sight.... [Moab oppresses Israel for 18 years.] ¹⁵ Then the Israelites cried out to YHWH, and He raised up a savior for them: Ehud son of Gera, the Benjaminite.... [Eglon is killed and the battle is fought and won.] ³⁰ Moab submitted to the hand of Israel on that day, and the land was quiet for 80 years.

Over and over again, history in the book of Judges is told in stories with just this kind of "once upon a time . . . happily ever after" setting. The pattern is predictable: Israel sins against YHWH; he permits a foreign country to dominate them; they cry out to him; he raises up a "savior" for them who defeats the enemy; and "the land is quiet"—that is peaceful and free of foreign interference—for twenty, forty, or eighty years. (See Judg. 2:11–23, where the Deuteronomistic Historian establishes the pattern of the book.) The Biblical Hebrew word customarily translated "savior" (and yes, this is the same word that underlies the name "Jesus") implies nothing more than a leader who brings military victory. Thus the NJPS translation of Judg. 3:15, putting the text in contemporary language, uses the English word "champion."

The Centrality of the Temple

This brief look at the two major historical voices in the Bible has shown us one thing they had in common. The Temple was central to both—but in very different ways, ways that help show us the essential nature of each of them. One easy method of demonstrating this is by experiment. Open a Bible and hold up the pages of the books of Chronicles; then separate the Temple chapters (1 Chronicles 22–2 Chronicles 7). You will find that you are holding a substantial chunk that appears right in the middle of the Chronicler's history. Now do the same for the Deuteronomistic History. First grab the books from Joshua through 2 Kings, and then separate out 1 Kgs 5–8. You will find yourself with just a few pages, well into the second half of a much longer story.

The Temple is just as central for the historian of Joshua–Kings as it is for the Chronicler, but in two different ways. First, it is central religiously, for it is the only legitimate option for any Israelite who wishes to make offerings to YHWH. Read the remarkable prayer of King Solomon in 1 Kings 8, and you will see that even prayer is centered around the Temple, which works almost like a radio antenna, not broadcasting but receiving the prayers of the Israelites wherever they might be. In fact, according to v. 48, the Temple's power to receive prayer works even for those outside the Land of Israel—as long as they pray in the direction of Israel, Jerusalem, and the Temple.

Why would this be important? We have said that the impetus for writing this history came during the reign of King Josiah. But the history was apparently not finished then, or else it was finished and reworked later, for (like Solomon's prayer) it ends with a scene of exile:

> 2 KGS. 25:27 In the 37th year of the exile of King Jehoiachin of Judah, on the 27th day of the 12th month, King Evil-Merodach of Babylonia, in the year of his accession to the throne, raised the head of King Jehoiachin of Judah from prison. ²⁸ He spoke kindly to him, and gave him a throne higher than the thrones of the other kings who were with him in Babylon. ²⁹ He changed [Jehoiachin's] prison clothes and [Jehoiachin] ate regularly before him all the days of his life. ³⁰ His meals were given to him regularly from the king—a daily allotment—all the days of his life.

This marks the second way in which the Temple is central in this telling of Israel's history. For, as you may remember, according to Kings the Temple was founded on a precise date—exactly 480 years after the Israelites left Egypt. A careful accounting of the chronology of Kings suggests that the editor who included this date thought that the return from exile took place exactly 480 years later—placing the founding of the Temple exactly in the middle of the history of the

Israelites in their own land, in between the years of slavery in Egypt to the west and their years of exile in Babylonia to the east.

Chronicles, we saw, removed this date. For the Chronicler, the Temple's centrality lay in its place in Israelite life. The Chronicler has so little interest in the larger story of Israelite history, and its possible meaning, that all of Israelite history up until David is covered in just nine chapters—and these chapters do not really even tell the history, they merely outline it with lists of names. Thus, the Chronicler sums up the first nine chapters of Genesis, with its familiar stories of creation, the Garden of Eden, Cain's killing of Abel, and the flood, in just twelve words:

1 CHR. 1:1 Adam, Seth, Enosh. ² Kenan, Mahalalel, Jared. ³ Enoch, Methuselah, Lamech. ⁴ Noah, Shem, Ham, and Japheth.

The Chronicler is so far from locating the center of Israel's history between the extremes of slavery and exile that he barely notices these events. The exile to Babylonia lasts a mere two verses (2 Chr. 36:20–21). As for Israel's years of slavery in Egypt, one could read Chronicles and barely realize that they had happened at all. The exodus is mentioned only once in Chronicles, in 2 Chr. 20:10, when King Jehoshaphat offhandedly mentions the time when Israel "came from" Egypt. In fact, as we have seen, one place in the first nine chapters where the Chronicler does tell a little snippet of a story, it seems to deny that the Israelites were ever in Egypt at all! 1 Chronicles 7:20–24 places Joseph's son Ephraim, and his sons, squarely in the Land of Israel, though Genesis and Exodus make clear that Ephraim and his sons were born, lived out their lives, and died in Egypt.

The "Priestly" History

There is one more way in which the Temple is central for the Chronicler. It seems to be his home base, the center of his own community—the world in which he is most comfortable. We saw a hint of this earlier in our discussion, when we looked at the two remarkable Passover celebrations. Just as the story of Josiah's Passover in Kings pointed us to the book of Deuteronomy, the story of Hezekiah's Passover in Chronicles will point us to another biblical voice too. In the case of Josiah's Passover, he is the only official figure involved in the celebrations. But the Chronicler's comparable story brings into clear focus the involvement of the priests and the Levites. Just as Kings is oriented to the theology of Deuteronomy, it seems plausible that one source of the Chronicler's view is the book of Leviticus and the other writings in the Torah that describe the role of those who served in the Temple.

In this chapter, we've seen that the Bible does not recount Israelite history from a single, objective point of view. Instead, the two long historical works in the Bible—Joshua through Kings on the one hand, and Chronicles on the other—understand Israelite history from particular perspectives. The more you learn to distinguish the different biblical voices, the more you will begin to understand what's behind any particular statement of "fact" about Israel's history in the Bible.

When we turn from Kings and Chronicles to the Torah, though, we leave the explicitly historical voices and must begin to listen for the original, theological voices that guided the Deuteronomistic Historian and the Chronicler. These theological voices will be the subject of our next chapter.

— 3 —
Theological Voices

It ought to be no surprise to anyone that there are "theological voices" throughout the Bible. We have already seen, in chapter 1, the argument between Jeremiah and the Judeans who fled to Egypt. Jeremiah claimed that all the disasters that had overtaken Judah were due to their abandonment of YHWH, while the refugees insisted that the true cause was their abandonment of the Queen of Heaven and concentration on the exclusive worship of YHWH—two exactly contradictory arguments about the nature of the Israelites' relationship with the divine powers.

In this case, both arguments are given to us by a single authorial voice that strongly suggests—though it doesn't state—that one of the explanations is right and the other is wrong. But in other cases, two differing and sometimes contradictory theological ideas are expressed that do not reflect a dramatic situation like the one with Jeremiah in Egypt but rather an apparent dispute among the various biblical writers about this or that idea. In this chapter, we'll be looking at two of the loudest and most distinctive theological voices of the Bible, Deuteronomy and the priestly writings. But first, to begin to sensitize our ears to theological questions, let's look at a theological dispute that's embedded in a single story in the Deuteronomistic History.

Regrets... God's Had a Few

Consider the following excerpt from 1 Samuel 15. Samuel has just told Saul that God has rejected him as king of Israel:

> 1 SAM. 15:24 Saul said to Samuel, "I have sinned, for I transgressed God's command and your words, because I feared the people and heeded them. 25 Now, I beg you, forgive my sin, come back with me, and let me bow down to YHWH." 26 Samuel said to Saul, "I will not come back with you, for you have rejected the word of YHWH, and YHWH has rejected you as king over Israel."
> 27 Samuel turned to go, and [Saul] seized the skirt of his robe, and it tore. 28 Samuel said to Saul, "YHWH has torn the kingship of Israel from you today, and given it to a better man than you. 29 Besides, the Eternal One of Israel does not lie or have regrets, for He is not a human being, to have regrets." 30 Saul said, "I have sinned; but please show me this respect before the elders of my people and before Israel, and come back with me. Then I will bow down before YHWH your God." 31 So Samuel came back with Saul, and Saul bowed down before YHWH.

One verse in this story is a little bit jarring—v. 29, where Samuel explains to Saul that God has no regrets, or, as some translate it, never changes his mind. In context, it might seem like a warning to Saul not to expect God to change the decision to take the kingship away from him; but Saul has said nothing about this. The truth, of course, is that God *has* changed his mind. For this whole episode began with Samuel receiving the following prophetic word from God: "I regret that I made Saul king, for he has turned aside from Me and not fulfilled My word" (1 Sam. 15:11). Again, the episode ends, in the last verse of the chapter, by summarizing the story this way: "YHWH regretted that He had made Saul king over Israel" (1 Sam. 15:35). How could Samuel say that God has no regrets when God himself admits that he has them? Was Samuel simply lying to Saul?

It seems more reasonable to assume that a later reader or editor of this story was uncomfortable with the idea that God might change his mind the way human beings do. Changing one's mind, after all, implies that the original decision—in this case, making Saul the king—was a mistake. God seems to be saying that he has changed his mind and will make a better choice this time: David. Samuel's remark implies that there was no mistake: Saul's ultimate replacement by David was the plan all along. It is easy to see that whether God changed his mind about making Saul king (as God says in vv. 11 and 35) or not (as Samuel says in v. 29) is not just a historical argument. It addresses a basic question about God's actions in history, and indeed about God's fundamental nature.

We saw in our last chapter that each of the two major historical works within the Bible, the Deuteronomistic History and Chronicles, not unexpectedly had a deeply religious understanding of Israelite history. We also saw that the two histories led us back to two different sections of the Pentateuch. When we begin to distinguish these two different voices in the Torah, we will get a clear picture of two different systems of belief that coexisted in ancient Israel. Eventually, we will see that a third voice attempts to harmonize the earlier two voices. It was this voice, apparently, that was responsible for blending the Deuteronomic and the priestly voices (along with the famous "J" source and another called "E") into the work that we know as the Five Books of Moses. But first, a bit of background.

The Documentary Hypothesis and the Sources of the Pentateuch

Most biblical research during the past century or more has operated under the assumptions of what scholars call the Documentary Hypothesis. To simplify somewhat, this theory suggests that the Pentateuch (that is, the first five books of the Bible, sometimes known as the Torah) was not written at a single time by a single author, but instead was based primarily on separate earlier sources.

One of these (D) is basically the same as today's book of Deuteronomy. A second is a source that is clearly very interested in everything to do with the priests who (among other duties) officiated at temple rituals; hence, for convenience, it is labeled P. A third is called J, because it refers to God by the personal name YHWH, which in older English was sometimes transliterated as Jehovah; a fourth, called E, simply uses the Hebrew word for "god," *elohim*.

Many scholars think that J and E came from different geographical areas: the J source, conveniently, from Jerusalem and the kingdom of Judah, and the E source from Ephraim, a name that is frequently used in the Bible for the Northern Kingdom of Israel. The J and E sources tell a lot of the well-known legendary kind of stories, like the one about Adam and Eve in the garden; P and D, though they also tell (or retell) some of the biblical stories, are more explicitly ideological. Some scholars prefer to think of the combination of J and E as a single source, since their voices are less distinctive than those of P and D. Others are confident they can hear even these more subtle differences.

In recent years, the Documentary Hypothesis has lost the near unanimity of support it once had among biblicists. This is partly due to a recognition that understanding the unified biblical text is at least as important as understanding the prehistory of the text (perhaps more so), and partly due to the fact that there are places in the Pentateuch (for example, the story of God's appearance at Mount Sinai) where it is not clear that the Documentary Hypothesis provides the best answer of how the text came to be. Nonetheless, the voices of P and D in particular are so distinctive that even someone who believes that God directly composed the Pentateuch must try to understand why it was written in these different "voices." For present purposes, the easiest assumption to make is that the different voices represent different writers, whose words were combined to make the text we have today.

The Pentateuch itself, after all, mentions sources for the writing of the Pentateuch. For example, Num. 21:14–15, in a discussion of the battles between Israel and the other nations in Canaan, says, "Therefore it is said in *The Book of the Wars of YHWH*," and offers an obscure geographical description. It's a citation—almost a footnote like what we use in modern books—which was copied out of a different book, which the writer identifies. By "book," of course, I don't mean a modern book with a spine and pages, since in biblical times these did not yet exist. *The Book of the Wars of YHWH* was presumably written on a scroll, but it was a book in the sense that it was an identifiable text with a particular title. So this is an earlier source of the Pentateuch that the Pentateuch itself identifies. The similar lines of poetry quoted just a bit further on, in vv. 27–30, are identified as something that "the bards" say, suggesting that there may well have been oral sources for the Pentateuch as well.

Some other written sources are also identified in the Pentateuch, at least one more of them by name. That one is in Genesis 5, following the story of Cain and Abel. It is the famous list of "begats" that describes the descendants of Adam all the way down to the flood. In Gen. 5:1, this list is identified as a "book" of its own, *The Book of the Descendants of Adam*. It is a genealogical record copied into the text at this point to bring us down to the next character of major significance for the story, Noah.

Other separate parts of the Pentateuch are also identified as written sources, even though they may not be given specific names. For example, in Deuteronomy 31, Moses is told to teach the people the poem "Give ear, O heavens," found in today's Bibles as Deut. 32:1–43. According to Deut. 31:22, however, he does not merely teach it to them, he writes it down. In fact, this is one of the few parts of the Pentateuch that the Pentateuch itself says was written down.

Another is found in Exodus 34, in the description of the second set of tablets of the Ten Commandments. (Moses had destroyed the first set in a fit of temper in Exod. 32:19, when he came down from Mount Sinai and discovered that the people were worshiping a golden calf.) Here, in v. 1, God says to Moses, "Carve yourself two stone tablets, like the previous ones, and I will inscribe upon the tablets the words that were on the previous tablets, which you shattered." Further on, in v.

27, God says (in contrast to v. 1), "Write down these commandments," and in v. 28 we are told that what Moses wrote on the tablets was the Ten Commandments.

So according to this part of the Pentateuch, the text that Moses carried down from the mountain was not the entire Pentateuch, but only the Ten Commandments—which would, of course, have been one of the sources of the Pentateuch. Moses is also instructed (in Exod. 17:14) to write down a threat against Israel's enemy the Amalekites, and (in Num. 33:2) to record the various stages of the Israelites' trek through the wilderness. There are a few more passages in Deuteronomy (17:18, 28:58, 28:61, 29:20 [29:21 in Christian Bibles], and 30:10) that talk about a written text, but they do not make clear just what that text is. Some of them at least may have been used in composing the Pentateuch as we have it today.

Distinguishing the Sources in the Flood Story

One thing that gives scholars reason to think that the Pentateuch might have been composed from earlier sources is that different terms are used to refer to God in different places in the Pentateuch. Perhaps the most famous example of this is the beginning of Genesis, where the first version of the story of creation (Gen. 1:1–2:3, which scholars consider part of the P source) refers to "God," while the second version (Gen. 2:4 ff., considered part of the J source) talks about "YHWH God"—that is, the personal name of Israel's God is missing in the first version but present in the retelling. In the first eleven chapters of Genesis, "YHWH" is usually indicative of J, and its absence is usually indicative of P.

When this distinction was first noticed, however, no one knew about P or J. How then did we deduce what lay behind these different names for God? You can understand the process by performing a little detective work on your own, with the following passage from the story of Noah. First, distinguish between the parts that talk about God and those that talk about YHWH. Then see what other differences you can find between those parts:

GEN. 6:9 This is the story of Noah. Noah was a righteous man, perfect in his generation; Noah constantly walked with God. **10** Noah fathered three sons: Shem, Ham, and Japhet. **11** The earth was corrupt before God, and the earth was filled with lawlessness. **12** God saw that the earth was defiled, for all flesh had defiled its way upon the earth.

13 God said to Noah, "I have decided to put an end to all flesh, for the earth is filled with lawlessness on their account, and I am going to destroy them along with the earth. **14** Make yourself an ark of gopher-wood; make the ark with compartments, and cover it inside and out with pitch. **15** This is how you shall make it: The ark shall be 300 cubits long, its width 50 cubits, and its height 30 cubits. **16** Make a skylight for the ark, and finish it to within a cubit on top, and put the entrance to the ark in its side. Make it with bottom, second, and third decks. **17** As for Me, I am bringing the Flood, waters upon the earth, to destroy all flesh in which there is the breath of life from under heaven. All that is on the earth shall perish. **18** But I shall establish My covenant with you, and you will come into the ark; you, your sons, your wife, and your sons' wives with you. **19** And of all life, of all flesh, bring two of everything living into the ark, to preserve it alive with you; they shall be male and female. **20** Of each kind of bird, of each kind of beast, and of each kind of creeping thing, two of each shall come to you to preserve alive. **21** As for you, take yourself all kinds of edible food, and store it so you and they shall have it to eat." **22** Noah did all that God had commanded him; just so did he.

7:1 YHWH said to Noah, "Come into the ark, you and your household, for it is you whom I find righteous before Me in this generation. **2** Of every pure beast, take seven males and their seven mates, and of every beast which is not pure, take two males and their mates. **3** Of the birds of heaven, too, take seven males and seven females, to keep alive offspring over the face of the whole earth. **4** For in another seven days, I will make it rain upon

the earth for 40 days and 40 nights, and I will wipe out from upon the surface of the earth all the existence which I created."
⁵ Noah did all that YHWH had commanded him.

It's easy to see that the chapter break is exactly the break between the sources. Based on what we saw in the creation stories, the first two paragraphs would be part of the P source because they use the word "God," while the last paragraph would be part of J because it uses the name YHWH.

Naturally, there are many similarities between the two parts. In both, Noah is "the righteous man of his generation." In both, we are told that Noah does as he is commanded. In both, Noah is told to take male and female animals on board to keep a sample of each species from drowning. Notice, though, that there are two particular differences *besides* the way God is referred to—differences that correspond to the differences in the names. In P, God tells Noah to bring one pair of each kind of animal; in J, he is instructed to bring seven pairs of certain animals. In P, God announces that he is going to bring a Flood upon the earth (I capitalize the word because the unusual Hebrew word here is used only for this special flood, Noah's flood), "waters upon the earth"; in J, God says simply that he is going to make it rain for forty days and forty nights.

Although it may not be obvious at first look, this last point, like the differences in the divine name, also matches the differences in the two creation stories. The same verb that is used in Gen. 7:4, "make it rain," also appears in Gen. 2:5, at the beginning of the J creation story. In both stories, one can see that J has a fairly naturalistic view of the world. The P creation story, however, is quite scientific, at least according to the scientific understanding of its day. There, life is created in a deliberate order of increasing complexity: plants, birds and fish, animals, humans. Even the universe is clearly framed according to the ancient Near Eastern understanding of cosmology, which we know in detail from Babylonian texts. At the beginning of creation, the world is made up of water. God first separates this into upper and lower waters by means of the firmament (that is, a solid shell of sky), and then forces the lower waters aside and below so that the dry land can appear.

This is important because it's a significant part of what the P version of the Flood story is trying to tell us.

The Flood: Weather, or Something More?

Let's look a little further along in Genesis 7, to see how the two versions make the Flood happen:

> [11] In the 600th year of Noah's life, in the 2nd month, on the 17th day of the month—on that day all the fountains of the great Deep burst open, and the floodgates of heaven were opened. [12] And the rain was upon the earth for 40 days and 40 nights.

Verse 12, as you can easily tell by comparison with v. 4, is from the J version of the story, describing the forty days and nights of constant rain. But v. 11 is clearly based on the P understanding of the universe (note that the "Deep" is also mentioned in the P version of the creation story, in Gen. 1:2). What happens in v. 11 is much more complicated, and more serious, than forty days of rain. Not that forty days of constant rain could not cause a massively destructive flood; of course it could. The P description, however, is constructed to show the observant reader that there is more to the Flood than just a lot of water.

What God is doing in Gen. 7:11 is deliberately reversing the process of creation described in Genesis 1. The structural integrity—so to speak—of the earth and the sky is compromised, and when holes are opened in each, the water that has been confined beneath the earth rushes up to meet the water that has been held above the solid "firmament," threatening a return to the state of watery chaos that characterized the world when God began his work of creation.

In both versions, of course, the ark will be floating on water. But where the water comes from makes a huge difference. In J, the story of Noah is "merely" an incredible adventure. In P, it is a critical moment in the history of the cosmos, almost like reversing the video to run the process of creation backward and start again at zero.

Let us look for a moment at what we have gained by temporarily "dissecting" the text so that we can hear a single one of the voices. It is not just that we have disassembled a biblical text into its constituent parts. We have a deeper insight into a story that we thought we knew. The Flood story becomes not merely a wiping out of humanity but—in one of its versions—a reversal of planetary physics to start creation afresh. For J, the revival of humanity after the flood is like starting with a clean slate. For P, it is like starting with the *original* slate before it got dirty. The composite biblical text we have now first gives the cosmic explanation, and then shows how the process looks to an observer who is not in on the behind-the-scenes explanation of the phenomenon. This is the same way the creation story is told.

Offering Sacrifice (Part One)

Now for the other difference we noticed between the two stories, the number of animals. In the P version God tells Noah to take two of every animal; in J, YHWH tells him to take two of most animals, but seven of the "pure" animals. The Hebrew word I have translated as "pure" does not mean genetically or hygienically pure, but pure in a ritual sense—that is, fit for sacrifice to God. The presumption is that, after being saved from the flood, Noah will offer a sacrifice of thanksgiving, and this, in fact, is the case:

> GEN. 8:15 God spoke to Noah as follows: [16] "Get out of the ark, you and your wife, your sons and your sons' wives with you, [17] every living thing that is with you, of all flesh—bird, beast, and everything that creeps upon the earth—bring them out with you, and let them swarm on the earth, and be fruitful and multiply upon the earth." [18] So Noah came out of the ark, and his sons and his wife and his sons' wives with him. [19] Every animal, every creeping

thing, every bird, all that creeps upon the earth, by families, came out of the ark. **20** Noah built an altar to YHWH, and he took of the pure beasts and the pure birds and offered up burnt offerings upon the altar. **21** YHWH smelled the sweet smell, and YHWH said to Himself, "Never again will I curse the earth on account of humanity. . . ."

Again, the differences between the two voices line up as we have come to expect. "God" tells Noah to come out of the ark, with his wife, sons, and daughters-in-law (did you notice that in the J version of the story, in Gen. 7:1, they are simply called "his household"?), and to bring out the different kinds of animals according to their categories, just as they were created by God in Genesis 1. As soon as the text shifts to using God's personal name, YHWH, as in the J version, we also see Noah sacrificing the "extra" pure animals and birds that, according to that version, he had brought along. It seems to be the pleasure YHWH gets from this sacrifice that makes him decide that he ought never again to destroy all life because of his displeasure at human behavior.

The P voice did not need the extra animals because its version of the story includes no sacrifice. But this means that the promise never again to destroy all life by means of a flood could not be based on God's pleasure at the sacrifices. As with the story of creation, the P version of this promise (in Genesis 9) makes it almost a cosmic moment—essentially a revision of the basic conditions of life on earth. According to Genesis 1, human beings—like all other animals—were originally intended to be vegetarians:

> **GEN. 1:29** God said, "I hereby give all the seed-bearing grasses upon the face of all the earth, and every tree with seed-bearing fruit, to you to eat. **30** And to every animal on earth, every bird in the sky, and everything that creeps on the earth, whatever has a living soul in it, [I give] the green grass for food." Thus it was.

In Genesis 9, after the epidemic of violence that caused God to bring on the Flood, it is clear that man's intrinsic bloodlust needs some less destructive outlet:

> GEN. 9:1 God blessed Noah and his sons and said to them, "Be fruitful and multiply and fill the earth. 2 The fear and dread of you shall be upon every animal on earth, every bird in the sky, everything that creeps on the ground and every fish in the sea; they are given into your power. 3 Every living thing that moves shall be for you to eat; just like the green grass, I give it all to you. 4 But flesh with its life—its blood—you shall not eat."

After the Flood—the reversal of the original creation—we have what is essentially a new creation, with a different relationship between the various orders of life. Now, human beings may eat meat, albeit only in a highly sacramental manner, being careful not to consume the blood, which was understood to be the essence of animal life. It is, in effect, a compromise between God's original plan for creation and the intrinsically violent nature of humanity, which prevented that plan from succeeding.

Let's sum up what we know about P, the priestly source, so far:

- P will not use YHWH, the name of God.
- P forbids the consumption of blood.
- P avoids describing the act of sacrifice.*

Why? Why couldn't Noah bring along extra "pure" animals? Why would the priestly version of the Flood story not be willing to let Noah offer a sacrifice of thanksgiving after being saved from universal destruction? The explanation is simple: Noah wasn't a priest, and for P, only priests could perform sacrifices. The priests, however, and the

---

* Note that when Abel brings an animal sacrifice in Gen 4:4, he brings it to YHWH; this story is part of the J source.

priestly instructions about how to perform sacrifices properly, don't come along until the book of Leviticus.

The Theology of God's Presence

In distinguishing between the two voices in the flood story we saw a number of characteristics that are fundamental to P: a reluctance to describe sacrifices being performed by a non-priest; an avoidance of the use of God's personal name; a scientific, even cosmic perspective on events that take place on earth. But we have not yet discussed the *most* distinguishing characteristic of P: its theology of God's presence. To begin this important discussion, let's take a brief detour out of the Pentateuch for a look at a man who had a vision of God—the prophet Ezekiel.

Ezekiel prophesied from Babylon, where he had been exiled in 597 BCE, eleven years before the destruction of the First Temple and the massive exile that accompanied it. You will find his book immediately after those of Isaiah and Jeremiah, just a little past the middle of a Jewish Bible and not far from the end of a Christian Old Testament. In the first chapter of Ezekiel, the prophet recounts an extremely involved, almost psychedelic vision that he has of God and the heavenly creatures. (You remember the "wheel in a wheel, way up in the middle of the air" from the old gospel song.) The particular verse I want to look at for our immediate purposes is Ezek. 1:26: "Above the firmament which was over their heads, with the appearance of sapphire stone, was the semblance of a throne, and above the semblance of a throne was a semblance like the appearance of a human being on it, from above." Although Ezekiel does not say so in plain Hebrew, this is God on his throne.

The evasive language suggests two things. First, it seems that Ezekiel felt he could not quite describe exactly what he was seeing. Second, he probably meant to say that these things were different in some indefinable way from the things in the human world that they seemed to resemble. The sapphire, of course, is the sky—in this conception, a solid, sapphire-colored translucent surface on which God's throne sits. The description continues:

EZEK. 1:27 I saw what looked like an amber gleam, with something like the appearance of fire inside it all around, from the appearance of his loins upward; and from the appearance of his loins and downward I saw something like the appearance of fire, with a radiance all around, **28** like the appearance of the bow which would be in the clouds on a rainy day. Such was the appearance of the radiance all around. This was the appearance of the semblance of the *kavod* of YHWH. I saw and fell on my face and heard a Voice speaking.

I have left the word *kavod* untranslated above, for it is the key word in the theology of the priestly literature. Ezekiel himself, you see, though he was called to be a prophet, was a priest by descent. We know this from v. 3 of the first chapter of his book, where he is identified by name: "Ezekiel son of Buzi the priest." Priesthood was not a vocation but an inherited status. Ezekiel's father Buzi was a priest, and (though we think of him as a prophet) so was he. This goes some way toward explaining something that scholars have noticed—that the style of Hebrew used in the book of Ezekiel is very similar to that used in the priestly portions of the Pentateuch.

God's Glorious "Presence"

What exactly is *kavod*? Traditional translations usually put this word into English as "glory." It comes from a Hebrew root used to denote honor or respect, ultimately coming from the meaning "heavy." (Similarly, in Biblical Hebrew one belittles someone, or curses him, with a word whose original meaning is "light.") Some contemporary translations use "Presence" (with a capital P) for this word, and this gets at the theological significance of the word.

When the Bible uses this word in connection with God, what it really means is a kind of superhuman, atomic brightness, a light too powerful for the eye to look at. One is reminded of J. Robert Oppenheimer's reaction to seeing the flash of the first nuclear explosion in the New Mexico desert: "I am become Shiva, Destroyer of Worlds."

No doubt the original source of this religious imagery was the sun, whose brilliance, unlike that of an atomic blast, simultaneously holds great destructive power and is the indispensable source of all life on earth.

It is this bright light that Ezekiel saw when he had his vision of the heavenly throne. And this light, denoted by the word *kavod*, is regularly used in the Bible to indicate the literal presence of YHWH. (As we'll see shortly, the priestly voice avoids use of this name only until a particular point in the story.) Let us look at a passage from Exodus 24 that describes how God made his presence known at Mount Sinai:

> EXOD. 24:16 The *kavod* of YHWH dwelt on Mount Sinai and the cloud covered it for six days. On the seventh day He called to Moses from the midst of the cloud. [17] The appearance of the *kavod* of YHWH was like a consuming fire on the top of the mountain in the sight of all Israel.

The presence of God on top of Mount Sinai is confirmed by the fact that his "*kavod*" (more accurately, as in Ezekiel, the "appearance" of his *kavod*) could be seen by all Israel. We also have an added feature that becomes equally indicative of God's presence, the cloud. God's brightness, after all, is so intense that it cannot be looked at safely; hence it is regularly concealed inside a cloud, which makes its presence obvious but shields viewers from potential danger.

Moses does something similar in Exodus 34, when he begins to glow with a secondary radiance after communicating with God:

> EXOD. 34:27 YHWH said to Moses, "Write down these words, for in accordance with these words do I cut a covenant with you and with Israel." [28] He was there with YHWH forty days and forty nights; no bread did he eat, no water did he drink. He wrote on the tablets the words of the covenant, the Ten Commandments. [29] When Moses came down from Mount Sinai, the two tablets of the Pact being in Moses's hand, when he came down from the

mountain, Moses did not know that the skin of his face was glowing from speaking to Him. ³⁰ Aaron and all the Israelites saw Moses with the skin of his face glowing, and they were afraid to come near him. ³¹ Moses called to them, and Aaron and all the princes of the congregation came back toward him, and Moses spoke to them. ³² Afterwards all the Israelites approached, and he commanded them everything that YHWH had spoken with him on Mount Sinai. ³³ Moses finished speaking with them and put a veil over his face. ³⁴ When Moses would come before YHWH to speak with Him, he would put aside the veil until he came out. He would come out and tell the Israelites what he had been commanded. ³⁵ The Israelites would see that the skin of Moses's face glowed; and Moses would put the veil back over his face until he went in to speak with Him.

This text clearly puts Moses in a semidivine state. Notice that he does not eat or drink while he is on the mountain for forty days and nights; he has left the human realm and approached, at least temporarily, that of divinity. Moreover, direct contact with YHWH means that Moses too begins to give off light. (The verb used here for "glow" is connected to the Hebrew word for "horn," suggesting that beams of light came from Moses's face; a mistranslation of this word in the Latin Bible is the source of the horns on Michelangelo's "Moses.") The veil concealing the shining of Moses's face serves the same purpose, both symbolically and practically, as the cloud that covers God's *kavod*.

A prophet who lived a century before Ezekiel, Isaiah, had a similar, if somewhat more restrained, vision. (Jewish legend says that they saw the same thing but that Ezekiel, who was experiencing it for the first time, was overwhelmed; Isaiah, whose vision comes in chapter 6 of his book, was already more used to being in God's presence.) In Isaiah's majestic vision of God on his throne, God's attendant angels call out, "Holy, holy, holy is YHWH of Hosts; the whole world is full of his *kavod*," and in response the doorposts tremble and the building fills with smoke, protecting the human Isaiah from the impact of God's brilliant presence. The building in which Isaiah's vision is set is in fact the Temple in Jerusalem. According to P, God (in the form of his *kavod*) was literally present in the Temple.

The Kavod Moves In

Since the Temple was an ordinary (if particularly splendid) building, constructed by human workmen out of regular building materials, something had to happen to transform it into a location of more-than-human sanctity. We can follow the process by first looking at the Temple's desert precursor, the portable Tabernacle whose construction takes up a large chunk of the second half of the book of Exodus. Finally, at the end of that book, in Exodus 40, the last Tab A has been put into Slot B (the Tabernacle was essentially a kit, meant to be disassembled for transport and reassembled the next time the Israelites camped), and it is ready for occupation:

> EXOD. 40:33 . . . Moses finished the work.
>
> 34 The cloud covered the Tent of Meeting [here, another name for the Tabernacle] and the *kavod* of YHWH filled the Tabernacle. 35 Moses could not enter the Tent of Meeting, for the cloud dwelt upon it and the *kavod* of YHWH had filled the Tabernacle. 36 When the cloud lifted off the Tabernacle, the Israelites would set off on all their journeys. 37 If the cloud did not lift, they would not set off until it did. 38 For the cloud of YHWH was over the Tabernacle all day long, and fire would be in it at night, in the sight of all Israel throughout their travels.

At the moment the Tabernacle was finished, it was (one might say) "plugged in" to the electricity of God's literal presence, a current of powerful energy that begins to flow as soon as the facility constructed to house it is complete. This is the priestly notion not only of the desert Tabernacle, but also of Solomon's Temple, as we will shortly see—a human construction that is, as it were, engineered to provide the possibility of safe contact (for trained professionals, i.e., the priests) with the potentially destructive power of God. To observe this same process happening with Solomon's Temple, however, will lead us immediately into the second great theological voice of the Hebrew Bible, that of Deuteronomy. Before we can do this, we must prepare the ground by examining a question that we have left unanswered until now, the question of why the priestly writings in Genesis refuse to use the name YHWH, God's personal name.

Knowing God's Name

We saw that Ezekiel, a priest, had no problem identifying the God whom he saw in his vision as YHWH. The God whom Moses encountered in the Tabernacle was also identified as YHWH. In the creation and flood stories according to P, however, only the designation "God" is used. What happened between the beginning of Genesis and the end of Exodus that persuaded P to begin using that name? In other words, when, according to the P source, did God reveal his personal name to the world, and what is the significance of that revelation?

The answer takes us to a text we looked at briefly in chapter 1, a point early in the book of Exodus, where the story of Israel's escape from slavery in Egypt is told. Here, in the P version of this story, when Moses must confront Pharaoh in a show of power between the Egyptian god (Pharaoh himself) and the God of Israel, God makes his identity known to Moses for the first time. Let us pick up the story in Exodus 6:

> EXOD. 6:2 God spoke to Moses and said to him, "I am YHWH.
> 3 I appeared to Abraham, to Isaac, and to Jacob as El Shaddai,*
> but I was not known to them by My name YHWH."

Here, God for the first time (according to P) reveals his personal name to a human being. We know that the idea that Moses was the

* Often translated as "God Almighty."

first to learn God's name is restricted to the priestly literature because other voices in the Pentateuch contradict it. Just a few chapters earlier, in Exodus 3, when Moses asks the God whom he encounters at the burning bush how he should identify him to the Israelites so that they will believe he has been sent by their own God, God identifies himself by name and makes clear that the Israelites already know him by that name:

> EXOD. 3:15 God said again to Moses, "Thus shall you say to the Israelites: 'YHWH, the God of your ancestors, God of Abraham, God of Isaac, and God of Jacob, has sent me to you.' That is My name forever, My appellation in every generation."

It was only Moses, not raised as an Israelite but as an Egyptian, who did not know it!

We can go even further back, to Gen. 12:1, where (in a J text) it is YHWH who tells Abram, in the first encounter of the two, "Go forth from your land, your birthplace, and your father's house to the land which I will show you." If this is not clear enough, simply move forward to v. 8: ". . . He built there an altar to YHWH, and he called upon YHWH by name." Even this was nothing new, for we are told in Gen. 4:26, "To Seth too was born a son, whom he named Enosh. At that time was the beginning of calling upon YHWH by name." So some parts of the Bible assumed that God's name was widely known long before Noah. For one of the biblical voices, though—P—not merely God's name but the very revelation of it had special significance.

What's in a Name?

Why this preoccupation with a name? What does knowing someone's name do? In some sense, it confers power on the one who knows. Hence the expression that used to be current in English when a stranger addressed one by name: "You have the advantage of me"—that is, you know my name but I don't know yours. There are occasions in the Bible where the deliberate withholding of a name makes this aspect of relationship between characters evident. One example is in Judges 13, the story of the angel who foretells the birth of the great hero Samson. Samson's father, Manoah (who is presented in the story as something less than quick witted), has no idea that he is talking to a divine messenger:

> JUDG. 13:17 Manoah said to the messenger of YHWH, "What is your name? When your word comes true, we will honor you." 18 The angel of YHWH replied, "Why do you ask my name? It is unknowable."

This will remind some readers of the story of Jacob wrestling with "the angel" in Genesis 32. (Despite how we usually think of this story, Jacob's opponent is simply introduced in the Bible as "a man.") They struggle all night, but the stranger can neither overcome Jacob nor break free from him:

> GEN. 32:27 He said, "Let me go, for dawn is breaking."* He said, "I will not let you go unless you bless me." 28 He said to him, "What is your name?" and he replied, "Jacob." 29 He said, "No longer shall your name be called Jacob, but Israel, for you have struggled with God and men and have prevailed." 30 Jacob said, "Now tell me your name," but he said, "Why do you ask my name?" and he blessed him there.

Jacob readily tells his antagonist what his name is, and the mysterious stranger seizes on this opportunity to change Jacob's name because of the power Jacob has exerted over him. When Jacob attempts to redress the balance by asking the stranger's name, however, he responds as did the angel who spoke to Manoah. Jacob has "prevailed" in the physical sense of fighting to a draw and making the stranger—who

---

* The insistence on leaving at dawn is the clue that Jacob's opponent is no ordinary man, but some kind of supernatural being. Note that in Christian Bibles these verses are Gen. 32:26–29.

must leave at dawn—agree to yield. But in the battle of names, it is the stranger who prevails. Jacob has "won" a blessing, but has not fundamentally changed the power relationship between the two of them. Names convey power.

This is why the P source is so reluctant to reveal God's name until the appearance on the scene of Moses, who plays "God" to Aaron's "prophet" (see Exod. 7:1) in the struggle with the pseudogods of Egypt to release the Israelite people from slavery. YHWH's power has certainly lain dormant while the descendants of the Patriarchs have been enslaved in Egypt. But now a new era in history is about to begin. From this point on, God's actions return, as in the stories of creation and the Flood, to a world stage.

What does all this concern about names have to do with the Tabernacle? Remember that for P, the essence of the Temple and of the Tabernacle is that God himself is present there, concealed by the brightness of the *kavod* that makes it impossible to see, which is concealed in turn by the cloud that protects human eyesight from it. But the *name* of God figures even more prominently in the other great theological voice in the Pentateuch, which scholars call "D." It is the voice of Deuteronomy.

The Theology of God's Name

We have identified the source called "P" in a number of places in the Pentateuch, and its concerns showed us that it came from the ideology of the priestly caste in Israel. D's particular concerns, and even the nature of its language, are equally distinctive, but we cannot be quite as certain from which social group within Israel it came. Textually, however, it is quite easy to identify, since it is almost entirely concentrated within, and almost entirely comprises, the book of Deuteronomy (hence the name).

This book, the last in the Pentateuch, is presented as the farewell speech of Moses, who has been forbidden by God to cross over into the land promised to the Patriarchs. Framed within this farewell speech, after a recap of Israelite history up to this point in the story,

Moses leaves the people with a last set of instructions from God, chapters 12–26 of the book. The particular emphasis that is most central to Deuteronomy appears quite clearly at the beginning of this section, in chapter 12. P insisted that sacrifice could only be performed by one particular *group*, but D insists that it can only be performed in one particular *place*. When the Israelites enter the land, Deuteronomy 12 warns, they must destroy all the religious sites belonging to the current inhabitants of the land, for they practice idolatry:

> DEUT. 12:4 Do not do so for YHWH your God. ⁵ Instead, you shall seek out only the place where YHWH your God shall choose, out of all your tribes, to set His name and make it dwell.

For D, what is in the place that God chooses is not his *kavod*—his actual presence—but his name. If *kavod* is the key word for P, the key word for D is *shem*, "name." And just as *kavod* has a special meaning for P unlike its general use in Hebrew, so too does *shem* for D. We can illustrate this by pointing out something that may not have been quite obvious in the English translations. The Hebrew word generally translated as "Tabernacle" is *mishkan*, from the verb that means "to dwell."* Remember that earlier, in Exod. 24:16, we saw that God's *kavod* "dwelt" on top of Mount Sinai. P's Tabernacle too is in a sense the "dwelling" place of God's *kavod*, that is, of his living, powerful presence. If you look closely at Deut. 12:5, however, which we have just quoted, you will see that for D what "dwells" in the place God chooses is not his *kavod* but his name.

Immanence and Transcendence

The distinction between the theology of *kavod* (expressed in the Pentateuch in the P source) and the theology of *shem* (expressed in the Pentateuch in the D source) is, in fact, one of the eternal quandaries

---

* From this same Hebrew root we get the Rabbinic word (now found even in English dictionaries) Shekinah, the "visible manifestation of the divine presence" (*American Heritage Dictionary*).

of religion. Is God immanent, that is, present in some almost tangible way in the ordinary physical world, and to be thanked and propitiated by the manipulation of physical objects, or is he transcendent, that is, existent somehow only outside the realm of the material universe and accessible only in a spiritual way? By its nature, this is not the kind of question to which rational inquiry will someday provide the answer; it is one that individuals will always answer according to their own predilections. Rather than come down decisively on either side of this nondecidable question, the Bible includes two voices, each arguing strongly for one of the possibilities.

The inclusion of both voices resulted from the serendipitous genius of the compiler of the Pentateuch, which does not seem to have existed as a complete book before the exile to Babylonia in 586 BCE. (Jewish traditions that Ezra, the Jew who was Persian governor of Judea in the post-Exilic period, had to somehow recreate the Torah given by God to Moses suggest a Rabbinic awareness of this too.) But the two voices, looked at separately, give us a window also on two ancient streams of Israelite religion whose voices, ultimately, continued to shape Judaism (and, hence, Christianity and Islam) throughout the ages.

What Was in Solomon's Temple?

We saw at the end of the last chapter that these two theological streams were reflected in the historical books of the Bible as well. Deuteronomy in particular left its mark very strongly on the historical books of Joshua through Kings. To follow it further, let us return to 1 Kings 5, where we will hear King Solomon expressing his determination to build a Temple for God in strongly Deuteronomistic language. Solomon is writing to King Hiram for help in constructing the Temple that his father David could not build, but which Solomon will now construct:

> 1 KGS. 5:19[*] I have decided to build a House for the name of YHWH my God, just as YHWH said to my father David, "Your

[*] This is 1 Kgs. 5:5 in Christian Bibles.

son, whom I shall place after you on your throne—he shall build the House for My name."

This promise is the one made by God to David in 2 Samuel 7, when he promises David that his son will be king after him—up to that point in history, a most un-Israelite idea. Neither Moses, nor Joshua, nor the judges who ruled Israel after them were succeeded by their heirs, but now, for the first time, this is to become the premise of rulership. God gives David this pledge about his son: "He [not you] shall build a house for My name, and I will establish his royal throne forever" (2 Sam. 7:13)—not, as it might have said, a house for Me, or for My *kavod*, but "for My name," just as in the theology of Deuteronomy 12.

By contrast, a bit earlier in the same chapter, God protests indignantly, "I have not settled in a house since the day I brought the Israelites up from Egypt, to this very day. No, I have gone about in Tent and Tabernacle" (2 Sam. 7:6), and continues by reminding David that he has never asked, "Why have you not built Me a house of cedar?" (2 Sam. 7:7). Here, the assumption is that God himself, not merely his name, would be expected to dwell in such a house.

Because Samuel, as part of the Deuteronomistic History, was edited by someone who believed in the *shem* theology, that theology "trumps" the hint in the earlier part of the story of the theology of presence. When this "house" is actually built, in the book of Kings, the narrative struggle between the theology of presence and the theology of name resumes. This text is parallel, in some sense, to the inauguration of the Tabernacle, which we saw at the end of Exodus 40. Remember that, in the story told there, the *kavod* of YHWH filled the Tabernacle. If we turn to the story of the dedication of Solomon's Temple, in 1 Kings 8, we might expect to find something similar happening. And, in fact, we do:

> 1 KGS. 8:10 When the priests left the holy place, the cloud having filled the House of YHWH, 11 the priests were unable to stand

before the cloud and perform their service, for the *kavod* of YHWH had filled the House of YHWH.

¹² Then Solomon said, "YHWH has determined to dwell in a thick cloud. ¹³ I have surely built a stately House for You, a fixed place for You to inhabit forever."

Just as in the case of the Tabernacle, the moment of inauguration of the Temple seems to plug in a power source. This time, the cloud that hides the *kavod* that conceals God's presence materializes so rapidly that, like demonstrators breathing tear gas, the priests have to scatter from the place where God's energy is centered. But this story will be different from Exodus 40. For, like Samuel, Kings was put together by someone of Deuteronomistic outlook. So even though Solomon has just announced that God himself is now dwelling in the Temple, the long dedicatory speech he gives following the Temple's inauguration (in this telling) will say exactly the opposite:

1 KGS. 8:27 But will God really dwell on earth? Even the heavens and the heavens beyond the heavens cannot contain You. How could this house which I have built? ²⁸ But turn, YHWH my God, to Your servant's prayer, and to his plea, to hear the cry and the prayer which Your servant prays before You today, ²⁹ that Your eyes may be open toward this house night and day, toward the place of which You said, "My name shall be there"; to hear the prayer which Your servant will pray toward this place. ³⁰ Hear the plea of Your servant and of Your people Israel who will pray toward this place. Hear in the place where You dwell, in the sky—hear and forgive.

According to this passage, God is not in the Temple at all. He inhabits the heavens (or some unimaginable realm beyond them). There is, however, something essential and personal of his in the Temple—his name—and this is apparently enough to make it the preferred spot on earth for human access to him. In this view, there is no direct access to God. But there is a secure channel of communication to him.

What the "Name" Theology Means for Prayer

If God is not immediately present in the Temple to hear one's prayer, the next logical step to take would be to say that the worshiper too need not be physically present there to be heard. Logically, if "God's in his heaven," it ought not to matter where on earth one is when one prays. This is exactly the line of reasoning followed in the continuation of Solomon's prayer. Yet, just as God's attention is focused on the Temple, so too must be the worshiper's. The solution is for those who pray, *wherever* they are, to direct their attention to the Temple just as God does:

> 1 KGS. 8:44 When Your people goes forth to war against its enemy, on the path which You shall send them, and they pray to YHWH in the direction of the city which You chose, and the house which I built for Your name, [45] hear their prayer and their plea in heaven, and do them justice. [46] When they sin against You—for there is no one who does not sin—and You get angry at them and give them over to the enemy, and they bring them captive to the enemy land, near or far, [47] and they take it to heart in the land where they are captive and repent and plead to You in their captors' land, "We have sinned, we have transgressed, we have done evil," [48] and they return to You with all their heart and with all their soul in the land of the enemies who captured them, and they pray to You in the direction of their land which You gave to their ancestors, the city which You chose, and the house which I built for Your name, [49] hear in Your dwelling place in heaven their prayer and their plea and do them justice.

The prayer is carefully constructed, paragraph by paragraph, to move the potential worshipers farther and farther away from the actual Temple. By this point, they may be in any country on earth—"near or far"—and still maintain the connection to God by using the Temple as a transmission point for prayer. Note the progressive broadening of the point at which the worshiper is "aiming." Ideally, one comes to the Temple. The next best alternative is to pray *toward* it. Someone who is farther away needs, as it were, a bigger "target," and prays toward Jerusalem, the city where the Temple is. Finally, someone who is out of the country altogether simply prays toward the Land of Israel, in which (like following an image down the wrong end of a telescope) Jerusalem and the Temple are found diminishing in size. Yet, as we saw in 1 Kgs. 8:48, God is related to each of these geographical levels in a particular way:

- the *land* which You gave to their ancestors
- the *city* which You chose
- the *house* which I built for Your name

God is not bound to any of these locations and certainly does not "live" in any of them; that is, he is not immanent, but transcendent. Still, he most certainly has a definite *relationship* with each of them. Again, this is the ideology that animates the so-called Deuteronomistic History of the biblical books from Joshua through Kings.

The Theology of Centralization

There is a second plank in the Deuteronomic platform that is even more historically significant than the theology of God's name. Think about Solomon's prayer for a moment, and you will realize what it is. We have concentrated so far on the prayer's denial that God actually lives in the Temple. But notice that, wherever one is on earth, it is *this* land, and within it *this* city, and within the city *this* Temple, that is meant to be the focus of prayer. In terms of achieving contact with God (according to the Deuteronomic view), this spot—the Temple in Jerusalem—is the center of the world. If you pray toward any other spot, you are wasting your time.

Admittedly, this concept makes a certain amount of intuitive sense to us. Scholars of religion tell us that many cultures think of a particular spot on earth as the only location of contact with the divine. With regard to our particular text, Jews today still pray toward Jerusalem, just as Muslims pray toward Mecca. But we must remember that, in biblical times, prayer was not the only or even the major aspect of worship. Sacrifice was.

Offering Sacrifice (Part Two)

We saw Moses's announcement in Deut. 12:5 that God was going to choose a place "to set His name and make it dwell." But now let us think for a moment about the first half of the statement, that God will choose a place—*one* place. Here's what that means: "The place where YHWH your God will choose to make His name dwell— there you shall bring all that I command you: burnt offerings, sacrifices, tithes, contributions, and all the choice things that you vow to YHWH" (Deut. 12:11). It is one thing to pray in the direction of Jerusalem, and quite another to have to bring all your sacrifices and tithes there. (The fact that the same Deuteronomic ideal that denied God's immanence in the Temple also insisted on centralizing all of Israelite worship there is a conundrum that still lacks a solution.)

As you might expect, this was not the standard attitude throughout Israelite history. For example, let us look at the paragraph that intervenes between the giving of the Ten Commandments in Exodus 20 and the beginning of the Covenant Code in Exodus 21. It contains a warning against idolatry and some instructions about the proper way to build an altar. Here is the crucial verse for our purposes: "Make Me an altar of earth, and sacrifice upon it your burnt-offerings and your whole-offerings, your sheep and your cattle. In *every* place where I cause My name to be mentioned, I will come to you and bless you" (Exod. 20:21; v. 24 in Christian translations).

Notice the ways this verse is different from Deuteronomic theology. God does not cause his name to *dwell*, but to be invoked; rather than remaining in his transcendent, heavenly realm, he is somehow present to extend blessing; and finally, this happens not in a single place, but in *every* place where God's name is invoked. And these are the locations not just for prayer, but for sacrifices and tithing.

The Deuteronomist insisted that all these activities were to be restricted to a single location. And just as we saw in the case of the name theology, centralization is reflected not only in D itself, but also in the Deuteronomistic History—in fact, far more so. To see how, we must look for a moment at the framework of the book of Kings. We saw earlier that the kingdom was split after Solomon's death into the large kingdom of the ten tribes of Israel and the smaller kingdom, centered around Jerusalem, politically based on the tribe of Judah. From this point on, the Deuteronomistic History swings back and forth between the two kingdoms, beginning the story of each king's reign with a kind of encyclopedia entry. Here is an example:

> **1 KGS. 15:1** In the 18th year of King Jeroboam son of Nebat, King Abijam began to reign over Judah. **2** He reigned for 13 years in Jerusalem. His mother's name was Maacah daughter of Abishalom. **3** He followed all the sins which his father had done before him; his heart was not whole with YHWH his God like that of his ancestor David.

Notice the typical elements:

- dating based on the reign of the contemporary king from the other kingdom
- name of the new king
- length of his reign
- his mother's name (for kings of Judah only)
- religious evaluation of his reign

The religious evaluation is always present, and it works this way. For kings of Israel, they are declared to have followed in the steps of the founder of their kingdom, Jeroboam I, in luring the Israelites away from Jerusalem; for kings of Judah, they are evaluated on whether they did or did not follow in the righteous footsteps of their ancestor David. As you will recall from 2 Samuel 7, though David did not build the Temple himself, it was he who established Jerusalem as "the place YHWH your God will choose." Thus, while some of the kings of Judah are considered good and some are bad, all the kings of Israel are automatically considered bad. They led Israel away from Jerusalem, the one legitimate place of worship.

You may think we have wandered from the theological voices of the Pentateuch back to the historical voices of our previous chapter. In fact, though the Documentary Hypothesis applies only to the Pentateuch (some would apply it to Joshua also), the very name Deuteronomistic History reminds us that it was someone who was whistling a tune from Deuteronomy who put together the biblical books of Joshua, Judges, Samuel, and Kings.

One of the key pieces of information that help us put together the story of how the biblical texts were created, thereby giving us a window on ancient Israel, is in 2 Kings 22–23. (We glanced at this story in chapter 2, and I promised we would return to it here.) In this remarkable passage, a "scroll of Torah" is found in the course of renovations on the Temple. Its status as legitimately conveying God's word is confirmed by the prophetess Huldah. And here is how King Josiah reacts to the discovery of the scroll: he brings all the priests of Judah to Jerusalem, and he destroys and defiles all the places where they had offered sacrifice up until that time.

This is exactly the theology of the book of Deuteronomy. For this reason, scholars have long assumed that the scroll that was discovered was some form of Deuteronomy. If that is true, then we have a fairly precise date for one of the voices. Whenever it was written, D was "discovered" and began having an impact on Israelite religion in the year 622 BCE.

Josiah and the Deuteronomistic History

As you can guess, the Deuteronomistic History could not have been put together until Deuteronomy was around to influence it. But how soon after the discovery of Deuteronomy was it created? There are two clues that tell us quite plainly that the first version of it comes from the time of King Josiah himself. The first clue is 1 Kgs. 13:2, in which a man of God interrupts the inauguration of King Jeroboam's shrine at Bethel to proclaim that, three hundred years later, a descendant of David named Josiah would destroy it. As we will see in our chapter on prophetic voices, this kind of precise, far-future prediction is not the sort of thing that Israelite prophets did. Hence this story was most likely written after the fact, in the time of Josiah, and by someone in his employ.

The second piece of evidence linking the Deuteronomistic History to Josiah is a more subtle one. The book of Deuteronomy, unlike most of the rest of the Pentateuch, expresses a deep concern not only for what the Israelites were to do, but for what they should think. You must not merely serve God, you must do it "with all your heart and with all your soul"—an expression that occurs nine times in Deuteronomy. But one of those times a third element is added to the expression: "You shall love YHWH your God with all your heart, with all your soul, and with all your might" (Deut. 6:5). It sounds familiar to Jews because this verse is the beginning of the first paragraph of the *Shema*, but "with all your might" is not found anywhere else in the Torah.

The more common form of the expression, "with all your heart and with all your soul," also occurs five times in the Deuteronomistic History, but only once more with this third, extra element—in the story of Josiah:

> 2 KGS. 23:25 There was no king before him like him, who returned to YHWH with all his heart, with all his soul, and with all his might, following all the Teaching of Moses. And no one like him arose after him.

The incomparable Josiah, and he alone of all the kings, did what God required "with all his heart, with all his soul, and with all his might," just as the Teaching of Moses instructed. And where is that instruction found? It is found in Deut. 6:5. Again, the likelihood is that this praise of Josiah was written in his own days.

The book of Kings ends, though, with the Land of Israel occupied, the population of Jerusalem (and the last remaining descendant of David) exiled, and the House of God burnt to the ground. This, of course, all happened after the death of Josiah. So the Deuteronomistic History must have been updated after the destruction of Jerusalem. And it is easy to see why. Theologically, there had to be an answer for this. There had to be a reason and there had to be an explanation. The explanation could perhaps not contradict, but must at least supplement the promises made to David as the people of Israel understood them when Josiah was king. We have already seen, in Solomon's prayer at the original dedication of the Temple, one of the ways in which this was done:

> 1 KGS. 8:46 When they sin against You—for there is no one who does not sin—and You get angry at them and give them over to the enemy, and they bring them captive to the enemy land, near or far, ⁴⁷ and they take it to heart in the land where they are captive and repent and plead to You in their captors' land, "We have sinned, we have transgressed, we have done evil," ⁴⁸ and they return to You with all their heart and with all their soul in the land of the enemies who captured them, and they pray to You in the direction of their land which You gave to their ancestors, the city which You chose, and the house which I built for Your name, ⁴⁹ hear in Your dwelling place in heaven their prayer and their plea and do them justice.

You can recognize the Deuteronomistic voice in the expression in v. 48, "with all their heart and with all their soul," as well as in the assertion that the Temple was built not for God but for God's name. We did not ask, when we saw this text earlier, what made necessary the description of how to pray toward the Temple from outside the

Land of Israel. But it must be because this section of the prayer was added after the destruction of Jerusalem, when a new framework for understanding the relationship between God and the People of Israel was desperately needed. This is why the prayer of Solomon describes not just how to live with the conception that God is in heaven and not in the Temple, but also how to live when you yourself are on foreign soil and not in Israel.

Locating the Voices in History

Unfortunately, not all the biblical voices are as easy to locate in history as is that of D. There is general (though not unanimous) agreement that the voices of J and E are early, if only because they do not weigh in on the great issues argued by P and D. For example, the altar law of Exod. 20:21/24 does not *argue* that altars can be built anywhere, it just assumes this. So it could hardly have been written after the time, during the reign of Josiah, when the restriction of sacrifices to Jerusalem became a major political issue. Some have suggested that J, with its repeated stories that feature younger sons who supplant their older brothers, dates to the time of Solomon, who did the same in succeeding his father David as king. This suggestion is certainly plausible, but it is a long way from being conclusive "beyond a reasonable doubt."

P is even harder to place in time, since its most clear source is not a moment in history, but a particular social group—one that existed during many centuries of Israel's history. For a long time P was identified as a voice dating to the Second Temple period. This was done on the basis of a theory about how religion (in the abstract) develops: spiritual insights eventually degenerate into meaningless ritual. But this theory, to the extent that it's true at all, is a tremendous oversimplification in general, and a misreading of P in particular. More recent studies on the kind of Hebrew in which P is written suggest that it actually dates from the First Temple period. But these studies too, though carefully done, don't provide an airtight argument.

In fact it is just this problem that has led to today's situation, in which many scholars are questioning the validity of the Documentary

Hypothesis. This hypothesis traditionally included a specific outline of the historical settings of the various documents that were ultimately combined into the Pentateuch, an outline that (as we've seen) is no longer universally accepted. For our purposes, though, it is not the historical origins of the sources that are important, but the various voices. And even scholars who disagree on just how, in history, the voices entered the Pentateuch still acknowledge their existence. So let's conclude this chapter with a review of the differences between the two most distinctive voices, the priestly voice of P and the Deuteronomic voice of D.

Differences between the Deuteronomic and Priestly Outlooks

In Deuteronomy, God is in heaven, not on earth; but the Torah is down on earth: "it is not in heaven . . . nor across the sea . . . but very close to you" (Deut. 30:12, 13, 14). According to the Deuteronomistic view, you do not have to be in the Land of Israel or even be an Israelite in order to worship YHWH, the God of Israel. 2 Kings 5 tells the story of Naaman, the chief of staff of the Aramean army, who suffers from leprosy. (Aram was located in today's Syria.) A captive Israelite girl tells him there is a prophet in Israel, Elisha, who can cure him. He finds Elisha, is cured, and announces that as a consequence he intends to become a worshiper of YHWH—even when he returns home to Aram.

In P, as in the prophecies of Ezekiel (remember that he was also a priest), it is the land that is holy. If the Israelites' wickedness grows too great, Leviticus 26 threatens, they will be thrown out of the land for abusing it. Sin somehow defiles the land; like a spiritual Superfund site, it must be evacuated and purified before it is once again fit for human habitation. The priestly picture is of a land that is holy; a city, within that land, that is even holier; a building within that city that is even holier; and a spot within that building in which, somehow, God himself can be said to dwell.

The holiness of the land radiates, as it were, from that central holiness marked and created by the presence of God. More than people's behavior, an understanding of the nature of the holiness radiating from that spot is the key to an understanding of how people should live their lives and what the moral structure of the world is. You can see the ultimate expression of this point of view in Ezekiel 48, a detailed description of Jerusalem's location in the precise center of the Land of Israel, ending with the assertion (in v. 35) that in the ideal future Jerusalem will be renamed "YHWH is there."

Which is more important, the land or the people? Where one lives, or how one lives? These are arguments that are still going on today, not least, but certainly not only, among the Jews. This is essentially the difference between the priestly and the Deuteronomistic conceptions of the world, a theological tension that still animates life in our century and most likely always will.

Just as the history from Joshua through Kings, first compiled in the time of Josiah (ca. 600 BCE) was oriented toward the D school of thought, so the other great work of biblical history, Chronicles (most likely written ca. 400 BCE), with its intense concentration on the temple service, is oriented toward the P school of thought. It seems that what energized this history and the society that produced it was the return from exile—the condition of being back in the holy land, resettling the holy city, and rebuilding the holy Temple. As we saw earlier, this is the society that, for the first time, seems to have had the Pentateuch as a unified book.

At the end of our next chapter, we will meet one last voice from the Pentateuch, a voice that sought to reconcile these two opposing views. To get there, though, we must temporarily set theology aside and look at something that seems much more mundane: the rules by which Israelite society was to constitute itself. So let's turn our attention now to the legal voices of the Bible.

4
Legal Voices

The first five books of the Bible are often called by biblical scholars, just as we have done earlier in this book, the "Pentateuch." This is a reasonably neutral term, being simply made up of Greek words meaning "five books." But what is it that makes these five books a unit? Why might we not speak of a "Tetrateuch," meaning only the *four* books up through Numbers, or conversely a "Hexateuch," the first *six* books, up through Joshua? In fact, scholars actually have used these terms to suggest that, at some point in the history of the biblical text, those were indeed standard groupings. Why is it that specifically the first *five* books of the Bible, the "Pentateuch," are now considered to make up a unit?

The answer is that this is a case where Jewish religious tradition (out of which, of course, Christian tradition grew) has shaped our view of the Bible. The scrolls that are read from in synagogues to this day contain not a single biblical book each, and certainly not the entire Bible, but also neither four nor six books, but precisely five: the "Five Books of Moses"—Genesis, Exodus, Leviticus, Numbers, and Deuteronomy.*
Moreover, these scrolls, and hence this section of the Bible, have a

---

* I don't know who coined this mnemonic, but you can remember their order by learning the phrase "General Electric lights never dim."

particular Hebrew name, the "Torah." This word has often been translated into Western languages (starting with *nomos* in the Greek translation, the Septuagint) by words meaning "law." But this is a misleading translation. Before we turn to a better translation for this word, let us spend some time thinking about the problem from another direction. Does the Torah make up a book of law in the modern sense of that term? Clearly, it does not.

The fact that the Pentateuch is not really a law book comes as no surprise to anyone who actually reads it. Very few law books begin, as Genesis does, with the creation of a solar system and then a story about two naked people wandering around a garden; very few law books conclude, as Deuteronomy does, with a dramatic and mysterious death and a cliffhanger ending that clamors for a sequel. (More people might go to law school if they did.) Why then, mistranslation though it is, did the Pentateuch acquire the name "Law"?

The answer, simply put, is because it is full of dos and don'ts, and of catalogues of various actions for which punishments are prescribed. These are things that, to our modern sensibilities, are most easily described as "laws." Yet it is worth stopping for a moment to consider the differences between the laws of the Pentateuch and those in the contemporary world. Outside of humorous or metaphoric uses, like Murphy's Law or the "law" of gravity, laws in our modern world are published in "codes" that attempt to thoroughly define all actions that violate the standards of society and prescribe what punishment shall be meted out for them. For instance, in the Commonwealth of Pennsylvania, the law against murder is found in Title 18, Sections 2501 and following, of the Pennsylvania Consolidated Statutes. It comprises hundreds of pages altogether, but it begins this way:

> A person is guilty of criminal homicide if he intentionally, knowingly, recklessly or negligently causes the death of another human being.

Compare this to the commandment given in Exod. 20:13:

You shall not murder.*

The "voice" in which the Pennsylvania Consolidated Statutes speak is an exhaustive and impersonal one. Such-and-such an act is defined as such-and-such a crime and is to be punished by such-and-such a penalty. The biblical "You shall not murder" neither defines the crime nor establishes a penalty for it. Nor is it impersonal. It addresses the individual directly: *you* shall not murder. This is law spoken in a very personal, albeit divine, voice. Moreover, this is not the only biblical "law" against murder. As part of the Ten Commandments, the injunction against murder is repeated in Deuteronomy. The commandment makes no mention of the distinctions recognized in modern law regarding various "degrees" of murder that mitigate the crime. But the distinction between an intentional and an unintentional killing naturally existed in biblical times too, and it *is* recognized in the Bible, though in a different context—that of the "cities of refuge":

> DEUT. 19:4 This is the case of the killer who shall flee there [to a "city of refuge"] and live: one who strikes another man without intent, not being a long-time enemy of his; 5 [for example] one who goes into the forest with someone else to cut wood, and his hand swings the ax to cut a tree, and the metal part of the ax slips off the handle and happens to hit the other man, who dies. Such a person shall flee to one of these cities and live.

See in full vv. 1–13. A similar, more extensive description of the cities of refuge and who may flee there is found in Numbers 35. Yet the context of that chapter is not a comprehensive listing of crimes, but a geographical description of the land that the Israelites are meant to live in. If the laws of the Bible are neither comprehensive nor

---

* The word "you" is in the singular (not plural) form in Hebrew, hence "thou" of the older translations. Despite the familiar translation, the verb used here is more usually used to mean the specific "murder," not the more general "kill."

"Consolidated," just what are they doing there? The answer is that they are expressions of different worldviews. In this chapter, we'll begin to think about not merely *what* the Bible's laws say, but *why* they say it.

Law and Story

The biblical repetition of laws in different places and in different forms is surprising when viewed in the context of modern law, but it makes perfect sense in light of the various theological voices we began to recognize in chapter 3. Remember also that the Pentateuch is *not* a legal code like modern compilations of laws. Instead, it is a story. A prologue, Genesis, sets the stage for the main story, told in Exodus through Deuteronomy, of a people enslaved who escape slavery and travel through the wilderness to the border of a new home where (it is implied) they will live happily ever after. In the course of this story, they are given instructions at various times on how to live once they are independent and self-governing in their new homeland. Unlike any other document of "law" I am familiar with, these rules for living are woven into the plot of the story. There is not a particular moment at which all the laws are handed down and recorded. True, sometimes the chapters of laws go on at such length that we do seem to be reading a law "code." Even these collections of laws, though, come to us, through the different theological voices of the Pentateuch, at different points in the plot of the exodus story. And some laws are actually given by God to Moses to settle individual cases. Consider, for example, the following from Numbers 15:

> NUM. 15:32 While the Israelites were in the wilderness, they found a man gathering wood on the Sabbath day. 33 Those who found him gathering wood brought him near to Moses and to Aaron and to the whole assembly. 34 They put him in custody, for it was not clear what should be done to him. 35 YHWH said to Moses, "The man must be put to death. The whole assembly shall pelt him with stones outside the camp." 36 The whole assembly took

LEGAL VOICES 137

him outside the camp and pelted him with stones, and he died, as YHWH had commanded Moses.

Here is an incident in which a "crime" (in our modern terminology) appeared to have been committed, yet despite the fact that many chapters of "law" have already been included by this point in the story, the leaders of the people are faced with an apparently simple case where they have no idea what to do. Fortunately, God provides the answer. Notice that the text does not say how or even whether they approached God with their problem, merely that he resolved the situation for them. Notice too that God's response is not formulated as a general law—"Anyone who gathers wood on the Sabbath day must be put to death"—but is framed as an instruction on how to handle this particular case. It seems reasonable to assume that the specific ruling implied a general application, but this is never stated.

Zelophehad's Daughters Stake Their Claim

A bit later on in Numbers, we do find a particular incident, this time involving a matter we would call civil rather than criminal law, where gaps similar to those in the woodcutter story *are* filled in. Numbers 26 describes a census of the various tribes, after which YHWH instructs Moses that the land should be divided proportionately by tribe. At the beginning of Numbers 27, as in the case of the woodcutter, a judgment on a particular point is sought:

> NUM. 27:1 The daughters of Zelophehad son of Hepher son of Gilead son of Machir son of Manasseh, of the clans of Manasseh son of Joseph, drew near. (These are the names of his daughters: Mahlah, Noah, Hoglah, Milcah, and Tirzah.) ² They stood before Moses and before Eleazar the priest, and before the leaders and the whole assembly at the entrance to the Tent of Meeting and said this: ³ "Our father died in the wilderness. He was not among the crowd who assembled against YHWH in the assembly of Korah; rather, he died for his own sin. And he had no sons.

⁴ Why should our father's name be excised from his clan because he had no son? Give us a land-holding in the midst of our father's brothers!" ⁵ Moses brought near their case before YHWH.
⁶ YHWH said to Moses, ⁷ "Zelophehad's daughters speak rightly. You must give them a holding of property amongst their father's brothers, and transfer their father's property to them. ⁸ And to the Israelites speak as follows: 'A man who dies and has no son—you must transfer his property to his daughter. ⁹ If he has no daughter, give his property to his brothers. ¹⁰ If he has no brothers, give his property to his father's brothers. ¹¹ If his father had no brothers, give his property to his closest kin from his own clan to inherit.' And this shall be a legal statute for the Israelites 'as YHWH commanded Moses.'"

Here we see that, just as Zelophehad's daughters brought their case "near" to Moses for judgment, so Moses brought it "near" before YHWH to provide a solution for this individual case. (To our disappointment, the text still does not tell us exactly how he did this; perhaps it was simply by entering the Tent of Meeting and speaking to YHWH, just as Zelophehad's daughters had spoken to him.)

YHWH renders judgment, but goes beyond what we saw in the woodcutter incident. This time not only is this particular case given its resolution, but a general rule is established. *Anyone* who dies without sons—not just Zelophehad—from now on leaves his property to his daughters. Nor is this all. YHWH takes the occasion to provide a complete hierarchy of inheritance that has nothing to do with the specific case at hand. Moreover, we are explicitly told (it is not completely clear in whose voice, whether YHWH's or the narrator's) that this is to be an Israelite "legal statute."

Zelophehad's Daughters: The Aftermath

Looking at the larger literary context, the clarification of inheritance rules has a certain logic at this moment in the "plot" of the Pentateuch.

In the next two verses of Numbers 27, Moses is told that he must climb a mountain from which he will view the Land of Israel from a distance and then die without leading the Israelites into it. Thus the division of the land among the various tribes and clans, as outlined in Numbers 26, is indeed topical at this point in the story. But even though Moses is about to die, the affair is not quite finished.

In Numbers 36, at the very end of the book, the other litigants in the case appear and persuade Moses to rule that Zelophehad's daughters must marry men from the tribe of Manasseh so that the property of their father will not pass over to a different tribe. Yet, appropriate as it is, the ad hoc nature of this judgment leaves someone who thinks of law in the modern sense somewhat uneasy. Still, the inheritance rules and the judgment about the woodcutter are somewhat peripheral issues from the wider perspective of biblical "law." So why are they here? At least in the case of Zelophehad's daughters, where the inheritance of land that has not yet even been distributed is so fiercely contested, we might well suspect that the two halves of the judgment were added to the narrative at a time when the land had already been settled. A later voice, interested in establishing a legal precedent about inheritance, might well have chosen a story framework to emphasize the effects of the problem on real people. But we would expect to find the more basic biblical commandments presented as part of YHWH's instructions to Moses, as a kind of constitution for Israel—not simply as individual laws casually introduced into the plot.

Manna and the Sabbath

Amazingly, the Sabbath, which in the ancient world was considered the feature that of all things most characterized and constituted the Jewish people, is also first introduced as an integrated part of the story and not a formal commandment. Although the very beginning of the Bible hints at the Sabbath when God creates the world in six days and then rests on the seventh, there is no explicit mention of it there. No instructions whatsoever regarding observance of a Sabbath are given to the Israelites until, in between the crossing of the Red Sea and their arrival at Sinai, they begin to eat manna. Exodus 16 tells the story. Each day, they collect just enough for that day—miraculously, everyone collects the same amount, one omer.* They eat as much as they collect and make no provision for the future; whatever is left over until the next morning breeds maggots. But the sixth day is different:

> EXOD. 16:22 On the sixth day, they gathered a double portion of food—two omers each. All the leaders of the assembly came and told Moses. [23] He said to them, "This is what YHWH has spoken. Tomorrow will be a day of rest, a holy Sabbath, to YHWH. Bake what you want to bake, boil what you want to boil, and keep whatever is left over for yourselves until the morning." [24] They left it until morning, as Moses had commanded, and it did not go bad, nor were there any maggots in it. [25] Moses said, "Eat it today, for today is a Sabbath to YHWH; you will not find it in the field. [26] You shall gather it for six days, but the seventh day is a Sabbath, on which there will not be any." [27] On the seventh day, some of the people went out to gather, but found nothing.
>
> [28] YHWH said to Moses, "How long will you refuse to keep My commandments and My instructions? [29] Look, YHWH has given you the Sabbath. Therefore, on the sixth day, He gives you two days worth of food. Sit, each of you, in your own spot. Let no one leave his place on the seventh day." [30] So the people rested on the seventh day.

We see, then, that even the law of the Sabbath, whose observance became one of the Ten Commandments, is not proclaimed in advance, but is integrated into the story of the manna. The Israelites learn its observance, and its importance, by experiencing it.

---

* We don't have precise equivalents for biblical measures. A reasonable guess for the omer would probably be about a quart.

Most of the laws in the Pentateuch, of course, are not found one at a time, in story contexts, but in larger groups that, by comparison with our own legal system, we sometimes call "codes." Yet even these larger groupings of laws are part of a story. They are given to the Israelites, and are encountered by readers of the Bible, at various times and places along the Israelites' journey out of Egypt and to the far bank of the Jordan River. This journey, a long one whether measured in distance or in time, provided room for the various different voices who told the story of it to include different sets of laws that fit their differing worldviews. To sort out the various voices of law in the Pentateuch, let us begin by looking at the two different versions of the Ten Commandments.

The Ten Commandments

According to the story line of the Pentateuch, of course, God only spoke the Ten Commandments once, in Exodus 20. But the book of Deuteronomy, which is essentially presented as a long farewell speech by Moses, gives him the opportunity to recap the entire story of the exodus and the wilderness wanderings. In the course of this recap, he retells the story of the giving of the Ten Commandments and, in Deuteronomy 5, recites them again. In Moses's repetition of the commandments, they are (naturally) essentially the same as in the Exodus 20 version, but not exactly so. The most obvious difference, and the most telling one, comes in the commandment about the Sabbath:*

EXOD. 20:8 Remember the Sabbath day, to sanctify it.	DEUT. 5:12 Keep the Sabbath day, to sanctify it, as YHWH your God commanded you.

---

* The commandments are divided into ten in different ways by Jews and by various kinds of Christians. For this reason, I refer to the Sabbath commandments by subject, not by number.

⁹ Six days shall you labor and do all of your work. ¹⁰ But the seventh day is a Sabbath to YHWH your God. You shall not do any work—you, your son or daughter, your male or female slave,	¹³ Six days shall you labor and do all of your work. ¹⁴ But the seventh day is a Sabbath to YHWH your God. You shall not do any work—you, your son or daughter, your male or female slave,
your animal,	your ox, your ass, or any of your animals,
or the stranger who lives in your town.	or the stranger who lives in your town, so that your slaves may rest as you do.
¹¹ For in six days YHWH made the heavens, the earth, the sea, and all that is in them, and he rested on the seventh day.	¹⁵ You shall remember that you were a slave in the land of Egypt, and that YHWH your God brought you out of there with a strong hand and an outstretched arm.
Therefore YHWH blessed the seventh day and sanctified it.	Therefore YHWH commanded you to observe the Sabbath day.

There are a few differences here that are fairly minor, of the kind that are found in the other commandments as well. For example, the words "As YHWH your God commanded you" are added after the very first sentence, and a couple of specific animals are added to the general rule that even animals should not be forced to work on the Sabbath. The more telling differences are a tiny but crucial one right at the beginning, a small addition in the middle, and then the large difference at the end. These are the differences that will enable us to begin to recognize the Deuteronomic voice in legal texts, just as we saw it in the previous chapter in theological ones. Let us take the differences in order.

The first difference between the two versions of the commandment is that in Exodus the Israelites are instructed to "remember" the Sabbath day, while in Deuteronomy they are instructed to "keep" it. The change is made because the word "remember" serves a special purpose in Deuteronomy. It is always used exclusively with historical events. In Deuteronomy, the Israelites are frequently told to remember what *happened* to them, but they are never told to remember what God has *told* them. They "remember" events, but "keep" God's commandments. Deuteronomy uses these verbs to distinguish two different kinds of knowledge, things that were *seen* and those that were *heard*. Most of the Bible is not interested in this distinction, which depends on a fairly sophisticated understanding of the human mind, but Deuteronomy is. Hence "remember" of the Exodus text was changed in the repetition to match Deuteronomic psychological terminology.

The second quite significant change is the addition to the long list of those who must be permitted to rest on the Sabbath of a clause emphasizing that, on this day, rest is not just for the masters but for the slaves as well. Since the Exodus version of the commandment already makes this entirely clear, the addition seems to serve as a kind of rhetorical emphasis, insisting that the commandment involves not just a day of rest, but a day when all people revert to their original equal status. Moreover, the emphasis that slaves must rest provides the justification for the rest of the verse, the Deuteronomic explanation of *why* the Israelites must observe the Sabbath.

The Exodus version of the Ten Commandments indicates that the special status of the seventh day of the week comes from the blessing God granted it when he finished the work of creation:

> GEN. 2:3 God blessed the seventh day and sanctified it, for on it He sabbathed from all His work that God created by making.

I have deliberately translated the verb "rested" here in accordance with its sound and its etymology, to show how the link with the Sabbath is all but explicit in this verse.

Though the explanation that the Israelites must observe the Sabbath because God blessed that day does not say so explicitly, it also implies something more: that observance of the Sabbath is an aspect of what theologians call *imitatio Dei*, "imitation of God." By imitating divine behavior, the human beings who (according to Genesis 1) were created in God's image can conform more closely to the divine model. In this case, since the process of creation involved not merely six days of labor but a seventh day of rest, they, like God, must work for six days but then rest on the seventh. Moreover, it would seem that according to this explanation the world was actually constructed in such a way that resting on the seventh day keeps one "in tune with the universe."

The Deuteronomic explanation is quite different. As we have pointed out, Deuteronomy adds an extra clause to the commandment, emphasizing that slaves rest equally with their masters, which makes the subsequent explanation of the commandment much more logical in context. The subsidiary "commandment" (not counted as one of the ten) to "remember that you were a slave in the land of Egypt" amounts almost literally to the insistence that each individual Israelite have a social conscience. This explanation presents the Sabbath commandment as inextricably tied up with the Israelites' experience in Egypt. Implicitly, God's redeeming them from slavery provides the justification for his issuance of commands to them, as their new master. Moreover, they are instructed to renew this awareness of their own experience as slaves every seven days. Seen in the perspective of Exodus 20, the Sabbath is an inherently cosmic phenomenon. In Deuteronomy 5, it is very much a social and historical one—a worldly one.

A Second Kind of Decalogue

One would think that including the Ten Commandments in the Bible twice would be enough. But in fact the Bible includes two *more* sets of "ten commandments." These are not repetitions of the commandments that were proclaimed in Exodus 20, as was Deuteronomy 5, but two different sets of commandments that, nonetheless, seem to have a special status. They are versions of what is called "the Ritual Decalogue."*

The reason it makes sense to think of these two sets of commandments as a second kind of Decalogue is the way they are woven into the story. Everyone is familiar with the image, made famous in art and so much a part of how we think of the Bible that it is used in movies and cartoons, of Moses coming down the mountains with two stone tablets that have the Ten Commandments engraved on them. But not everyone remembers that, when Moses finally did come down the mountain, he saw the Israelites worshiping the Golden Calf, lost his temper, and broke the stone tablets. (See Exod. 32:19. We will see later in this chapter why this happens so long after the giving of the Ten Commandments in Exodus 20.) Moses then goes back up the mountain and (after forty days) returns, in Exodus 34, with a *second* set of tablets. In fact, it is here (in Exod. 34:28) that they are first identified as the "Ten" Commandments; in Exodus 20, the number is not mentioned. Yet the commandments in Exodus 34, presented (like the earlier ones) as the basis of God's covenant with Israel, are quite different:

> [17] You shall not make molten gods for yourself.
>
> [18] You shall keep the Festival of Unleavened Bread. For seven days you shall eat unleavened bread, as I commanded you on the occasion of the month of Abib; for in Abib you went forth from Egypt.
>
> [19] Everything that first breaches the womb is Mine, among all of your animals that bear a male, whether ox or sheep. [20] But an ass that first breaches the womb you shall redeem with a sheep; if you do not redeem it, you must break its neck. Every first-born of your sons you shall redeem. No one shall appear before Me empty-handed.
>
> [21] Six days shall you labor, and on the seventh day you shall rest. In plowing-time and harvest-time, you shall rest.

---

* "Decalogue" comes from the Greek for "ten words," which is how this text is described in the Bible.

²² You shall make for yourself a Festival of Weeks—the first-fruits of the wheat harvest—and a Festival of Ingathering at the turn of the year.

²³ Three times a year, every one of your males shall appear before the Lord YHWH, God of Israel. ²⁴ When I dispossess nations before you and expand your territory, no one will covet your land when you go up to appear before YHWH your God three times a year.

²⁵ You shall not slaughter My sacrificial blood with anything leavened, nor shall the sacrifice of the Festival of Passover remain overnight until morning.

²⁶ You shall bring the best of the first-fruits of your soil to the House of YHWH your God.

You shall not boil a kid in its mother's milk.

²⁷ YHWH said to Moses, "Write down these words, for in accordance with these words do I make a covenant with you, and with Israel." ²⁸ He was there with YHWH forty days and forty nights. He ate no food and drank no water. He wrote on the tablets the words of the covenant, the Ten Words.

It is after coming down the mountain with this set of tablets that Moses's face acquires the radiance that we learned in chapter 3 is associated with God's Presence; that story is therefore assumed to be part of the priestly source. Nevertheless, scholars have long considered the preceding passage, the one we have just seen, to be the otherwise missing J version of the Ten Commandments, woven into the story at this point. (It is difficult to figure out how to divide them into ten, suggesting that even the identification of this passage as a Decalogue [in v. 28] is not original.) But because of the section's content, scholars often note that this version must have a "cultic" origin. In biblical scholarship, "cult" is not a pejorative word; it simply refers to the technical aspects of any form of worship—how the rituals of that religion are performed. The technical aspects of the worship of YHWH, of course, were in the hands of the priests. Since our object here is not to categorize texts according to the Documentary Hypothesis but simply to recognize the different biblical voices, we can safely say that this version of the Ten Commandments is priestly, whether or not it comes from the sources called "P."

The Ritual Decalogue

Looking back at what is covered in this set of commandments, it is easy to see why scholars have given it the "ritual" label. By contrast with the famous Decalogue of Exodus 20, this one has no rules against murder, adultery, theft, witnessing falsely, or covetousness, and no injunction to honor one's father and mother. Certainly the voice that is speaking here was not in favor of murder and so forth, and their absence from the Decalogue should not mislead us into thinking that such horrendous crimes were of no consequence for this author. Rather, we must assume that such things were taken for granted as the basis of any society.

The Ritual Decalogue says that the special basis of the covenant between God and the Israelites involves their obligations to him—to offer sacrifices to him according to certain particular rules and at certain particular times and, most importantly, to come on pilgrimage to his Temple three times a year with offerings of the bounty of the land to which God was bringing them.

It is also easy to see why this Decalogue makes sense from a priestly point of view. From a strictly practical perspective, the offerings brought to the Temple provided the priests with their subsistence. Reading more generously, it makes sense that the priests would see the obligations of the Israelites toward God—for which they were ultimately responsible—as the essential basis of society. Neglect of these obligations would, presumably, place the Israelites as a whole, not just the priests, at risk. If the purpose of a decalogue was to distill the essence of law, the constitutional core (so to speak) that defined this particular culture, it makes sense that a version of this in a priestly voice would be of a ritual nature.

Scholars gave this group of laws the name Ritual Decalogue at a time when "ritual" was something of a pejorative word. Ritual was considered to consist of a series of formal actions that could be carried out by someone who was actually thinking of evil or, perhaps worse, of nothing at all. The realm of ritual behavior, in this sense, was thought of as the enemy of what was "spiritual," an attitude of love and awe toward God. But to think of the Ritual Decalogue like this is to hear the priestly voice in a distorted way. We would do better to take our cue from the contrast between the two versions of the Sabbath commandment in the Exodus 20 and Deuteronomy 5 decalogues, one linking Sabbath observance to divine concerns and one to human concerns. The priestly decalogue of Exodus 34 shows us that the priestly writers gave pride of place to the Israelites' obligations toward God. As we will see further on in this chapter, another version of the priestly voice would integrate both ritual and social concerns within the Israelites' religious obligations. First, however, let us step back from our examination of the Decalogue—in all its forms—and take a broader look at the Pentateuch's combination of law and narrative.

The Different Sets of Laws

How is it that the first and second sets of stone tablets, the decalogues of Exodus 20 and Exodus 34, could be so different? What made this possible is the nature of the Pentateuch not as law but as story, the integration of God's commandments to Israel within a historical narrative. The biblical voices agree that God revealed himself to Israel in the wilderness of Sinai, but this was not the only time God spoke to Moses. So various larger collections of laws might fit into the story at several points. Leaving aside individual laws like the law of inheritance from the story about Zelophehad's daughters, the following list summarizes the "decalogues" and the other sizable law collections and shows how they fit into the "plot" of the Pentateuch:

- **Exodus 20:1–14 (the Ten Commandments).** * Despite our image of

* These extend through v. 17 in Christian Bibles; Jewish tradition combines the commandments against murder, adultery, stealing, and false witness into a single verse. A similar numbering pattern occurs in Deuteronomy 5, the chapter where Moses repeats the commandments.

Charlton Heston, if you read carefully, you will see that in the text as it stands Moses is *down on the ground, not on the mountain* when these words are spoken. In addition, God speaks them not to Moses alone but to all Israel. Nonetheless, since they occur immediately after the preparations for revelation that we examined in Exodus 19, they have achieved pride of place as "the" Ten Commandments. Which biblical voice speaks them is not easy to say. Many scholars hear a very slight Deuteronomic accent in them. But as we saw with the Sabbath commandment, the actual Deuteronomic voice is different from this one.

• **Exodus 21:1–23:19 (the Covenant Code).** This is the first major law collection in the Pentateuch. It is introduced as if it, not the Ten Commandments, was the contents of the revelation to Moses on Mount Sinai. By the end of Exodus 20, Moses has indeed approached God, who tells him, "Now these are the rulings (*mishpatim*) that you shall set before them" (Exod. 21:1). What follows is a collection of civil, criminal, ritual, and moral laws, presented both as cases and as commandments. I mention the particular Hebrew word that is used because, as we'll see, this too differs among the different voices.

• **Exodus 25:1–31:18.** In a sense, this is the longest of the sections of ad hoc law in the Pentateuch. It has no commonly used name because it is not law in the usual sense of the word, but more like what we would call a set of instructions. Also presented as part of the revelation to Moses on the mountain, it consists entirely of the details of how the Israelites are to build and staff the Tabernacle: "Let them build Me a sanctuary so I may dwell among them" (Exod. 25:8). Complete plans for the Tabernacle are given, as well as instructions on how to equip and install Moses's brother Aaron and Aaron's sons as priests to serve there. Though these instructions are presented as something that will be carried out immediately, the implication is that what is commanded here will continue, presumably forever, once the Israelites enter the land of Canaan. The content of the section makes clear that it belongs to P. The instructions are essentially repeated when they are carried out, "as YHWH commanded Moses," in Exodus 35–40 (the building of the Tabernacle) and Leviticus 8–9 (the inauguration of the priesthood).

- **Exodus 34:17–26 (the Ritual Decalogue).** While Moses is on the mountain getting the instructions about the Tabernacle and priesthood from God, the Israelites, despairing of his return, make the Golden Calf and begin to worship it. When God warns Moses about this, he goes back down to them and, in his anger, shatters the stone tablets that God had given him. After handling the situation, Moses is told to return to the mountain, where God instructs him to carve a new set of tablets. He is then given a set of commandments often thought of as belonging to J, but clearly in a voice that is concerned with ritual. As we saw, this is the point in the text where they are first identified as the "ten words." He then returns to the people and proceeds to build the Tabernacle.
- **Leviticus 1–7.** These are the laws of sacrifice (though there is no commonly used name for this section). They are the first section of the heart of P, the priestly document. As the introduction to this section shows, the priestly assumption that after the Tabernacle was built God dwelt among the people meant that law-giving was not restricted to the theophany before the whole people at Mount Sinai: "He called to Moses, and YHWH spoke to him from the Tent of Meeting as follows" (Lev. 1:1). Now that the Tent is in action—we saw in chapter 3 how, at the end of Exodus 40, the Tent received its "electric charge"—God can speak to Moses whenever necessary, even as the Israelites continue traveling through the wilderness. Nonetheless, the laws of sacrifice presented here are not ad hoc, but represent a complete system.
- **Leviticus 11–16.** After the intervening chapters of narrative in which the priests are sanctified and two of Aaron's sons die in the midst of unauthorized ritual acts, the second half of the priestly corpus of laws is presented. The focus here is on the avoidance of various forms of "contamination"—in a ritual, not a medical, sense (though the two categories sometimes overlap). This was also a major concern of P, as evidenced by the fact that returning to a state of purity also involves bringing a sacrifice. Again, although it is not explicitly stated, we should probably assume that when God speaks these laws to

Moses (and, because it is P, sometimes also to Aaron), he is doing so in the Tent of Meeting.
- **Leviticus 17–26 (the Holiness Code).** This section, following immediately after the P laws of Leviticus 1–7 and 11–16, is presented in context as if it too is revealed to Moses in the Tent of Meeting. This is also a priestly voice, but because of differences in language, emphasis, and ritual, scholars agree that it is not the same as the voice we call P. Because of its concern with holiness, it is labeled H. Scholars long believed that H was an early text of the priestly school and P a more developed one, and many Christian scholars still retain this view. But most Jewish scholars are now convinced that H is in fact the voice that is responsible for the final editing of the Pentateuch. This is the view that I will present later in this chapter. We will see then why, though H begins as if it were transmitted to Moses in the Tent of Meeting, it shifts in the middle (see 25:1) to Mount Sinai, and concludes with the statement, "These are the laws, the rules, and the instructions which YHWH established between Himself and the Israelites on Mount Sinai at the hand of Moses" (Lev. 26:46).
- **Leviticus 27.** This chapter seems to be a sort of appendix that was added to the end of the book of Leviticus. Despite the summary verse that ends Leviticus 26, this chapter begins again with the words "YHWH spoke to Moses as follows," introducing technical material that describes a set tariff of how various things are to be valued when it is necessary to convert their worth into sacred donations. This chapter ends with a conclusion similar to that of Leviticus 26: "These are the commandments which YHWH commanded Moses for the Israelites on Mount Sinai" (Lev. 27:34).
- **Numbers.** This is the book in which the entire wilderness journey from Sinai to the east bank of the Jordan takes place. There is nothing in Numbers resembling a law "code," but there are many sections of law scattered through the book. Some (like the stories of the man gathering wood on the Sabbath and the daughters of Zelophehad) are presented in narrative form, while others (like the ritual of the red

cow in Numbers 19 and the festival offerings of Numbers 28–29) have a more legal flavor. These longer sections have a distinct priestly flavor but it is not clear just what priestly voice they belong to.

• **Deuteronomy 5:6–18 (extending through v. 21 in Christian Bibles).** As we have already seen, this is Moses's repetition of the Ten Commandments found in Exodus 20. Deuteronomy is presented as the farewell address of Moses to the Israelites just before he is to die and they are to cross the Jordan River into Canaan—whose location is specified in Deut. 1:5 as "beyond the Jordan in the land of Moab" (part of today's kingdom of Jordan). As an introduction to his final words, Moses recounts everything that has happened to the Israelites since their journey from "Horeb" (this is the Deuteronomic name for Sinai). He then reminds the Israelites of the covenant that God made with them. This is the D version of the Ten Commandments.

• **Deuteronomy 12–26.** The centerpiece of the book of Deuteronomy, and thus of the D source, is the Deuteronomic law code. Like the Covenant Code of Exodus 21–23, it is broadly concerned with all areas of life. Some scholars believe that it is a revision (and expansion) of the Covenant Code; it certainly treats some of the same subjects differently. As we saw in chapter 2, various clues make this the one biblical source that we can assign with some confidence to a particular period in history—the seventh century BCE.

The two versions of the Ten Commandments and the Ritual Decalogue each line up (albeit not precisely) with one of the larger groupings of law and in turn with one of the narrative sources of the Pentateuch, though the laws in Numbers complicate this picture somewhat. Thus the version of the Ten Commandments that is presented in Exodus 20 is generally thought to belong to E, and so do the laws of the Covenant Code that immediately follow them in Exodus 21–23. The version of the Ten Commandments that Moses repeats in Deuteronomy 5, like the laws of Deuteronomy 12–26, are woven into the D source as a whole. Similarly, the Ritual Decalogue of Exodus is in a priestly voice, matching the instructions for the Tabernacle, sacrifice, and the priesthood that surround it in Exodus and Leviticus.

Now let us look at the differences between these voices more closely by narrowing our focus to a particular topic.

The Laws of Slavery

When we read the Torah with the notion of law presented as an integral part of a story, we realize that the first full set of laws presented to the Israelites is the Covenant Code. Narratively, with Moses still on the ground warning the people about the theophany to come, God has suddenly proclaimed the Ten Commandments. Only then does Moses once again approach God. After announcing the conditions under which he is to be worshiped—the "altar law" of Exod. 20:19–23 (vv. 22–26 in Christian versions), which we saw in chapter 3. God instructs Moses about the "rules" under which the Israelites are to live. Remarkably, the very beginning of the Covenant Code is this:

> EXOD. 21:2 When you buy a Hebrew slave, he shall serve for six years and in the seventh he shall go free without payment. 3 If he came in single, he shall leave single; if he is a married man, his wife shall leave with him. 4 If his master gives him a wife and she bears him sons or daughters, the wife and children shall belong to the master, and he [the slave] shall leave single. 5 But if the slave says, "I love my master, my wife, and my sons, and I will not go free," 6 then his master shall bring him to God [some translate: "to the judges"] and shall bring him to the door or the doorpost; and his master shall pierce his ear with an awl, and he shall serve him forever.

How are we to understand the placement of this law? We all know that slavery was an accepted part of the ancient world. Yet even in a world where slavery was commonplace, it could not have been anything other than jarring to see that the first law presented to the escaping slaves is one about owning slaves.

Nonetheless, the nature of the law is instructive. At least in the case of a Hebrew slave, his term of service is automatically limited. Rather than being a slave as we now understand the word—someone who must buy his freedom or die in chains—he is an indentured servant who must serve a fixed term of six years but then is automatically freed. Still, somehow mixed into this notion of service for a fixed term is the concept of children who are born into slavery. The end of the paragraph harshly insists that a slave who has been "bred" by his master and wishes to stay with his wife and children must give up his freedom for life.

On the surface, this is a practical law, that is, one that could, in practice, have been carried out. A man's six years as an indentured servant are over, and here is the procedure to be followed. It seems, moreover, to be a law that is meant to apply not to the period of the desert wandering when, according to the narrative, it was given, but to the settled life that is expected to follow the Israelites' arrival in Canaan. In general, this settled condition is the framework for the Covenant Code. For example:

> EXOD. 21:33 If a man opens a pit or digs a pit and does not cover it, and an ox or an ass falls into it, 34 the owner of the pit must pay. He shall hand over money to its owner, and the carcass shall be his.

> EXOD. 22:4 If a man lets a field or vineyard be grazed bare by loosing his livestock into another's field to graze it bare, he shall repay with the best of his field and the best of his vineyard.*

It need hardly be said that there were no vineyards in the wilderness of Sinai. Moreover, the religious laws included here also implicitly look forward past the period of wandering:

> EXOD. 23:19a The best of the first fruits of your soil you shall bring to the house of YHWH your God.

At the point when the Israelites arrive at Sinai, there is no "house of YHWH," nor will there be one for centuries to come. Yet the Covenant Code concludes with a law instructing the newly freed slaves

---

* This is v. 5 in Christian versions.

on how to express their thanks to God once they have established themselves as landowners in Canaan. Indeed, these chapters of law conclude (in Exod. 23:20-33) with a passage that explains just how God intends to give the land of Canaan to the Israelites.

What this means is that, in its context in the book of Exodus, the Covenant Code is playing two roles. It is to serve as a kind of law code to shape Israelite society—the "rulings" (as its laws are called) that will ensure a just and stable society. This system is marked as just by being placed in the mouth of God in the awe-inspiring moment when he appeared to the entire people at Sinai. From the perspective of the overall story line, though, all these are things the Israelites will not need to know until they have settled their land. In the context of the narrative, the key to this set of laws—and its difficulty—is its very beginning. The first "rule" offered to the escaped slaves is one that will permit them to have slaves of their own—and, implicitly, to be enslaved again themselves. Their descendants, the settled Israelites who encounter these words as text rather than as revelation, among them slave owners, would be viscerally reminded by the juxtaposition that there is another side to the master-slave relationship.

The Slave Law of Deuteronomy

If we examine the law about freeing slaves in D, we will see two key things. First, it is explicitly pegged to the kind of social agenda that we saw in the Sabbath commandment from the decalogue of Deuteronomy 5. Second, Deuteronomy's slave law is clearly based on the text of the slave law from the Covenant Code:

> DEUT. 15:12 When your brother or sister Hebrew is sold to you, he shall serve you for six years and in the seventh year you shall let him go free from you. **13** When you let him go free from you, do not let him go empty-handed. **14** You must bestow a gift upon him from your flock, your threshing-floor, and your vat; give him of what YHWH your God has blessed you with. **15** Remember that you were a slave in the land of Egypt and YHWH your God

redeemed you. Therefore I command you this thing today. ¹⁶ If he should say to you, "I will not leave you, for I love you and your household," for he has it good with you, ¹⁷ then you shall take the awl and put it in his ear and in the door, and he shall be your slave forever. Do the same for your female slave. ¹⁸ Do not think it hard when you send him forth free from you, for he has given you double the service of a hired hand for six years, and YHWH your God shall bless you in all that you do.

This law follows that of the Covenant Code in its structure and its basic prescriptions about slavery. If we compare the two, we can see how D has altered the earlier law in ways that clarify it, expand it, and change it. Let's line them up next to each other, as we did with the Sabbath commandments.

EXOD. 21:2 When you buy a Hebrew slave, he shall serve for six years and in the seventh he shall go free without payment.	DEUT. 15:12 When your brother or sister Hebrew is sold to you, he shall serve you for six years and in the seventh year you shall let him go free from you. ¹³ When you let him go free from you, do not let him go empty-handed. ¹⁴ You must bestow a gift upon him from your flock, your threshing-floor, and your vat; give him of what YHWH your God has blessed you with. ¹⁵ Remember that you were a slave in the land of Egypt and YHWH your God redeemed you. Therefore I command you this thing today.

³ If he came in single, he shall leave single; if he is a married man, his wife shall leave with him. ⁴ If his master gives him a wife and she bears him sons or daughters, the wife and children shall belong to the master, and he [the slave] shall leave single.
⁵ But if the slave says, "I love my master, my wife, and my sons, and I will not go free," ⁶ then his master shall bring him to God [some translate: "to the judges"] and shall bring him to the door or the doorpost; and his master shall pierce his ear with an awl, and he shall serve him forever.

¹⁶ If he should say to you, "I will not leave you, for I love you and your household," for he has it good with you, ¹⁷ then you shall take the awl and put it in his ear and in the door, and he shall be your slave forever.

Do the same for your female slave.
¹⁸ Do not think it hard when you send him forth free from you, for he has given you double the service of a hired hand for six years, and YHWH your God shall bless you in all that you do.

Instead of asserting "when you acquire a Hebrew slave," D makes slavery something the person *does*, not something that he *is*. Second, the slave owner does not go out and buy a slave; rather, the slave "is sold," passively, suggesting (as Jewish tradition interpreted it) that the "slave" was working off a debt, and perhaps further implying that one should not go out of one's way to acquire slaves. Third, the essential kinship of the "Hebrew" slave with his Israelite owner is emphasized. Fourth, the verse makes explicit that the same laws apply to both male and female slaves. By contrast, the slave of the Covenant Code law is a male; he may or may not have a wife, who may or may not be the owner's permanent property. In D, the simple insertion of two small words—"or sister"—means that the confusing (and for D, obviously troubling) possibility of someone's being born a slave, as in Exod. 21:4, is completely eliminated.

Next we come to a Deuteronomic prescription that illustrates the complicated nature of the interaction between the different biblical voices. Up to this point, it might be possible to argue that D is only making explicit what the Covenant Code really "meant." We have seen that one result of this process, based on making explicit that the release law applies to female slaves as well as to male ones, actually had the far-reaching result of implicitly eliminating the notion that an Israelite could be a slave by birth. (Nor does D seem to envision non-Israelites who are slaves to Israelites; at least, the text is silent on this subject.) Now, however, D makes a more complicated interpretive move. It deliberately misreads the Covenant Code in order to change it.

Exod. 21:2 says that the slave must be freed after six years of slavery "without payment." In context, and following what we know about the general practice of human slavery, this is a bold demand. It asserts that the slave does not have to *buy* his freedom; he serves six years and is then freed automatically without having to make any payment at all. D, of course, has no argument with this procedure. It too provides for the slave's automatic release. But D deliberately reads the words "without payment" in Exodus to mean *without payment by the owner* of the slave for his years of work, and this D finds intolerable. Instead, the slave must be set free *with* payment, by the bestowal of a gift from the natural bounty with which YHWH has blessed the slave's master.

The slave laws of the Covenant Code create—no doubt deliberately—a tension with the narrative framework in which they occur, being given to a people that has just been freed from years of slavery. But this tension, strong as it is, is left implicit. For D, the experience of slavery in Egypt was a formative one. Certainly not every law in D is given an explicit justification. But in the laws about slavery itself, the Egyptian experience cannot be ignored. The freeing of the slave is not merely the resolution of an economic transaction. It also always involves the explicit recognition of *why* the slave must be freed. The slave's master remembers that he too was once a slave and that God "redeemed" him—that is, restored him to his natural condition. The implication is that, under the ordinary conditions of day-to-day life in Israel, the natural human condition is one of freedom. The economic pressures that may force someone into slavery should not be thought of as altering his essential nature or fixing his place in society.

The provision for eternal enslavement follows a similar trend. In Exodus, the male slave could be in some sense coerced into permanent bondage by being given a slave wife. Love for his children, born into (apparently permanent) slavery, may persuade the father to acquiesce in permanent slavery for himself as well. In D, there is no coercive aspect to this law. Only the slave's own realization that his situation is a good one can persuade him not to leave at the end of six years. Again, D makes clear that this provision too applies equally to male and to female slaves. Finally, D concludes by emphasizing an element of fairness in the freeing of the slave. The slave owner should not be upset, for the slave has already given him double service. Since it is easy to imagine a slave owner who would be upset at not *continuing* to receive this double service, the argument here must be that the slave owner has already somehow gotten more than he deserved and so should not complain about losing it, especially when releasing another human being to freedom is involved.

The Slave Law of the Holiness Code

We've said before, and will see again, that the biblical law "codes" should not be mistaken for comprehensive sets of rules that were enforced by governmental authority. But the comparison of the slave laws in the Covenant Code and in Deuteronomy shows clearly that a later legal voice with a very different perspective might be partly constrained to follow an older text closely. It is easy to see that the structure of the D text is modeled after that of the corresponding law in the Covenant Code, just as the Sabbath commandment of Deuteronomy 5 was modeled after that of Exodus 20.

It is difficult for us to judge just how much of a constraint the earlier text was on the later writer. The equalization of the status of male and female slaves and the insistence that the slave must be given a grubstake when he is freed are radically different from the earlier law in extending extra protection to the slave. One might think, then, that the slave who was not ready for freedom might be allowed to renew his indenture on, say, a yearly basis, until he was more confident of success in earning a living on his own. In this case, the earlier text may have been the decisive factor that reduced the slave's choices to two: six years and out or slavery for life.

P has no slave law, because the laws of P are almost entirely concerned with priestly ritual. Slavery, as essentially an area of economic regulation, did not fall under the priests' purview. But there is a slave law in the Holiness Code (H) that, in my view, combines some of the same social concerns found in D with a distinctly priestly viewpoint:

> LEV. 25:39 When your kinsman has become impoverished with you and is sold to you, you shall not work him with slave's work. [40] Like a hired man or an indentured servant shall he be with you. He shall work with you until the Jubilee year. [41] Then he shall go forth from you, he and his children with him, and return to his family and to his father's holding. [42] For they are My slaves, Who brought them out of the land of Egypt; they shall not be sold as slaves are. [43] You shall not rule over him harshly. Fear your God! [44] But your male and female slaves whom you shall have from the nations who surround you—from them you shall buy slaves, male and female. [45] Also from the children of the aliens who are resident among you, from them you may buy, and from their family

which is with you, which they begot in your land; and they shall be your holding. ⁴⁶ You may leave them to your children after you to inherit as a holding. Them you may always enslave. But with your brother Israelites, you shall not rule over each other harshly.

The Covenant Code has no hesitation in calling the subject of the slave law a Hebrew slave. D avoids the term until the slave has himself signified his willingness to be enslaved forever. H makes explicit that he is not and cannot be treated like a slave, but rather like a hired laborer. But this rule applies *only* to the Israelite, and not to the non-Israelite slave. This is because H is animated not solely by the humanitarian outlook of D, but by a concept of holiness as an overriding commandment that shapes the details of all others. Here is how (in Lev. 19:2) God tells Moses to present this commandment to Israel:

Be holy! For I YHWH your God am holy.

We saw a hint of this concept of *imitatio Dei*, the imitation of God, in the Exodus version of the Ten Commandments, when the Israelites were commanded to observe the Sabbath because God had created the world in six days and rested on the seventh. In H, the concept is made explicit and the particular quality to be imitated is given a name: holiness. I believe that H was responding to the imperative given as part of the narrative introduction to the Ten Commandments in Exod. 19:6a:

You shall be to Me a kingdom of priests and a holy nation.

This concept of an entire nation each of whose members must behave like and be treated like God's priests is the underlying background for the H slave law.

Note that, as in D, the *explicit* background to the slave laws is the Israelites' exodus experience. But by contrast with D's insistence that the Israelites remember what it was like to be enslaved and—now that they are free—treat their own slaves humanely, H views that episode in quite a different light. For H, the essence of the exodus event was the transferal of the Israelites from the service of an illegitimate master to that of their legitimate master, YHWH. (The temple "service," or *avodah*, performed by the priests is etymologically related to the Hebrew word for "slave," *éved*.) Hence they may enslave others, but not *each* other; nor may anyone else enslave them other than God, their true master.

LEV. 25:55 For it is to *Me* that the Israelites are slaves; they are *My* slaves, Who brought them out of Egypt; I am YHWH your God.

Words for "Law"

I said at the beginning of this chapter that "the Law" was a misnomer for the first five books of the Bible. There are actually a number of words for laws in Biblical Hebrew. In fact, H's use of some of these words to describe its own laws demonstrates how it has tried to combine priestly and Deuteronomic concerns. To understand this, let's look for a moment not just at how the laws sound in the different voices, but at what they are called.

In the Covenant Code

The laws of the Covenant Code are called *mishpatim*, "rules" or "rulings." Since this word comes from a root meaning "judge" or "rule," its use probably implies that the purpose of the Covenant Code is to tell decision-makers how to rule on cases. This would fit in nicely with its current location in the Pentateuch, as the first law code (besides the Ten Commandments) following Moses's establishment of a system of law courts. Jethro, Moses's father-in-law, has seen that Moses is overworked as sole ruler of the people, and (in Exod. 18:21–22) makes the following suggestion to Moses:

EXOD. 18:21 And you, look among the whole people for substantial men, God-fearers, honest men who hate ill-gotten gain, and place over them [that is, over the Israelites] rulers of thousands, of hundreds, of fifties, and of tens. ²² Let them rule the people at all times. Let them bring every great matter to you, and let them rule on every small matter. This will lighten the burden on you; let them bear it with you.

The Ten Commandments make an inspiring moral statement but are not practical for courtroom use. The placement in the story of the more extensive set of laws in the Covenant Code of Exodus 21–23 seems to mark them as a set of rulings meant to guide the subordinate magistrates who are to assist Moses—and, by implication, those who will enforce law in Israel after Moses's death.

In the Priestly Writings

The laws of P, as we have said, fall into a different category. Although they are meant to apply to all the people, they are not general laws, but apply to the specific realm of rules about the sacrifices and other ritual activities. As such, they do not come under the authority of secular judges chosen from the lay leaders of the people. Instead, these rules are exclusively the province of a class of experts who specialize in them—the priests. Each set of rules is called an "instruction" or a "teaching." Thus, after a long list of rules explaining which animals may be eaten and which may not, Lev. 11:46–47 concludes the section with this summary:

> ⁴⁶ This is the teaching about beast and bird, every living thing that swims through the sea and all that swarms upon the land, ⁴⁷ to distinguish the impure from the pure and the animal that may be eaten from the one that shall not be eaten.

The laws of P, Leviticus 1–7 (sacrifices) and 11–16 (purity), are full of such "teachings." The word I am translating this way is *torah*—the same word that is the Jewish name for the Pentateuch, so often translated as "the Law."

In Deuteronomy

D adds yet a third term to the lexicon, which it combines with the term from the Covenant Code. (Scholars have long assumed that there is a relationship between E, which was responsible for the Covenant Code, and D.) The most common way to refer to the laws in Deuteronomy is as "laws and rules." This sort of phrase occurs fourteen times in that book. In English we use the expression "that's not carved in stone," but *ḥukkim*, the word I have translated as "laws" in the phrase "laws and rules," seems to indicate D's understanding that not just the Ten Commandments but D's laws too *were* carved in stone. It is etymologically connected with the verb that means "chisel, engrave." The permanence of the laws is emphasized by Moses's insistence that this code is both complete and unalterable:

> DEUT. 13:1 Everything that I command you, you must be sure to do. You shall not add to it or subtract from it.*

In fact, when the Deuteronomistic History continues the story of the Israelites crossing into the land in the book of Joshua, the laws *are* put on stone:

> JOSH. 8:30 Then Joshua built an altar to YHWH the God of Israel on Mount Ebal, 31 as Moses the servant of YHWH had commanded the Israelites, as written in the book of the Torah of Moses—an altar of whole stones, against which no iron had been lifted. They sacrificed whole-offerings to YHWH and slaughtered offerings of well-being. 32 He wrote there upon the stones a copy of the Torah of Moses, which he [Moses] had written in the presence of the Israelites.

One of the things that goes along with this idea of the permanence of the law is a somewhat different attitude toward those who admin-

---

* This is Deut. 12:32 in Christian versions.

ister it. Remember that in Exod. 18:21 Jethro told Moses to "look among the whole people for substantial men, God-fearers, honest men who hate ill-gotten gain." In Moses's retelling of how the system of subsidiary judges was set up, in the D version, it is his idea, not Jethro's:

> DEUT. 1:15 I took the heads of your tribes, men wise and experienced, and made them heads over you: rulers of thousands, of hundreds, of fifties, and of tens, as officers for your tribes.

The difference between the Deuteronomy and Exodus versions shows one more facet of the difference between the conceptions of law in these two voices. The judges of Exodus (in the E voice) are meant to be honest, God-fearing men; those of Deuteronomy are chosen for their wisdom, not their piety. There is no similar scene in P, since the priests themselves are the "judges" for matters that fall under their purview. They, of course, are not selected on the basis of individual qualities but inherit their status. The difference between the three amounts to a range of possibilities for selecting a society's leadership: character, intelligence, or descent.

In the Holiness Code

Finally we turn again to H, the voice that seems to be trying to combine P's emphasis on the holiness of the sanctuary and those who serve in it with D's emphasis on social concerns. First, note that in Leviticus 17–24, the first eight chapters of the Holiness Code, God "speaks" to Moses just as he did earlier in Leviticus; the reader's assumption is that he is communicating with Moses in the Tent of Meeting, as in the priestly conception of Leviticus 1–16. But the last two chapters of H, Leviticus 25–26, are introduced by noting that God's message is given at a specific, and by now unexpected, location:

> LEV. 25:1 YHWH spoke to Moses on Mount Sinai as follows.

Again, this looks like an attempt to blend the priestly and non-priestly traditions. To be sure, E and D use the name Horeb rather than Sinai—but both assume that all the laws were given there, not at the Tent or Tabernacle. (D saves their public proclamation for Moses's final speech on the east bank of the Jordan River.) The Holiness Code summarizes and concludes its work with the following words:

> **LEV. 26:46** These are the laws and the rules and the teachings which YHWH set between Himself and the Israelites, on Mount Sinai, by the hand of Moses.

The "rules" of the Covenant Code, the "laws and rules" of D, and the "teachings" of P are all one unified revelation of the proper relationship between God and the Israelites, given at Mount Sinai through Moses. The voice that proclaims this—the voice of the Holiness Code—is the voice that shaped the Pentateuch and indeed still shapes what most of us think "the Bible says" about the nature of revelation. "The three-fold cord is not easily broken" (Eccl. 4:12), and the weaving together of these three distinct, sometimes contrapuntal, yet ultimately harmonious voices produced a work that is powerful indeed.

From the Priestly *Torah* to the Torah of Ezra

We have one more question to answer before we leave the subject of law: How did *torah*, the parochial word that P uses for the priestly regulations, become the traditional Hebrew name for the Pentateuch, "Torah" with a capital T? The answer is that there is one voice that uses this word (but in a much more general sense than P) to refer to all of God's words to Moses as a single "Teaching."

Here is what this voice says about God's Torah:

> **DEUT. 31:12** Assemble the people—men, women and children—and the foreigner within your gates, so that they may listen and learn to fear YHWH your God and to keep doing all the things in this Torah. [13] And their children, who did not know, will hear and learn to fear YHWH your God as long as you live on the land which you are crossing the Jordan to possess.

The word *torah* is etymologically related to the word *moreh*, which meant "teacher" in Biblical Hebrew (see Prov. 5:13 and Isa. 30:20), just as it does in Israeli Hebrew today. As a name for the Pentateuch, then, "Torah" could be translated as "the Teaching," with a capital T. When we remember that the Torah/Pentateuch is not primarily a book of laws, but a book that weaves laws into the framework of a story, "Teaching" seems a much more appropriate name for it.

We have seen that the first time such a book of "Teaching" (most likely some form of Deuteronomy) appears on the historical stage is during the reign of King Josiah. We know that in the Persian period the inhabitants of Jerusalem had a text that must have been more or less the equivalent of today's Pentateuch:

> NEH. 8:8 They read aloud from the scroll of the Teaching of God, giving the sense and making the reading comprehensible.

Indeed, the word "Torah" is common in Chronicles, which (though it describes the pre-Exilic period) was written during the period of Persian rule. Some have suggested that the compilation of the Torah was actually done under Persian auspices, to provide a constitution (as it were) for the Persian province of Yehud. By that time, the legal voices of the Covenant Code, the priestly writings, Deuteronomy, and the Holiness Code had been woven into a single, intricate sound.

Were the Laws Really "Codes"?

The difference between "You shall not murder" and the much more complicated set of laws governing murder in contemporary America makes it clear that the biblical laws are a long way from what we today would consider a comprehensive "code" of law. Nor does it seem likely that at any time in Israelite history one of the law books contained in the Pentateuch was actually enforced as such. (Incidentally, the same applies to the famous "Code" of Hammurabi and its companion texts from elsewhere in the ancient Near East.) Yet these laws, or something very much like them, certainly shaped the world in which the other events recorded in the Bible took place. We can see this by once again turning to the connection between law and story. But this time, the stories we look at will illustrate the laws obliquely, not directly.

Family Values (Part One)

Let's begin with the story of Judah and Tamar. Judah (the son of Jacob) had three sons, Er, Onan, and Shelah. He married Er to a woman named Tamar, but Er died before she could bear him any children. Here is what happened next:

> GEN. 38:8 Judah said to Onan, "Go to your brother's wife and impregnate her, and raise up seed for your brother. ⁹ Onan knew that the seed would not be his, so whenever he would go in to his brother's wife, he would waste it upon the ground, in order not to give seed to his brother.

The text is playing here on the double meaning of the Hebrew word *zera*: "seed" and "offspring." The word I have translated above as "impregnate," *yabem*, does not really mean exactly that; but there is no word in English for what it *does* mean. The best way to explain it is to offer a combination of two translations, that used by the KJV—"marry her"—and that offered by the NJPS—"do your duty by her as a brother-in-law." To understand this concept, we must go to Deut. 25:5–10, a section of law, where the process is laid out more fully:

> DEUT. 25:5 When two brothers dwell together and one of them dies childless, the dead man's wife cannot marry outside the family. Her brother-in-law must come to her and take her as a wife and *yabem* her. ⁶ The first to be born shall stand in the name of his dead brother, so that his name shall not be wiped out from Israel.

Onan's job was to father a son who would be called "son of Er." It is this procedure, technically called "levirate marriage" (from the Latin *levir*, meaning "husband's brother"), to which the verb *yabem* refers.

Since having sex with his brother's widow but refusing to procreate was biblically considered comparable to incest, Onan was killed by God (but not before leaving his name to the dictionary, albeit for masturbation and not for *coitus interruptus*, which is what he really did). The assumption of our story in Genesis 38 is that the duty of begetting Er's child with Tamar now lay with Judah's third son, Shelah. Judah told Tamar that Shelah was still too young to marry, but really he was afraid that his third son too would die. The assumption of the story, however, is that Tamar was not free to find whomever she liked, but that she would have to wait patiently ("in your father's house," as Judah tells her in v. 11) until Shelah was grown.

Eventually, seeing that Shelah was never going to be married to her, Tamar puts on a disguise and tricks Judah himself into sleeping with her. Once she becomes noticeably pregnant, Judah commands that she be burnt to death for having sex outside the line of Er's brothers. But while in disguise she managed to get possession of Judah's signet, something that essentially served in those days as an item of personal identification. Once Tamar proved to him that he was the father of the child, he agreed that she had acted rightly and rescinded the command to burn her. But he did not sleep with her any more.

Did the "law" of Deuteronomy 25 apply to the story of Judah and Tamar? The simple but unsatisfying answer is that we don't know. Certainly the story does not invoke the law (as sometimes happens, for example, in Chronicles). Since we don't know when this story was written, we don't know whether its creator assumed that those who read or heard it would take the specific verses from Deuteronomy as its background. The fact that Judah considered it natural to have Tamar killed for sleeping with someone outside the family certainly sounds as if it matches Deuteronomy 25—but not exactly. In some ways, it is more like the "honor killing" that is still part of some cultures in the twenty-first century. Such killing is obviously not mandated or even sanctioned by law, but in a culture that practices it, "everybody knows" how and when it applies. Was levirate marriage a legal requirement in ancient Israel, or was it just something that everybody knew about?

Family Values (Part Two)

We can look at this question from another angle, this time from a story that is found outside the Pentateuch, in the book of Ruth. The story begins with Naomi and Elimelech, a couple from Bethlehem who had two sons, Mahlon and Chilion. (Since the names in this story are mostly meaningful "Pilgrim's Progress" kinds of names, perhaps we should translate Mahlon and Chilion into English: "Sicko" and "Goner.") Famine drives them to move to Moab. There, Elimelech dies and then Mahlon and Chilion (true to their names) die too, both without leaving children. The brothers had both been married to Moabite women, and one of them, Ruth, returns together with Naomi to Bethlehem.

There, Ruth is favored by the owner of a field in which she has come to glean, that is, to collect the stalks of barley dropped by the professional harvesters. (You can do your own research into the links between biblical law and story by comparing Ruth's gleaning with the injunctions to leave something for the gleaners, found in Lev. 19:9–10, Lev. 23:22, and Deut. 24:19–22.) Boaz wishes to marry Ruth, but there is something about her situation that prevents it. Another man, the proper "redeemer," is ahead of him in line. But the other man does not wish to marry Ruth, a foreigner, and possibly interfere with his own children's inheritance.

The law in Deuteronomy covers this possibility, too:

DEUT. 25:7 If the man does not want to marry his sister-in-law, the sister-in-law shall go up to the gate, to the elders, and say, "My brother-in-law refuses to establish a name in Israel for his brother. He does not want to *yabem* me." [8] The elders of his town shall call him and speak to him. If he stands firm and says, "I don't want to marry her," [9] then his sister-in-law shall go up to him in front of the elders, take off his shoe, spit in his face, and declare, "Thus shall be done to the man who will not build his brother's house." [10] And his name shall be called in Israel "the house of the unsandaled one."

The story in Ruth seems to know some kind of similar procedure:

RUTH 4:7 (Formerly in Israel, in cases of redemption and exchange, to seal any action a man would take off his sandal and give it to the other man. This was the form of attestation in Israel.) **8** The redeemer said to Boaz, "Acquire [Ruth] for yourself," and he took off his sandal. **9** Boaz said to the elders, "You are witnesses today that I hereby acquire everything that belonged to Elimelech, and everything that belonged to Mahlon and Chilion, from Naomi. **10** Ruth the Moabite, too, Mahlon's wife, I have acquired as my own wife, to establish the name of the dead man on his property, so that the dead man's name shall not be cut off from among his brothers and from the gate of his town—you are witnesses today."

This certainly seems to be comparable to the situation described in Deuteronomy. In fact, our story itself adds a parenthesis to explain the legal nature of taking off one's sandal. The whole procedure is performed at the "gate," the central meeting place of the town, and in front of the "elders." But the differences between the story told in Ruth 4 and the law as laid out in Deuteronomy 25 are fairly significant:

- There are no surviving brothers; in Ruth, more distant relatives seem to still have some right and some obligation to marry the widow.
- Ruth does not perform the action of degradation that the sister-in-law does in Deuteronomy.
- The Ruth story involves a question of real estate, which is not mentioned in Deuteronomy.

The final spin put on the situation is that the child who is ultimately born is not called the son of Mahlon, or of Elimelech, nor even of Boaz and Ruth. All the neighbor ladies acclaim him: "A son has been born to Naomi!"

It is quite clear that the story of Ruth 4 would make no sense without the phenomenon of levirate marriage. But it is far from clear that the "law" of Deuteronomy 25 is the precise background of that story. From our perspective, it seems again that we must look at that law, the story of Judah and Tamar, and the story of Ruth as three voices that blend with each other but are not saying exactly the same thing.

The Slave Law in Action—or Inaction

Our last example returns to the theme of slavery, with a narrative passage not from the Pentateuch, but from the story of Jeremiah. Jeremiah 34 tells of an agreement brokered by King Zedekiah of Judah for all the people to release their Hebrew slaves, male and female, and no longer to enslave each other. They did release them, but then forced them back into slavery again. Jeremiah receives an outraged message from God, proclaiming that the people who pretended to "release" their slaves would themselves be "released" to the tender mercies of the Babylonian army. Here is the basis for God's outrage:

> JER. 34:13 Thus said YHWH, God of Israel: "I made a covenant with your forefathers on the day I took them out of the land of Egypt, from the house of slavery: ¹⁴ 'At the end of seven years, each of you must release his brother Hebrew who has been sold to you. When he has served you six years, you must let him go free.' But your forefathers did not obey Me nor bend their ears to Me."

We need not be concerned about God's saying that he gave this instruction "on the day" that he brought the Israelites out of Egypt; this is a Biblical Hebrew idiom meaning "at the time." God is reminding Jeremiah of one of the laws given to Israel during the wilderness experience, on their way to the land of Canaan. Remembering that Jeremiah lived in the time when the scroll of Deuteronomy was discovered in the Temple, perhaps this was the law God had in mind:

DEUT. 15:12 When your brother or sister Hebrew is sold to you, he shall serve you for six years and in the seventh year you shall let him go free from you.

The language is very similar: the slave is acquired by being sold, and he serves for six years and goes free in the seventh. Deuteronomy makes clear that this law applies both to male and female slaves, and the law describing King Zedekiah's release also emphasizes this aspect. But though God insists that the people have had this law since "the day" they themselves were released from slavery in Egypt, King Zedekiah did not command the release on that basis; it seems to have been more of a political gesture. (Other ancient Near Eastern kings proclaimed similar releases of slaves.)

In this chapter we've seen that the theological differences among the biblical voices found their practical expression in different legal formulations. Naturally, since the voices are expressing views that stem from an established society, the various laws of the Pentateuch focus overwhelmingly on Israelite life as it would take shape *after* the Israelites settled in Canaan. But when the Bible goes on to tell us what happens after they cross the Jordan, we don't find them turning to written laws for guidance.

After the return from exile, as we have said, there are more explicit texts saying that Judean society operated on the basis of a written Torah providing a set of rules for proper conduct, in both the religious and the social realms. The picture presented in Jeremiah 34, just before the Babylonian exile, shows God pointing to such a written law, but the society to which he means it to apply does not yet acknowledge that law. Until it does so, God (according to the biblical story) relies on prophets to convey his message. We will look at the voices of some of these prophets in chapter 5.

5
Prophetic Voices

We saw in the previous chapter that the written Torah was not generally acknowledged, certainly not as a legal document, until after the exile. The "scroll of Torah" that was discovered in 622 BCE came as a complete surprise to the people who were living in Jerusalem at the time. What, then, played the role in earlier Judean society that the Torah began to play in the sixth century and later? That is, how did people know (as Mic. 6:8 puts it) "what God requires of you"? At least one answer is self-evident from the way I've asked the question: Micah (and other prophets like him) told them. In this chapter, we'll examine what prophecy meant to the ancient Israelites by listening to some of the Bible's most famous prophets—and to some of the most obscure prophets as well. When you listen carefully, you will find that prophets in the Bible are not exactly what you might expect a "prophet" to be.

English speakers—particularly those of us who have seen headlines about "the prophecies of Nostradamus" on our way through the grocery store checkout line—tend to think of a "prophet" as someone who predicts the future. To understand the prophetic voices in the Bible, however, it is important to realize that, though the biblical prophets often spoke about the future, they were not fortune-tellers, and their "forecasts" were not always precise. For example, in the year 734 the king of Aram (Syria) and the king of (northern) Israel moved to attack

Jerusalem in a struggle called the Syro-Ephraimite War. (Remember that "Ephraim" is another name for the Northern Kingdom.) The prophet Isaiah, who lived in Jerusalem at the time, assured King Ahaz that the attackers would not succeed, and predicted, "In another sixty-five years, Ephraim shall be shattered as a people" (Isa. 7:8). Sixty-five years after 734 takes us down to 669, but in fact, as we saw in chapter 1, the Northern Kingdom was conquered in 722 and its people, "Ephraim," exiled to the hinterlands of the Assyrian Empire, where they vanished from history.

What Did the Prophets Do?

Isaiah's "prediction" was certainly not wrong, but neither was it precise. In fact, it was off by half a century. If Isaiah had made his living as a fortune-teller, he would have been in bad shape. But, as I said, this is not the function that the prophets had in Israelite society. Rather, they were messengers of God. One way to remember this is to think of the etymology of our English word "prophet," which comes from Greek words meaning something like "one who speaks out." Within Hebrew, there is a clue in the name of the prophet Malachi, whose book is the last one in the "Prophets" section of both Jewish and Christian Bibles. It is very unlikely that this was the name he was given by his parents; *malachi* is a Hebrew word meaning "My messenger." The function of the prophet in Israelite society was to convey God's word. Thus, the purpose of what Isaiah told King Ahaz was not to pinpoint the precise date of the Northern Kingdom's demise, but to make sure that the king held firm and defended the city.

Jonah's "Failed" Prophecy

The story of Jonah makes the point very clear. In the book that bears his name, Jonah is sent to Nineveh with a warning: "Forty days more, and Nineveh shall be overthrown!" (Jonah 3:4). Here is what happened:

> JONAH 3:5 The people of Nineveh believed in God and put on burlap, from the greatest of them to the least. 6 When the matter

reached the king of Nineveh, he got off his throne, took off his cloak, wrapped himself in burlap, and sat in the ashes. **7** The following proclamation was made throughout Nineveh, in the name of the king and his nobles: "Let neither man nor beast, cattle nor sheep, taste a morsel—let the animals not graze—and let them drink no water. **8** Let them cover themselves with burlap, man and beast, let them call out forcefully to God, and let each of them turn back from his evil ways and from the violence that is in their hands. **9** Who knows? If *he* turns back, perhaps God too will change His mind and turn back from *His* anger, and we might not perish." **10** God saw their deeds, how they turned back from their evil ways, and God changed His mind about the evil He had declared He would do to them, and He did not do it.

Here you have prophecy in a nutshell. (In fact, that may be why this story is included in the Bible. As we will see, there were many more prophets than those whose words are preserved.) Jonah's cry of "forty days" was not a news item, but a warning. Its purpose was to make the inhabitants of Nineveh turn from evil to good. Once they indeed changed their behavior, the destruction of the city was no longer necessary and was canceled. So what he "prophesied" did not actually come true. But the purpose of the prophecy was achieved.

In fact, Jonah 4 tells us something more about prophets. In it, Jonah becomes extremely upset. It seems that he is afraid that the fact that Nineveh was not wiped out after all would destroy his credibility. What this tells us is that Jonah himself did not really understand what he was doing when he prophesied. He knew only as much as God told him, and not more. To put it in contemporary terms, he was God's spokesman—not a policy maker.

Again, it is this function of "spokesman" that characterizes the biblical prophets, not that of foretelling the future. In Exodus 4, when God tells Moses that he must return to Egypt to take the Israelites out of slavery, he is reluctant: "I am thick of speech and thick of tongue" (Exod. 4:10). Moses's brother Aaron, however, was a good speaker; so God assigned him to do Moses's talking for him: "he shall be a mouth for you, and you shall be a god to him" (Exod. 4:16). When God speaks again to Moses in Exod. 7:1, he defines Aaron's role precisely: "Look, I am making you a god to Pharaoh, and your brother Aaron will be your prophet."

The Bible's Many Prophets

It may surprise you to hear Aaron called a "prophet," even if he is a prophet of Moses, not of God. But in fact those prophets who have biblical books named after them (the "literary" prophets, as scholars call them) are not the only people called "prophets" in the Bible. Even with these prophets there is some disagreement; remember that Daniel is considered a prophet by Christians, and his book is in the "Prophets" section of the Christian Bible, but not among Jews, whose Bible puts him in the "Writings" section, not that of the "Prophets." Both religions agree that Isaiah, Jeremiah, and Ezekiel (the "major" prophets; so called because their books are long) and a dozen other "minor" prophets (in reference not to their importance, but to the length of their books) belong in the "Prophets" section of the Bible. But beyond these fifteen or sixteen books called by the name of a biblical prophet, literally hundreds of other people are called "prophet" in the Bible.

Think, for example, of the prophet Elijah, for whom the original chariot "swung low" to take him up to heaven. (See 2 Kings 2; remember that Joshua, Judges, Samuel, and Kings are also part of the "Prophets" section of a Jewish Bible.) Everyone knows that Elijah was a prophet, but there is no "Book of Elijah" in the Bible. There is no "Book of Miriam," either, but she too, like her brothers Moses and Aaron, is called a prophet (Exod. 15:20; Moses refers to himself as a prophet in Deut. 18:15). So are Abraham (Gen. 20:7), Deborah (Judg. 4:4), and many others whose names are not as recognizable or who are not named at all (e.g., the hundred anonymous prophets who are saved from death at the hands of Jezebel by Obadiah, Ahab's palace steward, in 1 Kgs. 18:3–4).

I suggested earlier that Jonah's prophecy may have been included in the Bible because it demonstrated one writer's idea of what the purpose of prophecy was. Knowing that there were many more prophets in ancient Israel than the ones after whom books were named tells us that there must have been something special about those particular prophets that caused their prophecies to be preserved. Other prophetic voices may have been considered important for their time, but not worth preserving for the future. Still other prophetic voices, as we will see, told falsehoods and not truth. But it will take a while to get to that aspect of the story. To begin, let us listen to some different voices of prophecy than the ones we have heard up to now.

Prophetic Behavior

The idea of the prophet as God's spokesman may lie behind the term *navi*, which is the Biblical Hebrew word for "prophet." But there is also a verb related to this word that tells us something rather different about the Israelite idea of prophecy. To see its use, let us turn to the story of Saul.

As the first king of Israel, he is someone we do not ordinarily think of in connection with prophecy. But the Bible makes clear that the Israelites did think of him in that way. When Samuel anoints Saul to rule over Israel, he tells him that he will meet certain people on his way home and perform certain actions. Here is what happens:

> 1 SAM. 10:9 When he turned around to leave Samuel, God replaced his heart with a new one. All these signs came true on that very day. 10 When they got to Gibeah, a band of prophets came out to meet him. A spirit of God overtook him, and he began acting the prophet among them. 11 Everyone who knew him from before saw him prophesying with the prophets and they said to each other, "What's happening to the son of Kish? Is Saul too among the prophets?" 12 . . . That is how the expression "Is Saul too among the prophets?" came about. 13 When he stopped prophesying, he went into the shrine.

We don't really know what the Israelites meant when they used this proverb, but it must have been a well-known one, for the Bible also has another story explaining how it originated. According to the voice that tells this story, it occurred long after Saul had become king, when he was out to kill David:

> 1 SAM. 19:18 David fled and escaped to Samuel's, in Ramah, and told him everything that Saul had done to him. He and Samuel went and stayed in Naioth. [19] When Saul was told that David was in Naioth in Ramah, [20] he sent messengers to arrest David. They saw a company of prophets with Samuel standing there in charge of them. A spirit of God fell upon Saul's messengers, and they too began to prophesy. [21] Saul was told, and sent more messengers, but they too prophesied; then Saul sent a third set of messengers, but they too prophesied. [22] So Saul went to Ramah himself. When he came to the great cistern in Secu, he asked, "Where are Samuel and David?" Someone told him, "They are in Naioth, in Ramah." [23] He went there, to Naioth in Ramah, and a spirit of God fell upon him too, and he kept prophesying all the way to Naioth in Ramah. [24] He too stripped off his clothes, and he too prophesied before Samuel and fell down naked all that day and all that night. That is why people say, "Is Saul too among the prophets?"

If you look at these two stories, you will see a curious thing. The one person who accurately predicts something that is going to happen in the future, Samuel in 1 Samuel 10, is not called a prophet and is not referred to as "prophesying." The people who do prophesy, by contrast, do not say anything—or at least nothing that we are told. The second story makes clear that "prophesying" is something that can happen to you inadvertently. It is something that comes over Saul's messengers when they see a band of prophets. When it happens to Saul himself in the second story, one of the things he does is take off his clothes and lie naked in public for hours on end. (If public nakedness does not strike you as something befitting a prophet, have a look at Isa. 20:2–3.) Notice too that what makes Saul and his messengers begin to prophesy is that "the spirit of God" comes upon them. The equivalent in the first story is that "God gave him another heart." These two statements are the clue that we need.

The indication in these stories that people are "prophesying" is that they act in bizarre ways. They have "another heart," they aren't themselves. In the terms that we use today, we would say that they are exhibiting mental illness. Indeed, elsewhere in the story, when something like this happens to Saul, it *is* treated not as prophecy but as illness. 1 Samuel 16:14 tells us that when Saul was troubled with "an evil spirit from YHWH," his advisers suggested that he find someone to play soothing music for him. One of them knew that Jesse the Bethlehemite had a capable son who was good at playing the lyre, and this is how David entered Saul's court. "When the spirit of God came upon Saul, David would take the lyre in his hand and play it; Saul would regain his spirits and feel better, and the evil spirit would leave him" (1 Sam. 16:23). The "spirit of God" can make you ill, or . . . it can make you prophesy.

Other Means of Finding an Answer

We tend to think of prophecy as a spiritual or at least a religious matter, but it is clear from the Bible that this mysterious connection to the divine realm was put to much more practical uses. People have always wanted, and sometimes needed, to know what the future holds, and the ancient Israelites were no different. Thus, when Saul is looking for the missing asses of his father Kish (1 Samuel 9), his servant suggests they contact a "man of God" (v. 6) to help find them; such a person is also called a "prophet" (v. 9) or a "seer" (v. 11). To be sure, this source of information was not always available. When Samuel was young, as we are told in 1 Sam. 3:1, "the word of YHWH was rare; prophecy was not widespread."

Admittedly, prophecy was only one of the means by which the Israelites could seek God's word. Let us look in again at Saul, on the eve of his death, when desperation makes him turn to a woman who can bring Samuel up from the dead for him. All other means of receiving God's word have failed him: "And Saul inquired of YHWH, but YHWH did not answer him, either by dreams or by Urim or by prophets" (1 Sam. 28:6). God's word cannot be compelled; the prophets could not simply prophesy at the king's command. But the other methods of determining God's will have also failed Saul. No divine messages have been received by means of dreams, nor by manipulation of the Urim (more on these in a moment).

By this point in the story, God is no longer speaking with Saul, but with David. And though David's questions and God's answers are depicted as if they are simple conversation, something more complicated may really be going on. Let's listen in as David consults God after a party of Amalekite raiders have burned his home base of Ziklag to the ground and captured the families of himself and his men:

1 SAM. 30:7 David said to Abiathar the priest, the son of Ahimelech, "Bring me the ephod." Abiathar brought the ephod to David. 8 David inquired of YHWH, "Shall I pursue this troop? Will I catch it?" [YHWH] told him, "Pursue it, for you will definitely catch it and rescue them."

There are a number of similar "conversations" between David and God in the books of 1 and 2 Samuel, but this one adds a particularly revealing detail—the ephod. If you do not know what an ephod is, welcome to the club. In Exodus 28, the ephod is described as a kind of elaborately decorated garment to be made for Aaron, the High Priest, to wear when he officiates at the Tabernacle. But in Judges 17–18, there is a story in which an ephod is stolen along with "teraphim and a sculptured image and a molten image" (Judg. 18:14). Since teraphim are also divine images, it seems that the ephod here is also understood to be not an article of clothing but an object that represents a god. It would seem that when David "inquires of YHWH," he is not directly communicating, but using the ephod.

I translated this part of 1 Sam. 30:8 as "[YHWH] told him," but as you can see by the brackets, there is no separate grammatical subject in the Hebrew phrase. The subject is simply built into the verb form: "He told him." But since Hebrew, unlike English, does not have a neuter gender, the same verb might just as easily mean, "*It* told him"— that is, the ephod told him!

How was this done? The Urim, which failed Saul in 1 Sam. 28:6, may give us a clue. Like the ephod, the mysterious Urim and their companion Thummim were part of the High Priest's accoutrements (Exod. 28:30). To see them in action, let's go back to 1 Samuel 14, where Saul inquires of God and, for the first time, God does not respond to him (see 1 Sam. 14:37).

Saul has sworn the troops not to eat until they have taken revenge on the Philistines. Someone has done so nonetheless, so when Saul inquires whether the attack should proceed, God gives him the cold shoulder. This leaves Saul with no choice but to cast lots to find the culprit. It turns out to be his son Jonathan, who had not heard his father's command. The method used to find him is somewhat obscure in the Hebrew text of 1 Sam. 14:41, so some Bibles, like the NRSV (which I will quote) and the NEB, translate this verse from the ancient Greek version of it. Saul asks God: "Why have You not answered Your servant today? If this guilt is in me or in my son Jonathan, O LORD God of Israel, give Urim; but if this guilt is in Your people Israel, give Thummim." The text continues, "Saul and Jonathan were caught by the lot, and the people got cleared. And Saul said, 'Cast lots between my son Jonathan and me'; and Jonathan was caught" (1 Sam. 14:41b–42, back once again to my own translation from the Hebrew).

We don't know exactly what these objects were, or how they worked, but one thing seems clear—they could be used to get a yes-or-no answer from God. Saul could not simply ask, "Who is the culprit?" He had to present a series of binary choices, the way we flip a coin to let heads or tails determine an answer. It appears that the Urim and Thummim were a kind of biblical coin flip that was thought to provide an answer from God. When David calls for the ephod before inquiring of God in 1 Sam. 30:7–8, he seems to be doing the same thing. God tells David, "Pursue, for you shall overtake and you shall rescue," but this may simply be the biblical writer's shorthand for a casting of lots and its result. God's "voice" was heard in an omen: David's coin has come up heads.

Prophets and Kings

So it appears that one way David had of getting an answer from God was by the manipulation of sacred objects whose purpose was to channel divine communications. But David also had a prophet on his staff, and for exactly the same purpose. In 2 Samuel 7 (as we saw in chapter 2), David planned to build a "House" for YHWH. To whom did David confide his plan?—to Nathan the "prophet." And what happened? "That very night . . . the word of YHWH came to Nathan" (2 Sam. 7:4). Just as elsewhere David used an ephod to get answers from God, here he used Nathan.

In fact, keeping a prophet on staff became standard behavior for subsequent kings of Israel and Judah. For an example, let us turn to 1 Kings 22, where, a century and a half after the time of David, King Ahab of Israel is at war with Aram and asks King Jehoshaphat of Judah to join him as an ally. Jehoshaphat agrees, but with one proviso: "Please, first inquire of YHWH" (1 Kgs. 22:5). We see what "to inquire" of a god meant in those days by what subsequently happens:

> 1 KGS. 22:6 So the king of Israel gathered the prophets, about four hundred men, and asked them, "Shall I go to war against Ramoth-Gilead or not?" "Go up," they said, "and the Lord will deliver it into the king's hands."

The desire to tap into a source of divine information was a standard feature of Israelite kingship. The kings regularly provided themselves with people who had demonstrated an ability to prophesy in order to use them for political advice. We have records of similar behavior among the kings of Mari, in Syria, and it was probably standard practice throughout the ancient Near East.

You may be wondering at this point whether I was correct in saying that "prophecy" in ancient Israel did not mean foretelling the future. Isn't this exactly what the king of Israel expected his prophets to do? It is. But the ability to convey information via a message from God also implies that God, not the king, is the prophet's true master. We saw this with Nathan in 2 Samuel 7, when he told David that God did not want him to carry out his plan. The role of prophet, it seems, was a standard part of the ancient Near Eastern political system; but the presumed connection with God that gave it its power also made it unpredictable.

Balaam and Balak

We can see this by looking for a moment at a non-Israelite biblical character: Balaam. His story is told in Numbers 22–24. He is not explicitly referred to as a prophet, but he speaks under the influence of "the spirit of God" (Num. 24:2) and YHWH "puts a word in his mouth" (Num. 23:16). Moreover, an eighth-century inscription from the Jordan Valley refers to Balaam as a "seer," which 1 Sam. 9:9 tells us is another name for a prophet; the prophet's experience often involves having a vision as well as hearing words. Balaam's story is instructive for what it tells us about the varying demands on the prophet from his two masters—God and the king.

King Balak of Moab has a big problem. Six hundred thousand Israelite warriors (and their families) are about to cut the same kind of swath through Moab that General Sherman cut through Georgia. Balak's solution is to hire Balaam, a freelance prophet of YHWH, to curse them. Balaam's connection with God means that his words will not just be so much hot air; they will have real power, crippling the Israelite army and permitting Balak to drive them out of his kingdom. The king's assumption is that Balaam's only question will be who can pay him better. But Balaam—reminded who is boss after the famous incident of the talking ass (Num. 22:21–35)—cautions him: "I will make sure to speak what YHWH puts in my mouth" (Num. 23:12). The upshot, of course, is that (at God's direction) Balaam blesses Israel rather than cursing them.

Actions and Omens

Balak was right about one thing, though. Prophetic words and actions, in the biblical stories, can have actual power. Balak told Balaam, "I know that whom you bless *is* blessed, and whom you curse is cursed" (Num. 22:6), and this is the operative assumption of the story: Balaam is not *predicting* that Israel will be blessed; his words themselves are actually effecting the blessing. Like the voodoo priest sticking pins into the doll representing his enemy, a prophet's actions can be simultaneously symbolic and practical.

In fact, the symbolic action need not be performed by the prophet himself. Thus in Jer. 51:59–64, Jeremiah "sends" a symbolic action to Babylonia in the person of Seraiah, brother of Baruch, the prophet's secretary. Seraiah is to accompany King Zedekiah to Babylon as part of the exile of 597. When they get within sight of the city, Seraiah is to read out from a scroll Jeremiah's prophecies of Babylonia's destruction, then tie a stone to the scroll, throw it into the Euphrates, and say, "Thus shall Babylonia sink and not rise from the evil that I [that is, God] intend to bring upon it" (Jer. 51:64). Seraiah is no prophet; he was the Judean quartermaster general. But Jeremiah's words can empower him to effect Babylon's inevitable future destruction—by proxy!—even at the moment of her greatest power.

Jeremiah arranged for Seraiah to carry out this symbolic action because he himself was staying behind in Jerusalem; Babylon's doom had to be effected on-site. We can see a more intimate conveyance of the prophet's power in the story of King Joash and Elisha the prophet. Hearing that the prophet is on his deathbed, the king goes to visit him:

> 2 KGS. 13:15 Elisha said to him, "Take a bow and arrows," and he picked up a bow and some arrows. 16 Then he said to the king of

Israel, "Set your hand to the bow," and he set his hand to the bow. Elisha put his own hands on the king's hands **17** and said, "Open the east window." He opened it, and Elisha said, "Shoot," and he shot. [Elisha] said, "An arrow of victory for YHWH! And an arrow of victory over Aram! You shall hit Aram at Aphek and finish them off."

Elisha's arrow, like Jeremiah's scroll, is an omen of the future defeat of Israel's enemies. His hands convey to those of the king the power to shape history by symbolic action. The story continues with another, even more interesting, omen:

> 2 KGS. 13:18 He said, "Take the arrows," and [the king] took them. He told the king of Israel, "Hit the ground with them," and he hit the ground three times and then stopped. **19** The man of God, infuriated, said, "You should have hit them five or six times! Then you would have hit Aram and finished them off! But now you will [only] hit them three times."

Here, the dying prophet somehow has the power to convert the king's symbolic action into Aramean military defeat—but this power is limited by a chance element. The actual symbolic action must be performed by the king, Israel's military leader, who does not understand the significance of what he is doing and acts randomly.

True Prophets, False Prophets, and True False Prophets

What happened, though, when there was more than one prophet on the scene? We can get a picture of this complicated dynamic, and through it a broader perspective on the Israelite notion of prophecy, by returning to the complicated story of 1 Kings 22. We left this story with a group of four hundred prophets having told King Jehoshaphat of Judah and King Ahab of Israel that they should indeed go to war against Aram, for God would give them success. Jehoshaphat was somewhat suspicious of this advice, however, and asked for a second opinion. Ahab replied, "There is one more man by whom to inquire of YHWH, but I hate him, for he will never prophesy good for me, only evil—Micaiah son of Imlah" (1 Kgs. 22:8). Human nature was much the same in that day as in this. The king wanted yes-men. He did not want to listen to advice from someone who was likely to tell him no. At Jehoshaphat's urging, however, Micaiah is sent for.

Meanwhile the other prophets continue to prophesy—that is, to act in bizarre ways that suggest they are possessed by a divine spirit—and one of them performs a symbolic action of the kind that Elisha did for King Joash:

> 1 KGS. 22:10 The king of Israel and King Jehoshaphat of Judah were seated on their thrones and dressed in [royal] robes at the threshing floor at the entrance to Samaria, and all the prophets were prophesying before them. 11 Zedekiah the son of Chenaanah made himself iron horns and said, "Thus said YHWH: With these shall you gore Aram to death." 12 And all the other prophets prophesied the same: "Go up to Ramoth Gilead and triumph! YHWH will give them into the king's hand."

Micaiah, when he arrives, gives the same advice. But the king, not trusting a positive response from a prophet who he thinks has it in for him, admonishes him again to tell him the truth. At last Micaiah admits, "I saw all Israel scattered over the hills like sheep who have no shepherd. YHWH said, 'These have no master. Let them return each to his household in peace'" (1 Kgs. 22:17). But Zedekiah steps up, slaps Micaiah, and demands, "How is it that the spirit of YHWH shifted from me to speak with you?" (v. 24). Micaiah replies, "You'll see—when the day comes that you try to hide [from the victorious enemies] room by room!" (v. 25).

What's a poor king to do? One voice, Zedekiah's, assures the king that victory is inevitable. Another, Micaiah's, promises that the Israelite army will be scattered, and that their "shepherd"—the king himself—will be lost. Each stands up to the other and claims to be delivering the true word of God. In the event, the king makes what turns out to be a foolish decision:

> 1 KGS. 22:26 Then the king of Israel said, "Take Micaiah and bring him back to Amon, the governor of the city, and to Joash, the king's son, [27] and say, 'Thus said the king: Put this in prison and feed it scant bread and water until I come home safe.'" [28] Micaiah replied, "If you do come home safe, YHWH has not spoken through me."

In the end, the king is indeed killed and the army of Israel scattered. But do not blame Zedekiah for this. For I have left out a key element of Micaiah's story. As Micaiah had warned the kings—to no avail—Zedekiah and his four hundred colleagues were not false prophets, but true ones who had been given bad information to convey:

> 1 KGS. 22:19 [Micaiah] said, "All right, then; hear the word of YHWH. I saw YHWH sitting upon His throne, with all the host of heaven standing attendance to His right and to His left. [20] YHWH said, 'Who will entice Ahab, so that he goes up against Ramoth Gilead and falls there?' One said this and another said that, [21] until a spirit came forth to stand before YHWH and said, 'I will entice him.' YHWH said, 'How?' [22] And he said, "'I will go forth and be a lying spirit in the mouth of all his prophets.' YHWH said, 'You will entice him and succeed. Go and do it.' [23] So YHWH put a lying spirit in the mouth of all these prophets of yours, for YHWH has decreed evil upon you."

Here we see the same notion as we saw in the story of Saul: Prophecy involves being inhabited, as it were, by a divine spirit that conveys a message that comes from outside the prophet who utters it. Zedekiah was not a fraud, but, just as he claimed, a genuine prophet, and one who was true to his task. But the rule for computers applies to prophets, too: Garbage in, garbage out. Unbeknownst to Zedekiah, he had been selected to "channel" a spirit with a deliberately false message. God's intent was to lure Ahab to his doom, and the prophets on Ahab's staff were manipulated into doing so. Then, to be utterly fair, God lets another prophet reveal the ruse to the king, who apparently takes it as just more of the war of words between the two contending prophets.

Prediction as Confirmation

We've seen that, despite what the word "prophet" suggests to us, the purpose of biblical prophecy was not prediction. In fact, the one place where it is clear that the purpose of a pronouncement is pure "prediction" is so out of character for the Bible that scholars agree it is a *vaticinium ex eventu*—that is, a "prophecy" made *after* the event it predicts, but recorded as if it had been made in advance.

We have seen that the books of Joshua, Judges, Samuel, and Kings were first assembled into a history of Israel during the reign of King Josiah of Judah, at the end of the seventh century BCE; remember that (as we saw in chapter 3) 2 Kgs. 23:25 tells us, "There was no king like him before who turned back to YHWH with all his heart and soul and might, in full accord with the Teaching of Moses; nor did any like him arise after him." It is Josiah who is the subject of our prediction.

When King Jeroboam, founder of the breakaway kingdom of (northern) Israel, founds a temple at Bethel to rival the one in Jerusalem, a "man of God" cries out, "Altar! Altar! Thus said YHWH: A son shall be born to the house of David, Josiah by name, who will slaughter upon you the priests of the high places who send up smoke from you, and human bones shall be burnt upon you" (1 Kgs. 13:2). This is, in fact, what happened (see 2 Kgs. 23:16); but the fact that the king's name is actually predicted—a kind of prediction that is never made anywhere else in the Bible—gives us good reason to believe that these words were really written in Josiah's own time, and to redound to his credit.

No doubt a prophet whose predictions failed too often—or too spectacularly—would lose his credibility. But the editors of the biblical books had a perspective on prophecy that transcended the concerns of an individual prophet making a specific prediction at a particular moment in history. On this level, the purpose of correct prognostication was to persuade the public that a threat like Jonah's against Nineveh was to be taken seriously. The ultimate purpose, of course, as in the Jonah story, was to move people to righteous behavior. That is why the Deuteronomistic History included the Josiah incident—to show that prophecy was fulfilled.

A King and Two Prophets

For another example, we may return to the story of Ahab and Jehoshaphat. God's planned destruction of Ahab, which he achieved by his manipulation of the prophets who served as Ahab's national security advisers, was not a random act. Ahab's wife, the notorious Jezebel (a Phoenician princess), had falsely accused a man named Naboth of blasphemy against God and the king so that she and her husband could acquire his vineyard, which was in the midst of their own holdings. (An executed man's property was forfeit to the crown.) When Naboth was stoned to death, God issued the following prophecy:

> 1 KGS. 21:17 The word of YHWH came to Elijah the Tishbite: 18 "Up, go down to meet King Ahab of Israel, who is in Samaria; he is in the vineyard of Naboth, which he has gone down to take possession of. 19 Speak to him as follows: 'Thus said YHWH: Have you murdered and taken possession?' Speak to him as follows: 'Thus said YHWH: In the place where the dogs licked up the blood of Naboth, the dogs will lick up your blood, too.'"

And when Micaiah's prediction about the outcome of the battle of Ramoth Gilead comes true, this is exactly what happens:

> 1 KGS. 22:34 Then a man pulled his bow as far as it would go, and shot the king of Israel between the scales of his armor. He told his charioteer, "Turn around and get me out of the camp—I'm

hurt." ³⁵ The battle raged furiously on that day, and the king was propped up in the chariot, facing Aram, and died at evening. The blood from his wound flowed into the body of the chariot. ³⁶ As the sun set, a cry went up in the camp: "Everyone to his own city and his own land!" ³⁷ The king died, and was brought to Samaria, and they buried the king in Samaria. ³⁸ They washed out the chariot at the pool of Samaria where the prostitutes washed, and the dogs licked up his blood—precisely according to the word of YHWH which He had spoken.

This is the voice of a biblical prophet—not fortune-telling, but a grim warning that sin will be punished. The prediction that a king named "Josiah" would destroy Jeroboam's altar was merely the invention of one of Josiah's own courtiers to make his king, and himself, look good. What biblical prophecy really was is made much clearer to us by the story in 1 Kings 22, telling us not only what Micaiah saw and heard during his experience of receiving prophecy, but also what happened when he tried to convey that prophecy to the people whom it most concerned. The prophet's exhortation to behave as God demanded needed to be backed up by credible punishment for failing to do so. In this case, Ahab's naïve belief in predictive prophecy meant that real prophecy could be used to lead him to his own destruction.

Prophecies of Consolation

All this is not to say that the true voice of biblical prophecy is always one of warning. It can offer reward and consolation as well. We can see this in an incident involving Josiah himself, along with one of the lesser known prophets in the Bible, a woman named Huldah. As we saw in chapter 2, the discovery of a "book of the Torah" in the Temple during Josiah's reign was a watershed in the history of Israel. Most likely it was this discovery that first prompted the compilation of the Deuteronomistic History. Let us look more closely at the story of this scroll's discovery.

When the scroll is read to the king, he orders his staff to "inquire of YHWH" about its authenticity. You remember how one "inquires" of God in First Temple times—by consulting a prophet, if one is available. So Josiah's advisers pay a call on the prophetess Huldah, the wife of one of the king's courtiers, to find out whether the scroll is really God's word. (Conveniently, she lives in Jerusalem, on the other side of town.) Here is what she tells them:

> 2 KGS. 22:15 Thus said YHWH, the God of Israel: Tell the man who sent you to me: **16** Thus said YHWH: I am bringing evil on this place and its inhabitants—all the words of the scroll which the king of Judah read— **17** because they have abandoned Me and sent up smoke to other gods, just to make Me angry with all of their deeds. My wrath has been kindled against this place, and it will not be quenched. **18** To the king of Judah who is sending you here to seek YHWH, say this: Thus said YHWH, the God of Israel: As for the words you have heard, **19** because your heart was softened and you submitted to Me, when you heard what I declared about making this place and its inhabitants a ruin and a curse, and you tore your clothes and cried before Me, I too have heard—declares YHWH. **20** Therefore I am gathering you to your fathers, and you will be gathered to your grave peacefully. Your eyes will not see all the evil I am bringing on this place." They brought the reply to the king.

The prophecy consists of a warning that YHWH has determined to doom Jerusalem *and* of a promise that Josiah himself will be laid to rest in peace and not live to see the disaster.

Was Huldah's Prophecy Fulfilled?

Let us look for a moment at the predictive aspect of this prophecy. Jerusalem was indeed destroyed, within forty years or so, and Josiah did indeed not live to see it. But he did not die peacefully. As 2 Kgs. 23:29 tells us, he was killed by Pharaoh Neco of Egypt at Megiddo.

To be sure, he was indeed laid to rest in his tomb in Jerusalem, and this is all that the prophecy literally promised. But the promise that he would be laid in his tomb "in peace" surely implies a peaceful death as well. Given that Josiah is called the king without peer, one hates to think of God as tricking him with this bit of pettifoggery into thinking that he would die in his bed.

Again, it is the nature of biblical prophecy that the warning and the promise were paramount. The predictive details of the prophecy were incidental, not essential. When the Egyptians passed through the country on their way to attack the Assyrians, Josiah marched forth to stop them—and was killed trying to do so. But that was his business, not God's. Just as Huldah promised, the destruction of Jerusalem did not occur until after Josiah's time. The essential element of the prophecy was the promise of peace and safety for Jerusalem as long as Josiah reigned.

In fact, words of reassurance and promise make up a significant part of the Bible's prophetic voices. In chapter 1 we saw the majestic announcement that God had anointed Cyrus the Great, king of Persia and Media, to rule over the former Babylonian Empire as well:

ISA. 45:1 Thus said the LORD to Cyrus, His anointed one—
Whose right hand He has grasped,
Treading down nations before him,
Ungirding the loins of kings,
Opening doors before him
And letting no gate stay shut:
² I will march before you
And level the hills that loom up;
I will shatter doors of bronze
And cut down iron bars.
³ I will give you treasures concealed in the dark
And secret hoards—
So that you may know that it is I, the LORD,
The God of Israel, who call you by name.
⁴ For the sake of My servant Jacob,

Israel My chosen one,
I call you by name,
I hail you by title, though you have not known Me. (NJPS)

This is not a harsh call for repentance "or else," but a promise of success for Cyrus and a word of comfort and reassurance for Israel.

In fact, the voice of chapters 40 and following of the book of Isaiah are rich with words of comfort for Israel, beginning with the very first two words: "Comfort, comfort My people" (Isa. 40:1). Most likely, this is due to the date of these later chapters, which (as has been recognized since at least medieval times) is not the eighth century of the prophet whose name was Isaiah, but the late sixth century, a time when Cyrus had decreed that the Israelites who had been exiled to Babylonia by Nebuchadnezzar could return to their homeland. (Scholars call the prophetic voice of this section "Second" Isaiah.) The reassurance, judiciously offered, might be applicable at any moment of Israelite history; but the name Cyrus was not. This passage is not prediction, but reassurance that Israel's exile is over.

The prophecies of consolation are not based merely on the promise of reward or the promise that a punishment will end. They may even have an almost romantic aspect, with the genuine warmth of emotion that true consolation implies. Take, for example, these words from Second Isaiah:

ISA. 52:7 How beautiful on the mountains are the feet of the herald
Announcing peace, heralding good
Announcing victory, telling Zion
"Your God reigns!"

This is reminiscent, perhaps deliberately so, of a line like the following, from the Song of Songs (in the beautiful King James translation): "How beautiful are thy feet with shoes, O prince's daughter!" (Song 7:1 in the KJV; v. 2 in the Hebrew text and in Jewish translations). The biblical prophets frequently liken the relationship between God and

Israel to a human love affair or marriage, so it is not surprising that the prophecies of consolation at times take on the air of love poetry. (For a prophetic song of unrequited love, see Isa. 5:1–7.)

Oracles against the Nations

Many of the words of the Israelite prophets are warnings and calls for repentance, like the one we heard Jonah bring to Nineveh. Others are words of comfort and reassurance to Israel, like those we heard from Second Isaiah. But still others are ostensibly addressed not to Israel, but to the nations that surround her. You may have noticed that many of the prophetic voices preserved in the Bible comment directly on matters of war and international politics. This should not be surprising when you remember two things. First, as we've seen, many prophets were employed by the kings to provide advice on just such matters. Second, the many prophecies with a more personal dimension that must have been uttered were not preserved unless they fit into the story that the biblical editors chose to tell—and this story was primarily one of God's action in history.

The Israelite belief that God acted in history demanded that he control the fates of her neighbors as well as her own, and the prophets announced such fates in powerful poetry. Here (in the NJPS translation) is Ezekiel declaring God's wrath against Tyre, the Phoenician city (just north of Israel on the Mediterranean coast of today's Lebanon) that had gloated over the fall of Jerusalem:

> EZEK. 26:7 For thus said the Lord GOD: I will bring from the north, against Tyre, King Nebuchadrezzar of Babylon, a king of kings, with horses, chariots, and horsemen—a great mass of troops.
> 8 Your daughter-towns in the country
> He shall put to the sword;
> He shall erect towers against you,
> And cast up mounds against you,
> And raise [a wall of] bucklers against you.

⁹ He shall turn the force of his battering rams
Against your walls
And smash your towers with his axes.
¹⁰ From the cloud raised by his horses
Dust shall cover you;
From the clatter of horsemen
And wheels and chariots,
Your walls shall shake—
When he enters your gates
As men enter a breached city.
¹¹ With the hoofs of his steeds
He shall trample all your streets.
He shall put your people to the sword,
And your mighty pillars shall crash to the ground.
¹² They shall plunder your wealth
And loot your merchandise.
They shall raze your walls
And tear down your splendid houses,
And they shall cast into the water
Your stones and timber and soil.
¹³ I will put an end to the murmur of your songs,
And the sound of your lyres shall be heard no more.
¹⁴ I will make you a naked rock,
You shall be a place for drying nets;
You shall never be rebuilt.
For I have spoken
—declares the Lord GOD.

In fact, the third kind of prophetic style, the "oracle against the nations," in a sense combines the two other styles, blending God's threat to punish the wicked (here Israel's enemies) with the reassurance that everything will be all right in the end (for Israel). The message of an individual prophet might fall into a single one of these modes (like Obadiah's oracle against Edom) or, more often, a blend of them. This is especially true of the "major" books of the prophecies of Isaiah, Jeremiah, and Ezekiel. But it is worth remembering that these men were not faceless envoys bringing a divine message. They were men of flesh and blood, individuals, who communicated their messages in very different voices.

This brings up the question: What was it like to live in a society where prophets were common? Let us see what we can learn about this by looking at the career of the prophet Jeremiah, as presented in the biblical book named after him.

Jeremiah the Prophet

Just as Isaiah, whose book is first in the collection of the prophets in both Jewish and Christian Bibles, prophesied at a crucial time in the history of Israel—the conquest of the Northern Kingdom by Assyria—so too did Jeremiah, whose book comes second. Jeremiah lived in Jerusalem in the decades before 586 BCE, when the kingdom of Judah was uneasily poised between the rival superpowers of Egypt and Babylonia.* This was a period when the political cliché that the future of the country was at stake was literally true, and Jeremiah was no bystander; he played a major role in the events leading up to the destruction of Jerusalem.

When he first started to prophesy, though, Jeremiah was not predicting Jerusalem's downfall at the hands of Babylonia. His vision of God proclaiming the destruction to come is, as yet, vague: "For I bring evil from the north, and great disaster" (Jer. 4:6). Jeremiah warns of this "evil from the north" six times in the prophecies of the first fifteen chapters of his book. The same prediction is made in Jeremiah 47 (given here in the NJPS translation), which is dated "before Pharaoh conquered Gaza" (v. 1)—that is, before about 600 BCE:

---

* Rabbinic tradition asked why Josiah's men had consulted Huldah and not Jeremiah in 1 Kings 22 and concluded that Jeremiah must have been out of town.

> **JER. 47:2** See, waters are rising from the north,
> They shall become a raging torrent,
> They shall flood the land and its creatures,
> The towns and their inhabitants.
> Men shall cry out,
> All the inhabitants of the land shall howl,
> ³ At the clatter of the stamping hoofs of his stallions,
> At the noise of his chariots,
> The rumbling of their wheels. (NJPS)

We might think that the prophet was speaking poetically rather than geopolitically, but in fact he goes on, in vv. 4–5, to enumerate precisely the cities that will be destroyed: Tyre and Sidon, Gaza and Ashkelon. The "enemy from the north" is marching down the coast of the "Great Sea," as the Mediterranean is called in the Bible, leaving destruction in its wake. But the prophet did not yet have a specific name for this ravaging enemy.

In Jeremiah 19, the prophet goes to the court of the Temple in Jerusalem and issues a final condemnation: as a result of the people's idolatry, God has resolved to bring destruction down upon the city and its inhabitants. With this proclamation, Jeremiah's prophetic role changed from that of a sidewalk soothsayer to that of a political activist. He is arrested, flogged, and jailed overnight; released the next day, he warns his jailer:

> **JER. 20:4** For thus said YHWH: I am giving you and all your allies over to terror; they will fall by the sword of their enemies while your eyes watch. I will give all Judah into the hands of the king of Babylon, and he will exile them to Babylon or put them to the sword.

This prophecy of Jeremiah is not dated, but in Jeremiah 25, when he makes a similar prophecy, the date *is* given: "the 4th year of Jehoiakim son of Josiah, king of Judah." Ominously, that year was also "the 1st year of King Nebuchadrezzar of Babylon" (both phrases are from Jer. 25:1). By then, at least, the light has finally dawned on Jeremiah:

> JER. 25:8 Thus said YHWH of Hosts: since you have not heeded My words, ⁹ I am therefore sending to take all the clans of the north—oracle of YHWH—and to Nebuchadrezzar the king of Babylon My servant. I shall bring them upon this land, its inhabitants, and all these nations around, and I shall destroy them and make them a ruin and an object of hissing*—and eternal ruins.

The "evil from the north" is . . . Nebuchadrezzar. (As we saw in chapter 1, the book of Jeremiah generally prefers to call him by this more accurate transliteration of his name, not by "Nebuchadnezzar," the transliteration found most everywhere else in the Bible, which we commonly use today.) True, Babylonia is east of Israel, not north of it. But don't think that Jeremiah's geography is off base. Remember that Babylonia and Israel were separated by many miles of waterless desert that an invading army could not cross. The Babylonian attack would have to come from the only direction where an army could find water—from the north, via the Fertile Crescent. Jeremiah's visions had not misled him.

Indeed, had he been more politically aware at the beginning of his prophetic experience, he might well have realized that the enemy he was proclaiming was Babylonia. But to repeat: politics was not his prime concern. Only because of the intersection of religion and history did Jeremiah concern himself with politics. His own concern—beyond the personal one of discharging his prophetic duty—was to proclaim the theological reason for the political and military disaster that Judah was facing. So his proclamation of Jerusalem's destruction was preceded by the following announcement:

---

* The implication of this word is not clear. It may be a sign of contempt, or perhaps a superstitious reaction to the ruin, a kind of "whistling past the graveyard."

> **JER. 25:3** From the 13th year of the reign of Josiah son of Amon king of Judah until this day—these 23 years—the word of YHWH has come to me, and I spoke it to you over and over again, and you would not listen. **4** YHWH kept sending you His servants the prophets, over and over again, but you would not listen nor turn your ears to hear **5** when they said, "Turn back, each one of you, from your evil ways and from your evil deeds; and return to the land that YHWH has given eternally to you and to your ancestors."

Jeremiah insists with exasperation that, just like Jonah, *all* the prophets, no matter what their claims about the future, had come with a single purpose: to warn the people to follow God's ways and turn from evil.

Turmoil at the Temple

Now that we have Jeremiah in our sights, let us spend a few more minutes following him through the last doomed years of Jerusalem. In doing so, we will get a rare opportunity to hear some of the voices that filled Jerusalem in the fateful years before it fell to Nebuchadnezzar. Along the way, we will also hear the voices of two other prophets: one with a book of his own in the Bible and another whose voice is heard only here.

We begin with Jeremiah 26, a text we first looked at in chapter 1. At God's instruction, Jeremiah goes to the courtyard of the "House of YHWH"—that is, the Temple—and repeats a warning whose terms are by now familiar to us:

> **JER. 26:4** Say to them: Thus said YHWH: If you do not heed Me— by following My teaching which I have given you, **5** and by heeding the words of My servants the prophets, whom I have been sending before you over and over again, and whom you have not heeded— **6** then I will make this House like Shiloh, and this city I will make a curse to all the nations of the earth.

Shiloh (the battle site in Tennessee was named after it) was the site of another House of YHWH; see 1 Sam. 1:24. (The story of its end is not told in the Bible, but it is referred to in Ps. 78:60.) I was willing to let that Temple of mine become a ruin, God threatens, and I will destroy this one too, if I have to. But Jeremiah's listeners would rather accuse him of blasphemy than change their ways:

> JER. 26:8 When Jeremiah finished speaking all that YHWH had commanded him to speak to all the people, the priests, the prophets, and all the people seized him, saying, "You must die! 9 How could you prophesy in the name of YHWH that this House will be like Shiloh and this city be left an uninhabited ruin?!" And all the people crowded around Jeremiah in the House of YHWH.

If you were thinking of the Temple as an awesome place of quiet and decorum, think again. It was the great central meeting place of ancient Jerusalem, and when tempers ran high, it could become a place of violence. (Six and a half centuries after Jeremiah, during the years 66–70 CE, Herod's rebuilt Temple on the same Jerusalem site would be the fortified headquarters of the First Jewish Revolt against Rome.)

And notice one more thing: among those screaming in anger at Jeremiah are not only "the priests" who staffed the Temple, but also . . . "the prophets." By now you realize that "prophet" in Biblical Hebrew is not so much a spiritual term as it is a job description. Many others who claimed the title of "prophet" lived in Jerusalem at the time of Jeremiah—we will meet another of them shortly—and here we see these other "prophets" joining with those who find Jeremiah's ranting offensive.

But a certain faction of the government officials, those who felt sure that Judah's future depended on submission to Babylonia, believed that Jeremiah's political stance was in line with their own. They wanted him protected, hoping that his influence would help them prevail in the political struggle. Now they too appear on the scene:

JER. 26:10 When the Judean officials heard these words, they went up from the palace to the House of YHWH. They sat at the entrance to the New Gate of YHWH. **11** The priests and prophets told the officials and all the people, "This man deserves the death penalty, for he prophesied against this city, as you heard with your very ears."

Jeremiah insists that God has sent him and that if the people repent there is still a chance for the city to be saved. Now "the people" switch sides, and they and the officials tell the priests and prophets, "This man does not deserve the death penalty, for he spoke to us in the name of YHWH our God" (v. 16).

At this point comes the most intriguing part of the argument:

JER. 26:17 Some of the elders of the land rose up and said to the assembly of the people, **18** "Micah the Morashtite, who prophesied in the days of King Hezekiah of Judah, said to all the people of Judah, 'Thus said YHWH of Hosts:
Zion shall be plowed as a field,
Jerusalem shall become heaps of ruins
And the Temple Mount a shrine in the woods.'
19 Did King Hezekiah of Judah, and all of Judah, put him to death? No, he [Hezekiah] feared YHWH, and entreated YHWH, and YHWH changed His mind about the evil He had declared against them. We are doing great evil to ourselves!"

Through the elders' persuasion, and perhaps more practically by the intervention of one of the officials (see v. 24), Jeremiah was saved. Another prophet, Uriah, was not so lucky. Verses 20–23 of our chapter tell how he prophesied the same things as Jeremiah, fled to Egypt for his life, and was kidnapped, brought back to Jerusalem, and executed.

The Bible "Quotes" the Bible

Despite the sheer dramatic interest of this scene—of all the stories in the Bible, this may be the one that is easiest to imagine going viral on

YouTube—in one way the most exciting of the voices here is that of Micah. As the elders point out, he had prophesied over a century earlier, in the time of King Hezekiah, when the ostensible threat was from Assyria, not Babylonia. When they repeat his words, they are, for the first time in recorded history, quoting the Bible.

Let me be clear about just what I mean. There was, of course, no "Bible" as we find it in churches and synagogues (and in hotel rooms) today; as you realize, many of the books in today's Bible had not yet even been written. Even the idea of sacred writings was fairly new— remember that a "book of Torah," probably a version of Deuteronomy, had been found in the Temple only a few years before, within living memory of many of the participants in our dramatic scene. What I mean is that the words the elders quoted are in the Bible today, in our Bibles.

Seven chapters of Micah the Morashtite's prophecies are included among the twelve minor prophets in our Bibles, and you will find exactly the words quoted by the elders in Mic. 3:12. I don't think it is likely that all seven chapters had been remembered for over a hundred years. But this verse, at least, was still current on people's lips. No doubt there was a scroll somewhere, perhaps more than one, that preserved Micah's words.

The idea of sacred writings was still so new, though, that the discoverers of the "book of Torah" had had to consult Huldah about it. It will take another four hundred years before we find a reference to sacred "books of the prophets" (in the Greek translation of the book of Ben Sira, by his grandson). Nonetheless, the historical consciousness of the elders in Jeremiah 26, in the middle of a Jerusalem riot, gives us a quick glimpse into one of the earliest stages of the Bible's formation. As I said in the introduction, I believe that the fulfillment of Jeremiah's prophecy of destruction is a key reason we have such a thing as a Bible at all.

Jeremiah Meets His Match

I promised you the voices of two other prophets in addition to that of Jeremiah. We have heard Micah's, but Uriah was silenced without our being able to hear him. (Jer. 26:30 tells us that he prophesied "the same things as Jeremiah.") The second prophet I had in mind was not a colleague of Jeremiah's, but one of his rivals. In 594, God told Jeremiah to put a yoke on his neck, and went on to tell him that God had given dominion to King Nebuchadnezzar. The story is told in Jeremiah 27:

> **JER. 27:9** Pay no heed to your prophets and your diviners, your dreams and your soothsayers and your sorcerers, who are telling you, "You must not serve the king of Babylon." **¹⁰** For they are prophesying a lie to you, in order to remove you from your soil. I shall scatter you and you will perish. **¹¹** But the nation that puts its neck in the yoke of the king of Babylon and serves him, I shall leave them on their soil—oracle of YHWH—and they will work it and dwell on it.

And here is how Hananiah son of Azzur of Gibeon, Jeremiah's rival, responded:

> **JER. 28:2** Thus said YHWH of Hosts, the God of Israel: I have broken the yoke of the king of Babylon. **³** In two more years, I am bringing back to this place all the utensils of the House of YHWH that King Nebuchadnezzar of Babylon took from this place* and brought to Babylon. **⁴** And King Jeconiah son of Jehoiakim of Judah, and all the exiles of Judah who came to Babylon, I am bringing back to this place—declares YHWH—for I will break the yoke of the king of Babylon.

"Amen!" said Jeremiah (v. 5). But he questioned Hananiah's bona fides: "The prophet who prophesies good fortune—when the prophet's word comes true it can be known that YHWH really sent him" (v. 9). This is what had happened with Isaiah in the days of King Ahaz, and again in the days of King Hezekiah, when he prophesied confidence against

---

* In 597 BCE; see 2 Kgs. 24:13.

the military attacks of Israel, Aram, and Assyria. But Hananiah was undaunted, and he trumped Jeremiah's own dramatic proclamation:

JER. 28:10 But Hananiah the prophet took the yoke off the neck of Jeremiah the prophet, and broke it; 11 and Hananiah said before all the people, "Thus said YHWH: So shall I break the yoke of King Nebuchadnezzar of Babylon, in another two years, from off the neck of all the nations." Jeremiah the prophet went on his way.

Eight years later, far from seeing his yoke broken, Nebuchadnezzar had what was left of Jerusalem destroyed. But Hananiah had already died and did not live to see the fulfillment of God's cruel promise to him: "You broke bars of wood, but you shall make bars of iron instead" (v. 13). Indeed, his death was prophesied by Jeremiah (v. 16).

What Hananiah said was neither true nor predictive. It did not take place, and v. 13 makes clear that God did not trick him into uttering this falsehood. Yet it is equally clear that he believed he was telling the truth. Indeed, Jer. 28:10 explicitly calls him "Hananiah the prophet." Prophecy was a phenomenon of biblical times, and nothing but the unfolding of events could establish whether a particular prophecy was true or false.

The Prophets' Conversation

We cannot part from Jeremiah, or from our chapter on prophetic voices, without a last look at the book of Isaiah. The specific passage I mean occurs in the voice of Second Isaiah, the comforting prophet of the return from exile, at the beginning of chapter 40 (in the NJPS translation):

ISA. 40:1 Comfort, oh comfort My people,
Says your God.
2 Speak tenderly to Jerusalem,
And declare to her
That her term of service is over,

> That her iniquity is expiated;
> For she has received at the hand of the LORD
> Double for all her sins.

This instruction to the prophet to speak tenderly to Jerusalem is indeed an oracle of comfort to Israel, and it is beautiful poetry besides. There is more here, though, than meets the eye. The prophet of these chapters is one of the finest literary stylists among the biblical writers. (We don't know how prophecy worked technically, but, as we have said, the prophet's individual human voice is not silenced as part of the process.) But it is not just poetic craft that makes the voice of this prophet stand out. This is a new kind of prophecy—it is prophecy written in response to the words of an earlier prophet.

Remember that by the time the return from exile took place, the idea that God's word might also be found in a scroll was beginning to gain currency. A close reading of these chapters shows that our prophet had mastered the earlier literature of prophecy. Here, at the beginning of his message, he is alluding to a verse from the book of our old friend Jeremiah, from a passage that threatens Israel:

> JER. 16:18 First, I shall pay them double for their iniquity and their sin, for their profanation of My land with the corpses of their disgusting idols and their filling up My possession with their abominations.

The announcement in Isa. 40:2 that Israel's iniquity had been expiated by paying "double for all her sins" is not mere rhetoric, as if to say, "You have paid your debt and more." It is a specific reference to the prophecy of Jeremiah that threatened Israel with just this, double punishment for their crimes. Second Isaiah is not merely offering vague comfort. He is saying (to those who can hear the different biblical voices) something much more powerful: God's threats of doom all came true just exactly as they were prophesied—and so will his promises of redemption that I am bringing to you now.

The ancient Israelites, and the kings especially, were faced with a clamor of prophetic voices, each trying to outshout the others. Today, we can hear these confrontational voices from a perspective that lets us know which prophecies were fulfilled and which were not. But we have also heard Micah in Jeremiah's book, and (more subtly) Jeremiah in Isaiah's. The prophetic voices, like the other biblical voices we've heard, provide a richer music than may be evident on first hearing.

6
Women's Voices

We have discussed many different voices so far, but the prophets were the first of them that could be considered the individual voices of real human beings. Listening carefully to individual voices like these will provide us with a means to hear some voices that are less prominent in the Bible: the voices of women. As we'll see in this chapter, women's voices are more audible in the Bible than most people think. But because relatively few women in the Bible play prominent *public* roles, we must first think about how it might be possible to hear the voices of real individuals through the biblical texts, and not just those of the writers and editors who created the biblical writings. Then we can begin to tune in to the individual voices of biblical women.

It's true that writers and editors too are generally individuals and not committees, but the characteristics of style and the theological views that permit us to identify these voices make it hard to attribute them to anything other than "the Deuteronomic school," "the priestly writers," and so forth. If these are individual voices that we hear, they are nonetheless the voices of ideologues, for all practical purposes indistinguishable from the voices of others who shared their political and religious ideas. They are Republicans, but not Lincoln; Democrats, but not Jefferson.

With the prophets, though, we do have real individual voices. One might have thought the prophets would be the least individual of all the biblical voices—their individuality uniformly obliterated by the voice of God that "possesses" them—but, as we saw in chapter 5, that is far from the case. Even the anonymous prophet of Isaiah chapters 40 and following, who submerged his identity (or had it submerged for him) within that of the eighth-century BCE prophet Isaiah, possesses a unique voice and a well-defined set of ideas. (To my ear, there are occasional hints of this voice in the book of Job; I have often wondered whether the prophet, disillusioned by the failure of the return to Zion to take on the miraculous quality he had foreseen, ended by writing the great poem questioning God's justice.)

Then as now, however, most people were not prophets. But of course all through the period of a thousand years during which the biblical texts were written, ordinary people like you and me were getting up in the morning (or having trouble getting up—see Prov. 6:9), going to work, and doing all the other ordinary things that human beings have done each day since time immemorial. Are the voices of any of these ordinary people preserved in the Bible?

If they are, they are few and far between. To be sure, the biblical stories are full of conversations and quoted remarks. But there were no tape recorders in those days. More to the point, there is no reason to expect from the Bible the kind of insistence on absolute precision that we try to demand today when scholars, lawyers, or journalists quote someone else's words. The literary voices of the biblical writers, and the real voices of the many people who told some of the biblical stories aloud before they were written down, inevitably reshaped the original wording.

We can see a simple example of this process in operation within the biblical text itself. In Genesis 24, Abraham sends a servant back to his family in Hebron to get a wife for his son Isaac. He instructs him carefully: "Do not get a wife for my son from the women of the Canaanites in whose midst I dwell" (Gen. 24:3). When the servant meets the family of Rebecca, daughter of Abraham's cousin Bethuel, he repeats the command that Abraham had given him: "'Do not get a wife for my son from the women of the Canaanites in whose *land* I dwell'" (Gen. 24:37). Even though the servant introduces Abraham's instructions with the Hebrew word that denotes direct quotation, he is not concerned with repeating Abraham's wording mechanically, merely with accurately conveying his meaning.

On the other side of the coin, most of the unidentified voices we hear in the Bible are really those of types, not of unique, real individuals. Among these are the illiterate person who says, "I don't know how to read" (Isa. 29:12), the lazy Alibi Ike who says, "There's a lion out there! I'll be killed in the streets!" (Prov. 22:13), and the scoundrel who thinks, "There is no God" (Ps. 14:1). No doubt there were real individuals who said or thought these things. But the biblical writers are not trying to depict these individuals for us, but to show us that *type* of person. Few of the real people whose lives or characters led them to say these things have managed to leave their individual portraits in the biblical text.

It's true that a few biblical stories do seem to open for us a window, however small, on personal experience from the biblical era. The chapters narrating the career of the prophet Elisha give us one of them:

> 2 KGS. 4:8 One day, Elisha passed through Shunem, where there was a wealthy woman who insisted that he stop for a meal. From then on, whenever he passed by, he would stop there to eat. ⁹ She said to her husband, "Look, I know that this person who is always stopping by our place is a holy man of God. ¹⁰ Let's make him a little loft and put a bed, a table, a chair, and a lamp for him there, so that whenever he comes to our part of the country he will stop off there." ¹¹ One day, he came there, stopped off at the loft, and lay down there. ¹² He said to his servant Gehazi, "Call this Shunammite woman." He called her, and she stood before him. ¹³ He said to [Gehazi], "Ask her, 'You have gone to all this trouble for us—what is to be done for you? Do you need someone to speak on your behalf to the king or the commander of the army?'" She replied, "I live among my own people." ¹⁴ So he said,

"What is to be done for her?" Gehazi said, "You know, she has no children, and her husband is old." ¹⁵ He said, "Call her," and he called her and she stood at the entrance. ¹⁶ He said, "At this season next year, you will be holding a child." She replied, "Don't, O man of God, sir—don't make empty promises to your maidservant." ¹⁷ But the woman got pregnant and bore a son at the same season the next year, as Elisha had said to her.

The story goes on to tell that the child subsequently died, but was brought back to life by Elisha. We are never told the names of the woman, her husband, or their child; for the biblical writer, the purpose of the story is to demonstrate Elisha's miraculous power. But something of the woman's personal story does manage to touch us. We feel that somehow an ordinary (if well-off) life has bridged the gap of three millennia and, more significantly, sneaked past the Bible's relentless focus on God and the Israelites en masse to say, "I'm a woman of ancient Israel, and here is what my life is like." Put aside theology and what you see is a person we can relate to: a farm woman who is eager to listen to someone who can bring news of the outside world; a woman who builds an addition to her house and furnishes it; a woman who wants a child but is anxious about what might happen if she has one.

You may be wondering whether this woman is "real." That is, is our story objective reporting of something that actually happened to an actual woman in ancient Israel, or is it simply a tale showing what a wonder-worker Elisha was? For our purposes in this chapter, though, that question isn't much different from asking whether the Iliad was written by Homer or by another man with the same name. To make the same point in biblical terms, did Mahlah, Noah, Hoglah, Milcah, and Tirzah, the daughters of Zelophehad, really challenge Moses about their father's inheritance (see chapter 4), or did some unnamed man's unnamed daughters raise this challenge at some unknown time in Israelite history?

If the story of the Shunammite woman is true (and accurately told), we are of course hearing the voice of an authentic woman of ancient Israel. But even if it is fiction, it is realistic fiction. I'm not speaking here about the prophet bringing the boy back to life—utterly unrealistic even if it is true—but about the scene we just saw. Supposing the Shunammite woman is just a character, she is nonetheless a realistic character, giving us an idea of what the authentic voice of a woman of her day sounded like.

Women in Official Roles

It goes without saying that the overwhelming majority of characters in the Bible are male, as were most (not all!) of the biblical writers. The relative silence of women in the biblical record is not primarily caused by an ideological blindness to women among the biblical writers, but by their focus on the political and religious leadership to the exclusion of ordinary people. As in most of the ancient world—and in today's world, for that matter—leadership roles were primarily, and in some sectors exclusively, occupied by males.

Some women did play religious roles; we have already seen the women who sacrificed to the Queen of Heaven, and there are a few female prophets as well. But the official roles in the religion of YHWH with its center in Jerusalem, those of the priests and the Levites, were reserved exclusively for men. (Exod. 38:8 and 1 Sam. 2:22 describe women performing certain tasks at the entrance to the Tent of Meeting, but whatever these were, their location shows that they were peripheral, not central, to the cult.) Again, though a non-Davidic queen usurped the throne for half a dozen years just after the middle of the ninth century BCE, even so, both before, during, and after the monarchy, political leadership was almost always in the hands of men. The simultaneous exception to the rule in both the religious and political spheres was Deborah, the prophetess and judge who ruled Israel in the twelfth century; we will take a closer look at her story shortly.

Still, most of the women we meet in the Bible are the wives, mothers, or daughters of the men whose stories are told there. Nonetheless, one such mother will show us something important about women's voices in the Bible. She appears in Prov. 31:1, a seemingly quite unrevealing verse that serves as the heading to the short section of the book made up by Prov. 31:2–9. Here it is: "The words of King Lemuel of Massa,* with which his mother admonished him."

You mustn't think that Lemuel's mom was nagging him to clean up his room. She was giving him the kind of advice that rulers would do well to follow in any age: "Open your mouth, rule justly, [heed] the case of the poor and needy" (Prov. 31:9). We know from the book of Kings that there was a recognized position of queen mother—the mother of the ruling king. As we saw in chapter 3, using the example of 1 Kgs. 15:1–3, one of the formulaic elements in the encyclopedia-style entry that introduces each king of Judah is the name of his mother. The heading of this tiny book of wisdom that identifies it as being in a woman's voice may tell us that the queen mother's voice did, indeed, carry some weight in the royal council. As we will see later in this chapter, it is not unusual for women's voices to occur among those who provide sage counsel.

Egalitarian Language

Another aspect of the biblical text may superficially point, if not certainly to the voices of women themselves, at least to women's concerns: the use of egalitarian language. This is not easy to achieve in Biblical Hebrew, because every noun and verb is grammatically marked as either masculine or feminine—including inanimate objects. Take as an example Exod. 26:3, which describes how the curtains of the Tabernacle are to be connected to each other. Since the word for "curtain" is grammatically feminine, the original Hebrew says not "to each other" but literally "a woman to her sister." A language in which curtains are female is a language in which egalitarian formulations are difficult

---

* An unknown country (if we are correctly understanding the text here). The Hebrew of this section has a slight Aramaic flavor, as if to accent its foreignness.

to achieve! Thus, the example I'm about to offer of a case that I think is egalitarian will take some explaining.

It comes from Deuteronomy, written in a voice that is concerned to insist that each individual has a personal relationship with God. Here is the instruction in Deuteronomy to observe the Feast of Booths:

> DEUT. 16:13 You shall observe for yourself the Feast of Booths for seven days, when you gather in from your threshing-floor and your vat [of wine or oil]. 14 You shall rejoice on your festival—you, your son and daughter, your male and female slaves, the Levite, the alien, the orphan, and the widow who is in your locality.

"You" and "your," which sound neutral in English, are grammatically marked as masculine (and singular) in Hebrew. Notice, though, that in the laundry list of people who are supposed to observe this holiday, one is missing: "your wife." By contrast, look at what God told Noah after the flood was over:

> GEN. 8:16 Go out of the ark, you and your wife and your sons and your sons' wives with you.

The words "your wife" (four letters in Hebrew) would have been easy to add in the Deuteronomy text as well. Why aren't they there?

I think the answer must be that Deuteronomy is trying its best, within the limited capabilities of Biblical Hebrew, to speak directly to women as well as to men. The missing "wife" of Deut. 16:14 is not an adjunct to the head of the household, as are his children and his slaves, or as Noah's wife is in Genesis 8. Deuteronomy wanted her to understand herself as "you" just as much as her husband did. The same formulation is found in the Ten Commandments (in both Exod. 20:10 and Deut. 5:14), in the commandment to observe the Sabbath.* It

---

* This is one of a number of aspects of the Ten Commandments that lead some scholars to think that even the Exodus version of them is on its way to developing a Deuteronomic accent.

seems plausible that the absence of "your wife" from these expressions is meant to suggest that they are directed to men and women equally.

Theological Equality

We must be careful, of course, not to rely too much on contemporary sensibilities that might lead us astray in understanding the biblical voices. An example of what I mean is found in Numbers 30, the chapter which gives the rules about vows. (This chapter begins in Christian Bibles with the equivalent of Num. 29:40 in Jewish Bibles. So if you are using a Christian Bible, subtract one from each of the verse numbers below: Num. 30:3 = Num. 30:2 in Christian Bibles, and so forth.) Here we find a biblical writer maintaining a careful balance between the social notion that males must play a superior role and the notion that men and women are equal—a notion that is *not* social, but theological. If the rule about vows were only one verse long, I would translate it this way:

> NUM. 30:3 Anyone who makes a vow to YHWH or swears an oath to impose a restriction on himself shall not profane his word. He shall do everything that comes out of his mouth.

The verse begins with the Hebrew word *ish* (say the vowel like "ea" in "each"). Like the English "man," this can refer both to human beings in general or to a male human being in particular. Thus in Num. 19:20, the NJPS translates, "If *anyone* who has become unclean fails to cleanse himself" whereas the King James Version has "But *the man* that shall be unclean, and shall not purify himself." The more literal KJV translates *ish* as "man"; the more colloquial NJPS uses "anyone." "Himself" sounds masculine, of course, but that is an artifact of language; neither Hebrew nor English has a gender-neutral pronoun that can be used for a human being, and both languages historically use the masculine pronouns by default.

In Numbers 30, however, v. 4 begins with the word *ishah*, "woman," for the rules about vows offer a concession to social reality:

NUM. 30:4 But when a woman who makes a vow to YHWH or imposes a restriction on herself while in her father's house, during her youth, 5 if her father hears about her vow or the restriction she imposed on herself and her father says nothing to her, then all her vows and every restriction she imposed on herself shall stand. 6 But if her father forbids her on the day he hears of it, then all her vows and the restrictions she has imposed on herself shall stand. YHWH will forgive her, for her father forbade her [to fulfill her vow].

When a girl's father, or a woman's husband (see vv. 7–16), hears about her oath, he has the right to object *as long as he does so by the next day* (see v. 15). If he does not, or if the woman is not living in a man's home—something v. 10 assumes could only apply if she is widowed or divorced—then she is bound by her vow just as a man would be by his. The bottom line is that a woman's oath binds her just as a man's binds him. But the escape clause shows a concession to social realities. As important as the sanctity of an oath made to YHWH is to the priestly writers, the male who in practical terms may also be bound by a woman's oath is given a twenty-four-hour window to nullify it; the woman bound by her father's or husband's oath has no such opportunity. So "anyone" is not really correct in Num. 30:3. Rather, that verse presents the situation when "a man" takes an oath, followed in v. 4 by the case when "a woman" takes one.

Precisely because the priestly point of view focused on the relationship with God, however, that perspective had room for a certain backdoor egalitarianism. We can see this in Numbers 6, the chapter that gives the rules about how to be a Nazirite—a person who dedicates himself completely to God in a particular ritual way. Ordinarily one would do this only for a limited period of time (typically thirty days, if postbiblical tradition is any guide). There is one biblical story, though, about someone who was a Nazirite for life, actually starting while he was still in his mother's womb. If you don't know who this is, you'll remember him as soon as I tell you the rules for being a Nazirite: never go near a source of ritual impurity; never drink alcohol or consume any kind of grape products; and never, ever, cut your hair. That's right—the famous biblical strongman Samson was a Nazirite. (See Judges 13–16 for his story; according to a version of 1 Samuel found among the Dead Sea Scrolls, Samuel too was a lifelong Nazirite.) But Numbers 6 supposes that anyone might want to experience this special state of holiness for a while. So it declares that the rules apply to "any man or woman who pronounces a Nazirite's vow, to be a Nazirite for YHWH" (Num. 6:2). A Nazirite was performing a religious action, but a private one, not a public one. So there was no reason a woman could not do so as well as a man, and the text makes this explicit.

Even in the priestly writings, this is not a unique occurrence. There are definitely realms in which temple ritual practices made a distinction between females—who give birth and have menstrual bleeding—and males. And of course (as we've said) the priests and Levites who perform specific tasks in the Temple must be male, by definition.

"When a Soul . . ."

But on other occasions, in the book of Leviticus, great care is taken to clarify that certain rules apply to both men and women. One way this is done is with a very unusual Hebrew expression, one that occurs eight times in Leviticus and nowhere else in the Bible. To examine it, let's look at the very first occurrence, at the beginning of the chapter on meal offerings ("meal" in the sense of ground grain, as in our expression "corn meal"). Here are four translations of the first words of Lev. 2:1:

> And when any will offer a meat offering unto the LORD (KJV, using "meat" in an archaic sense)

> When a person presents an offering of meal to the LORD (NJPS)

> When anyone presents a grain offering to the LORD (NRSV)

A person—when he brings-near a near-offering of a grain-gift for YHWH (Everett Fox)*

And here is the most literal translation I can offer:

And a soul, when she offers a meal offering to YHWH

The Hebrew word *nefesh*—which in later Hebrew means "soul" (as opposed to "body")—more often refers in Biblical Hebrew to the self, to one's life, or simply, as here, to "a person." (See, e.g., the "souls" that Abram and Sarai brought with them when they first arrived in Canaan, according to Gen. 12:5.) But *nefesh* is a feminine noun in Hebrew, and Hebrew distinguishes feminine from masculine verb forms as well. So this idiom literally reads as if "she" is bringing the offering. Replacing *ish* with *nefesh* permits "anyone" to sound feminine instead of masculine.

Precisely because Hebrew verbs are marked for gender, the "he or she" alternative is even more awkward in Hebrew than it is in English. Nonetheless, in addition to the eight occurrences of "a soul, when she [does something]," another eight—scattered through Exodus, Leviticus, Numbers, and Deuteronomy—do use the alternatives *ish o ishah*, "a man or a woman," precisely specified:

LEV. 13:29 If a man or a woman has a skin disorder on the head or the beard . . .

The biblical writers who use the expression "a man or a woman" took unnecessary pains to make clear that, despite what social norms might call for, some of the most basic aspects of Israelite religion invoke instead divine norms that sometimes call for no distinction between men and women—a point of view that some people today will be surprised to find emphasized in the Bible.

* Everett Fox, *The Five Books of Moses* (New York: Schocken, 1995), 513.

Women's Literature

We know for certain that the priestly literature was written by males; so an ostensibly egalitarian text does not necessarily mean that we are hearing a woman's concerns. But thinking about the priestly literature does point us to another, perhaps surprising, way to look for women's voices in the Bible. Sometimes, a society in which men and women play very distinct social roles also has distinct literary roles for them to play. The Bible does in fact offer hints that in ancient Israel particular kinds of writing were primarily female. In such cases, we need to consider the possibility that the anonymous voices speaking to us when we read these pieces are those of Israelite women.

For example, when Saul is killed and the news is brought to David, he recites the lament "Tell it not in Gath" (2 Sam. 1:19–27), ending with the famous expression, "How are the mighty fallen!" Gath, where David did not want the news of the death of Israel's king to be heard, was one of the major cities of the Philistines, at the time Israel's most dangerous and hated enemy. But look at how David goes on to phrase his wish: "Tell it not in Gath, lest the daughters of the Philistines rejoice." Why the daughters and not the sons? The old joke about the Sunday school kid who keeps hearing about the "Children of Israel" and wonders what happened to the grownups reminds us that this is a Biblical Hebrew idiom. Just as "the Children of Israel" means (in contemporary English) "the Israelites," so too "the daughters of the Philistines" means "the Philistine women."

But the question remains: Why would the women, and not all the Philistines, perhaps even particularly the men who were fighting, rejoice? The implications of David's statement is that it was the women who would sing the songs of victory, just as Deborah sings her song of victory in Judges 5 after the Israelites defeated Sisera and the armies of Hazor back in the period of the judges. (The male judges who win similar victories do not recite songs of triumph.) Similarly, some scholars think that the Israelites' song of triumph in Exodus 15, after the pursuing Egyptians have drowned, should perhaps be called "the Song of Miriam" (see Exod. 15:20–21). Whether or not this is correct, it is worth remembering that the creation of this *kind* of song may well have been the province of women, not of men.

This was true in the case of David himself after the Israelites had successfully routed their enemy, the Philistines:

> 1 SAM. 18:6 When David and they [the troops] returned from slaying the Philistines, the women came out from all the cities of Israel singing and dancing, to greet King Saul with tambourines, jubilation, and cymbals. 7 The women who were playing declared,
> "Saul has slain by the thousand,
> And David by the ten thousand!"
> 8 Saul was furious and took the matter extremely badly. He said, "They give ten thousand to David and only a thousand to me? All he needs now is the kingship!" 9 Saul kept a suspicious eye on David from that day forward.

It was women who created the chant that annoyed Saul so much, along with the victory dance that accompanied the song of triumph. The song and the dance made David famous; see 1 Sam. 21:12 (v. 11 in Christian Bibles) and 29:5, where the Philistines themselves identify him with this refrain. But it's instructive to note Saul's reaction. Although the women could certainly not have threatened his kingship politically or militarily, Saul seems to have assumed that their reaction was an accurate gauge of popular sentiment. The women could not overthrow him, but their song was a serious warning.

The Song of Deborah

An earlier and much longer song of victory that can also be presumed to have been sung by women is found, as I said, in Judges 5, the poetic version of the story of Deborah. The song is introduced this way:

> JUDG. 5:1 Deborah and Barak the son of Abinoam sang on that day—

This sounds very much like the introduction to another song of victory:

EXOD. 15:1 Then Moses and the Israelites sang this song to YHWH. They said—

This, of course, is the "Song of Miriam," as some like to call it. More significant for our current purpose is a comparison of the verbs in the two verses.

In the Hebrew of both verses, the verbs actually precede the subjects; this is the normal word order in Biblical Hebrew. When there is a compound subject (Moses and the Israelites, Deborah and Barak), the verb should be plural, to match. But occasionally the verb simply matches the first noun of the compound, the one that directly follows it. In this case, the effect is exactly opposite what the English sounds like—not "(Moses and) the Israelites sang," but "Then sang Moses (and the Israelites)." Judges 5, the prophetic reading that accompanies Exodus 15 in synagogue readings, works in exactly the opposite way, with a feminine singular verb: "Then sang Deborah (and Barak the son of Abinoam)." This is not the song of "Deborah and Barak"; he is very much secondary here.

The song concludes with verses of praise for Jael, the woman who killed Sisera, the military leader of Israel's enemies, and a final stanza mocking Sisera's mother as she and her ladies-in-waiting peer through the window, speculating that he is so late in returning home because he is distributing the captive women to his soldiers. But the bulk of the song is praise for the Israelite tribes who participated in the victory and scorn for those who did not show up. If this, like the chant celebrating the defeat of the Philistines in the days of Saul and David, was a women's victory song, then here too the women's voices were the voice of the nation: *vox feminarum vox populi*.

Songs of Lamentation

The same may have been true for the opposite category of literature, the dirge or lament. As with songs of victory, lamentation over defeat or death is also a women's role in many traditional cultures. To be sure, 1 Samuel tells us that the lament for Saul was written by David, and Jeremiah wrote one for King Josiah:

> 2 CHR. 35:25 Jeremiah bewailed Josiah, and all the singers, male and female, have repeated it in their lamentations to this day. It became a rule for Israel, and they are written down in the lamentations.

But even this very verse tells us that there were female singers of dirges. It may be that some of the laments in the books of Psalms or Lamentations (the collection of dirges bemoaning the fall of Jerusalem to the Babylonians in 586) were written by women. (Tradition assigns Lamentations too to Jeremiah.)

The Reversals of Ruth

Besides the various *kinds* of literature that may have been written by women, though, two specific *books* of the Bible do seem to be written in a woman's voice. Since there is no reason to think it would have been impossible for a woman to write a biblical book, it is reasonable to assume that these books were written by women until it can be proven otherwise.

One of these is the book of Ruth. Anyone who teaches Biblical Hebrew grammar knows that Ruth is a great place to find the feminine, especially feminine plural, grammatical forms that are scattered much more sparsely through most of the Bible. Of course there is more to it than just that.

A man could certainly write a book about women. But there are other indications, too, that point as well to the book of Ruth being written in a women's voice. One of them is the realization of who *isn't* getting much attention here: the men. Contrast the famous passage in Exodus 19, where God tells Moses, "Go to the people and sanctify them today and tomorrow; let them wash their garments and be ready for the day after tomorrow. For on the day after tomorrow YHWH will come down in the sight of all the people on Mount Sinai" (vv. 10–11). "All the people" sounds quite inclusive to modern ears, but Moses seems to interpret it differently: "He said to the people, 'Be ready for the day after tomorrow; do not approach a woman'" (v. 15). We do not know whether it is the author of this text who assumes "people" means grown males only—there are other places in the Bible where the Hebrew word used here means "army"—or whether it is Moses who is being made to say this. (Notice that God's original instructions do not say it this way.) Still, there is a voice here in the crucial scene of the theophany at Mount Sinai that seems to be saying that "the people" is a male group.

Women and "the Queen of Heaven"

Even when "the people" really is a female group, there seems to be some reluctance to point this out. In chapter 1, we saw in Jer. 44:16–18 that the Judahites who fled to Egypt after the assassination of the Babylonian puppet ruler Gedaliah told Jeremiah that Judah had been destroyed because King Josiah had made them stop worshiping the Queen of Heaven. This time, let us look at the verses that introduce and conclude that passage:

> JER. 44:15 They answered Jeremiah, all the men who knew that their wives had been sacrificing to other gods and all the women who were standing there—all the people who were living in Patros, Egypt: 16 "We will not listen to you in the matter about which you spoke to us in the name of YHWH. 17 On the contrary, we will do everything that we have vowed—to make offerings to the Queen of Heaven and to pour libations to her, as we used to do, we and our fathers, our kings and our officials, 'in the towns of Judah and the streets of Jerusalem.' For then we had plenty to eat, we were well-off, and suffered no misfortune. 18 But ever since we stopped making offerings to the Queen of Heaven and pouring libations to her, we have lacked everything, and we have been consumed by the sword and by famine. 19 And is it just we who

were sacrificing to the Queen of Heaven and pouring libations to her? Did we make cakes in the image of the crescent moon for her, and pour libations to her, without our husbands?"

Verse 15 is careful to say that *all* the people were speaking, both the men and the women, and repeats: "all the people." Yet as the quotation ends (Jeremiah's reply begins in v. 20), it becomes clear that "all the people" have husbands. It is only the women who have been speaking, but we are told in v.15 that the men are speaking too—perhaps because the writer was uncomfortable with the idea that a group of women would challenge the prophet with their husbands standing silently by.

When Tout le Monde *Is Female*

Just the opposite happens in the book of Ruth. In the first chapter of this story, a man from Bethlehem named Elimelech is driven by famine to take his wife and his two sons to Moab, in today's Jordan, in search of food. The family stays for ten years in Moab, where the boys marry Moabite girls. Subsequently, all three of the men die. (That much of the story takes only five verses.) At this point, the widow Naomi returns to Bethlehem with one of her daughters-in-law, Ruth.

Here is the scene: "The two of them walked on until they came to Bethlehem. When they came to Bethlehem, the whole town was abuzz, saying 'Can this be Naomi?'" (Ruth 1:19). The word translated here as "saying" is a feminine plural form of the verb. It cannot be Naomi and Ruth who ask the question, "Can this be Naomi?" So the speakers must (since the verb is feminine) be the women of Bethlehem. Yet they are referred to earlier in the verse as "the whole town," as if this were the most natural thing in the world. This, then, is a writer for whom "everybody" means women, not men. This is the flip side of Moses's instructions to "the people" in Exodus not to "approach a woman."

There are other reversals of this kind in Ruth. For example, there is the case of the son born to Ruth and Boaz at the end of the book.

Although the biblical legal background to this is not entirely clear, Boaz is presented in the book as a "redeemer," that is, a relative of Naomi's late husband who has the duty to see that Elimelech's land stays in the family, and apparently also to produce a son who will be considered Elimelech's male heir. This represents a version of the custom of levirate marriage.

As we saw in chapter 4, the situation here does not exactly match that of Deut. 25:5–10, where levirate marriage is explicitly commanded, since both brothers, as well as their father, are dead. But the text clearly presents Boaz as taking on the role of "closest surviving male relative." Nonetheless, it is not Elimelech who is saved from childlessness by his actions:

> RUTH 4:13 Boaz took Ruth and she became his wife. He came to her and God gave her pregnancy and she bore a son. . . . [16] Naomi took the boy and held him to her breast and became his nurse. [17] And all the neighbor women named him, saying "A son is born to Naomi!" They named him Obed. He was the father of Jesse, the father of David.

We know that Naomi is too old to literally nurse a child, for she has told us so herself (see Ruth 1:11). But we also know, from examples in other cultures, that Naomi's action of embracing the child was symbolic of her adopting him, and this is just what the words of the "neighbors" (again, a feminine plural word referring to people who are otherwise unidentified) say. Biologically, this child is the son of Ruth and Boaz. But culturally, the child is the son not of Ruth's first husband, Mahlon (as Deuteronomy would have led us to expect), or of her original father-in-law, Elimelech (as we might have thought from the example of Genesis 38), but of her *mother-in-law*, Naomi. Elimelech's line is being carried on, but that is not what is important for this writer. What is important is that *Naomi* is being saved from childlessness.

The Anonymous Male

There is another reversal in Ruth that is both significant and clever. Whereas many of the female characters in the Bible, even individual and important ones, are anonymous, in Ruth it will be a male whose name we never learn. The textbook example of an anonymous female is found in Judges 13, the story of the birth of our Nazirite friend, Samson. Samson's mother-to-be is visited by an angel, who informs her of his coming birth and how he should be raised so that he can save Israel from the Philistines. Her husband, Manoah, is presented as something of a dolt. It is his wife who receives the angel's revelation and who acts quickly and competently. But the text never tells us her name.

Once again, Ruth reverses the pattern. The ostensible reason for marrying your late husband's brother is to make sure that his *name* does not die with him. We have already seen how our author reversed this by way of the declaration that "A son is born to Naomi!" But I left one character out of my summary of the story. The book of Ruth is full of cliffhangers, and at the end of chapter 3, just when we think the marriage between Ruth and Boaz is set, it turns out that Boaz is not the closest surviving male relative after all.

The other relative is eager to acquire Naomi's land, but when he discovers he is meant to sire someone else's child—and with an immigrant Moabite woman, to boot—he backs down. Measure for measure, the author leaves the man who refused to perpetuate his relative's name without a name of his own. In fact, the insult is pointed. When Boaz summons the man to discuss the situation, he says, "Come on over and sit down here, So-and-so" (Ruth 4:1). Like the "no-name" restaurant on Boston's Fish Pier, this character has had his lack of identity immortalized. He is "Mr. So-and-So" for eternity. His refusal to help preserve the names of Naomi, Elimelech, and Mahlon did not prevent us, after all, from knowing anyone's name but his own.

Sexual Harassment in the Ancient Israelite Workplace

Yet another piece of evidence points to this book's focus on women's concerns—the scene of Boaz and Ruth's first meeting, in chapter 2 of

Ruth. Ruth is gleaning behind the reapers in a barley field that happens to belong to Boaz. The right to glean (to pick up what the reapers had dropped or neglected), like the law about levirate marriage, is part of the assumed background of the story on which a text from Deuteronomy sheds some light:

> DEUT. 24:19 When you harvest the crop from your field, if you forget a sheaf in the field, do not go back to retrieve it. Let the stranger, the orphan, and the widow have it, so that YHWH your God shall bless you in all the work of your hands. 20 When you beat the fruit down from your olive trees, do not pick over them when you are done; let the stranger, the orphan, and the widow have it. 21 When you pick the grapes from your vineyard, do not go through it again when you are done; let the stranger, the orphan, and the widow have it. 22 Remember that you were a slave in the land of Egypt. That is why I command you to do this thing.

See also Lev. 19:9 and 23:22 in the Deuteronomy-inspired Holiness Code.

The sociological assumption of the Ruth story, like that of the passage from Deuteronomy, is that anyone who did not control agricultural land was without economic resources. Naomi, as a widow, could not support Ruth; and Ruth, as a woman, a widow, and a foreigner, was in a triply precarious position.

The Hebrew text is difficult here, so it is not entirely clear what has just occurred when Boaz arrives at the field, some while after work has begun on the day Ruth first shows up to glean. But *something* certainly has. And from his first words to Ruth we have a fairly good idea of what it was:

> RUTH 2:8 Listen here, young lady, don't go to glean in another field. Don't leave here. Just stick close to my girls. 9 Keep your eyes on the field where they are harvesting and stick close to them. I'm ordering the boys not to touch you.

After the lunch break, he warns the male harvesters:

> **RUTH 2:15** Let her glean amongst the sheaves and don't hassle her. **16** Drop a few stalks for her out of the bunches. Leave them for her to glean and don't harass her.

In short, this is an example of what today we would call sexual harassment, and of at least one Israelite employer who had a strict policy against it. There is no reason why a male might not have written this—as you remember, the gender-neutral language in Leviticus, Numbers, and Deuteronomy was almost certainly written by men—but in the context of the other indications of female authorship, it's reasonable to think that sexual harassment is part of the story because it was one of the author's concerns as a woman.

The Song of Songs

The other book in the Bible that may well have been written by a woman is the Song of Songs. If you read the Song of Songs, you can clearly hear a woman's voice and of course a man's as well. But the woman's voice is more frequent than the man's—most of Song 4 is his, and about half of Song 6, and outside of that his voice is scattered through the book, while hers is constantly recurring. Most often, the voice that says "I" or "me" or "my" in the book is the woman's, not the man's (three times as often, by my rough count). More significantly, the *imaginative* voice of the book is the woman's. The man describes her beauty (as is common, for example, in ancient Egyptian love poetry) or responds to what she says; but she describes her thoughts, her dreams, her fantasies. We may even guess that the male voice that speaks in the book is sometimes a voice that she is imagining:

> **SONG 5:2** I was asleep, yet my mind was awake—Listen! My beloved is knocking at the door! "Open up for me, my sister, my bride, my dove, my perfect one! My head is full of dew, my curls are damp with the night." **3** "I have taken off my dress—am I sup-

posed to put it back on? I have washed my feet—am I supposed to dirty them again?" ⁴ My beloved put his hand through the latch-hole and my innards were stirred for him. ⁵ I got up to open for my beloved; my hands dripped with myrrh and my fingers with flowing myrrh on the handles of the lock.

I hope to present another case of the woman imagining her lover's voice, that of Song 2:8–13, in a book on biblical poetry that will be a companion volume to this one.

To be sure, writing that centers on a woman's imaginative life is not *necessarily* written by a woman; but, all things being equal, this is certainly the likelier scenario. Moreover, we find in the Song of Songs two more of the female "reversals" that we saw in Ruth. The first is the numerous references in the book to the woman's mother—not, as would be usual in the rest of the Bible, to her father (who does not appear in the book at all). Perhaps you remember from earlier in this chapter the law in Numbers 30 in which a woman's vow could be canceled by her husband or by her father if he did so within twenty-four hours of hearing it.* The premise of this law is that a woman lives in a household headed by a man, either her husband or, if she is not yet married, her father. There is no reason a woman's home before marriage could not be referred to as "her mother's house," but it is always and only referred to as the "father's house," except for two biblical books.† One is here in the Song of Songs, where we twice find the unmarried heroine eager to bring her lover to "my mother's house" (Song 3:4, 8:2). The other, as you may already have guessed, is Ruth. When Naomi's two sons die, at the beginning of the story, she decides to go home to Bethlehem. Her Moabite daughters-in-law make as if to accompany her, but she does not want to be a burden to them and tells

---

* For the complete passage, see Num. 30:4–16; 3–15 in Christian Bibles.

† The one exception is Gen. 24:28, when Rebecca runs to tell her *mother's* household that Abraham's servant has arrived (and see v. 55 there). It has been suggested that this too is a story originally told by women.

them that they should each return to "her *mother's* house." (Ruth, of course, does not listen, but follows Naomi home to Judah.) So this is not only a reversal of standard male biblical language, but one that Ruth and the Song of Songs share.

The second such reversal in the Song of Songs is slightly different, but in some ways even more fascinating, for it shows our author to be aware not just of standard biblical language but of a particular biblical story. To set the stage for this second reversal, please follow me on a quick detour back to the story of Cain and Abel. You may remember that Eve's first two sons brought offerings to YHWH and that Abel's offering was accepted but Cain's was rejected. Cain gets extremely upset at this rejection, and God warns him not to do anything drastic: "Sin crouches at the door—its desire is for you, but you can rule over it" (Gen. 4:7). It's too bad Cain did not listen to the advice, but that's another story. For now, our concern is with the word *teshukah*, "desire." This seems to be an important word in the stories of the Adam family, for exactly this same word is used when YHWH tells Eve what her punishment will be for eating the "forbidden fruit" of the tree of knowledge of good and evil: "I shall greatly increase your labor pains; in pain shall you bring forth children. Your desire will be for your husband, and he will rule over you" (Gen. 3:16).

There is only one other place in the entire Bible where this word *teshukah* occurs, and that is in the Song of Songs. In Song 7:11 (7:10 in Christian Bibles), ready to invite her lover to the orchard where she will give him her love, the woman says, "I am my beloved's, and his desire is for me." I don't know what form the Genesis stories were in at the time the author of the Song of Songs was writing, but I am convinced of this: she knew the traditional saying that, though women would find childbirth painful, they would nevertheless have desire for their husbands—and she flipped it 180 degrees. In the Song of Songs, the Genesis statement of the woman's desire for her husband is reversed, becoming the lover's desire for the woman, and leading not to the trauma of a difficult labor but to a romantic invitation to sensual and mutual love. This is a woman's voice, not a man's, and it is the voice of a writer who is as talented, and as well read, as any in the Bible.

Women's Voices in Wisdom

For our next source of women's voices in the Bible, let us follow the heroine of the Song of Songs back to her mother's house, where we will find what used to be called "mother wit." The Bible describes three sources of knowledge. Jeremiah's enemies summarize them, explaining that it would be no great loss if he were done away with: "Teaching shall not vanish from the priests, nor counsel from the sages, nor oracles from the prophets" (Jer. 18:18). The priests were certainly all male. We have seen that some prophets were female: Miriam, Deborah, Huldah. (For good measure, there is a presumably false prophetess, too, named Noadiah; see Neh. 6:14.) So far we have seen only one female sage, Lemuel's (anonymous!) mother in Prov. 31:1, but she turns out to represent the commonest type of all. It was not only the king's mother who could offer wisdom to her son—it was *everyone's* mother.

The book of Proverbs tells us this when it begins (after the book's title and introduction) with the following words:

> **PROV. 1:8** Heed, my son, the instruction of your father,
> And do not reject the teaching of your mother.
> ⁹ For they are a graceful wreath for your head
> And a necklace for your throat.

The same pairing of father and mother occurs a total of twelve times in Proverbs—far out of proportion to its occurrence elsewhere in the Bible. In expressions like this, grammar does not force us to assume that the speaker is the child's father; in Hebrew, the first-person voice, the speaker who says "I—me—mine," carries no indication of gender.

Biblical proverbs are written in poetic form, and biblical poetry is frequently written in parallel couplets, where synonyms or antonyms are paired to repeat a thought. It is easy to see that our verses from Proverbs work exactly that way:

Heed	//	do not reject
instruction	//	teaching
father	//	mother

"Father" and "mother" are an obvious pair, after all. But we should not, as some scholars suggest, dismiss this as something mechanical, and deny that "mother" in this Proverbs verse (and in Prov. 6:20 and 23:22, which are similar) is to be taken seriously. The biblical poets are quite happy to use unusual words, and (just as "hear" is paired with "give ear" in Deut. 32:1), "your father" might have been matched with "the one who sired you," as in Job 38:28, "Does the rain have a father? Who sired the dewdrops?" Our poet in the Song of Songs too did something similar: "I seized him and would not let him go until I had brought him to my mother's house, to the chamber of her who conceived me" (Song 3:4). So there is no reason "father" had to be automatically matched with "mother." If we think for a moment about what biblical wisdom is, we will realize that "mother" here in Prov. 1:8 is in its rightful place.

The prophet's knowledge is that of revelation; the priest's, that of tradition. The prophet gets his knowledge at God's discretion; the priest, from a guild into which he is born. But the knowledge of a sage is knowledge developed by human experience. It is offered to all who are willing to listen, and can be added to by everyone. This kind of wisdom, though by now (in modern, scientific form) it has taken us to the farthest reaches of the universe, begins at home when we are very young, just learning how to behave. And that, of course, is something we really are taught by both our fathers and our mothers.

The Wise Woman

Did women really make a significant contribution—let alone a *distinctive* contribution—to the Bible's wisdom? It's true that none of the texts in the book of Proverbs look specifically like wisdom texts that must have been developed by a woman rather than a man. It has often been said, for example, about the warning to the young man in Proverbs 7 to stay away from the "strange woman" that a man must be giving the advice. However, the case of Benjamin Franklin should warn us against making the assumption that this must be a *father's* warning to his son. In chapter 2 of his autobiography he tells the following story:

> At Newport we took in a number of passengers, among whom were two young women traveling together and a sensible, matron-like Quaker lady, with her servants. I had shown an obliging disposition to render her some little services, which probably impressed her with sentiments of good will toward me, for when she witnessed the daily growing familiarity between the young women and myself, which they appeared to encourage, she took me aside and said: "Young man, I am concerned for thee, as thou hast no friend with thee and seems not to know much of the world or of the snares youth is exposed to. Depend upon it, these are very bad women: I can see it by all their actions; and if thee art not upon thy guard they will draw thee into some danger; they are strangers to thee, and I advise thee, in a friendly concern for thy welfare, to have no acquaintance with them."

The young women turned out to be thieves, and Franklin was glad to have taken the motherly advice of the Quaker lady.

Franklin calls the sensible lady on the boat "matron-like," implying that he saw her as standing in for his mother; as we've seen, it is natural to learn from both parents. But there was an entire category of women who were recognized as sages outside the domestic setting of the home. We may reasonably assume that women were included among the "sages" of Jer. 18:18.

"Wise Women" in the Story of David

The book of Samuel tells us the stories of two such women (both anonymous). The story of the first is told in 2 Samuel 14. A woman from Tekoa comes to King David in Jerusalem with the following tale:

2 SAM. 14:5 I am a widow woman whose husband has died. ⁶ Your servant [a polite way of referring to herself] had two sons, and the two of them got into a fight out in the fields. Since there was no one around to stop them, one of them struck the other and killed him. ⁷ The whole family has risen up against your servant, demanding, "Hand over the one who slew his brother so we can put him to death for taking the life of the brother whom he killed—even though [by doing so] we wipe out your last heir."

The story is a ruse, however. When David promises that he will make sure nothing happens to the boy who killed his brother, the woman reveals her true intent, in a speech of six verses that essentially boils down to this: "The king pronounces his own guilt in not bringing back the one he has banished" (v. 13). The "banished" one is Absalom, one of *David's* sons, who has had another of David's sons, Amnon, killed (see 2 Samuel 13). The woman's story is a clever way of making David see the situation without his own family feelings being involved.

In this particular case, it was not the woman herself who came up with the ruse; according to v. 3, Joab (David's army commander and his first cousin) "put the words into her mouth." Even though it was Joab who thought up the scheme, it is not he whom the text refers to as clever, but the woman who carries out his plan. Her "wisdom" lay both in her acting skill and in the native wit and eloquence to play her part ad lib, for high stakes, before King David himself.

The other wise woman who appears in the story of David lives in northern Israel, in the town of Abel-Beth-Maacah. Sheba son of Bichri, who has rebelled against David, takes refuge in the town, which finds itself besieged by David's army, under the command of none other than Joab. As the troops begin to batter down the wall of the city . . .

2 SAM. 20:16 A wise woman of the town called out, "Listen! Listen! Tell Joab to come here so I can talk to him!" ¹⁷ Joab came over to her, and the woman said, "Are you Joab?" "Yes," he replied. "Listen

to the words of your servant," she said, and he replied, "I'm listening." [18] She said, "Whenever people say, 'Let them ask in Abel,' that has always been the end of the matter. [19] I am one who is whole-heartedly faithful to Israel. But you are seeking to put to death an Israelite metropolis! Why would you swallow up a possession of YHWH?" [20] "God forbid!" said Joab in reply. "God forbid that I should swallow it up, or destroy it! [21] That's not it at all! But a man from Mount Ephraim, Sheba son of Bichri, has rebelled against King David. Hand him over, and I will leave the city alone." The woman replied to Joab, "You'll see—his head will be flung to you over the wall." [22] The woman came to the townspeople with her plan, and they cut off the head of Sheba son of Bichri and threw it down to Joab.

Here, of course, the wise woman is not merely persuasive but actually initiates the plan. We do not hear how she persuaded the townspeople, only her negotiations with Joab, because the authorial point of view is with David's army, *outside* the city. But the wise woman's ability to persuade the others that her plan would save them is something that the story takes for granted. It seems, then, that it was precisely the voices of these women—their powers of persuasive speech—that qualified them as "wise." This wisdom was enough to preserve their individual voices for us to hear three thousand years later.

We ask once more: Are these voices really those of genuine individuals, or are they invented characters? Let us assume (for the sake of argument) that these are *not* the voices of real Israelite women, but voices created by a writer. Perhaps it was King David's court historian, or perhaps another writer who lived long after David. There is no obvious reason why these two "wise" individuals would have to be female, although Nathan, who tricks David with a similar story in 2 Samuel 12, is *not* called wise. Indeed, in the story from 2 Samuel 14 where the woman with two sons stands in for King David, it would have made more sense for a man, standing for David, to play the role: a father, not a mother. But our supposed author chose women to fill these roles and speak these words. They must be either real or at least authentic; if not live, then certainly true to life.

Jephthah's Daughter

Let us conclude with a final story that will let us listen briefly to the voice of one last biblical woman, who will give us a tantalizing look at another aspect of women's experience in biblical times. As with the wise women from Tekoa and Abel-Beth-Maacah, I will leave it to you to decide whether the voice we hear is really her own, or whether this is merely an imitation of a woman's voice. She is yet one more woman whom the Bible leaves without a name, one we know merely as "Jephthah's daughter."

The situation is this: The Gileadites—Israelites who live not in the Israelite heartland, but in the wild, wild East, on the far side of the Jordan River—are under military pressure from the Ammonites, whose base was the area where Amman, the capital of Jordan, is today. Without a competent military leader of their own, the Gileadites turn to Gilead's illegitimate son, Jephthah, who has been thrown out by his legitimate brothers and is now the chief of a band of outlaws. He takes a mighty vow to God:

> JUDG. 11:30 Jephthah vowed to YHWH, saying, "If only you put the Ammonites in my power, 31 then the very first thing that comes out of the door of my house to welcome me when I come home safe from the Ammonites shall be YHWH's—and I will offer it up as a sacrifice."

The Israelites are victorious and Jephthah does indeed come home safely, but (as you can imagine) his vow has tempted fate:

> JUDG. 11:34 Jephthah came back to his home in Mizpah, and there was his daughter, dancing out of the door with timbrels to greet him! She was an only child; he had no other son or daughter besides her. 35 When he saw her, he said, "Alas, my daughter! You

have brought me to my knees, you have become one more of those who would ruin me! I have opened my mouth to YHWH, and I cannot take it back!"

But Jephthah's daughter has exactly the attitude toward her father's vow that we saw in the priestly passage of Numbers 30: you said it, YHWH heard it, and that settles it.

JUDG. 11:36 She said to him, "Father, if you have opened your mouth to YHWH, then do to me what came out of your mouth—now that God has given *you* revenge on your Ammonite enemies." 37 She said to her father, "Let this one thing be done for me. Let me alone for two months so that I can wander about the mountains and bewail my virginity, I and my girlfriends." 38 He said, "Go." He sent her off for two months, and she and her girlfriends bewailed her virginity on the mountains. 39 At the end of the two months, she returned to her father and he fulfilled the vow he had made about her. She had never known a man. And it became the rule in Israel: 40 Every year the Israelite girls go to lament for the daughter of Jephthah the Gileadite—four days a year.

This four-day women's festival is utterly unknown to us from any other source. But it was clearly still a living event in the time of our author.

As we've seen, it is in such tiny textual details that we must look to find a reflection of women's lives in ancient Israel. Whether in poetry, in history, or in religious law, careful attention can still let us tune in to female, and sometimes even feminist, concerns. We have encountered, in Ruth, a poor, immigrant widow; in the Song of Songs, a girl on the brink of love; in Deborah, a woman holding the reins of power; in Leviticus and Numbers, women who are significant individuals in the eyes of God. Now, in the calm, rational, religious voice of Jephthah's daughter, and in the wordless voices of the girls who mourned for her year after year, the Bible gives us (if we are willing to hear) two more living voices of Israelite women.

7
Voices of the Wise

In the last chapter, we encountered a verse from Jeremiah that listed, in a nutshell, the three sources of knowledge as the Bible understood it: "Teaching shall not vanish from the priests, nor counsel from the sages, nor oracles from the prophets" (Jer. 18:18). We have devoted several long discussions to the priestly literature, and an entire chapter to the prophets. Now it is time to turn our attention to the remaining category, the sages.

We have already met two sages in the "wise women" of 2 Samuel, and a third in King Lemuel's mother from Proverbs 30. But as we will see, three entire books of the Bible come to us not from priests or prophets, but from sages. We do not know the names of any of the biblical "wise women," but you might expect that we would know the names of the "wise men." In fact, two of the three most famous wise men in the Hebrew Bible are also anonymous. So let's begin by meeting the famous wise man whose name we do know: Solomon.

The Wisdom to Rule

Though it is not as familiar as the stories of Adam and Eve or David and Goliath, you most likely do already know the biblical tale in which Solomon first displays his great wisdom, and you probably even remember the punch line: "Cut the baby in half!" (1 Kgs. 3:25). But where did Solomon get this great wisdom? Certainly not from his father. David was clever enough, at least earlier in life, but the Bible never describes him as wise. Solomon's wisdom was not a genetic inheritance, and it was not the product of an elite education (in fact, the Bible has no mention whatsoever of anything we would recognize as a school). Solomon's wisdom was a gift to him from God—and it was a gift that he himself requested, when suddenly given the opportunity, at the beginning of his reign:

1 KGS. 3:4 The king went to Gibeon to offer sacrifice, for that was the great high place [in those days]. Solomon sacrificed 1,000 burnt offerings on that altar. 5 While Solomon was at Gibeon, YHWH appeared to him at night, in a dream, and said, "Ask! What shall I give you?" 6 Solomon replied, "You did such great kindness to my father David, who followed You truly, righteously, and honestly, and You have continued that kindness by giving him a son sitting on his throne this very day. 7 Now, O YHWH my God, You have made Your servant king in place of my father David—but I am just a little child. I do not know how to exercise leadership. 8 Yet Your servant is among Your people, whom You have chosen: a people too great to be numbered or counted. 9 So give Your servant a 'hearing heart' [a mind capable of comprehension] in order to be able to rule Your people, to understand what is good and what is bad."

Things turn out even better than Solomon has wished, for God is so pleased that Solomon has asked for wisdom that he gives him some bonus gifts: wealth, glory, and (if Solomon too will follow God's commandments as David did) long life.

Solomon's Legendary Wisdom

Was the historical Solomon really this wise? The famous story about the baby that immediately follows the gift is the *only* time we see Solomon exercising his wisdom. And we already know that Deuteronomy, which had such a great influence on the historian of the book of Kings, has a particular admiration for wisdom as a character trait. Remember that when Moses chooses the lower ranks of Israelite leaders, Jethro tells him to look for "substantial men, God-fearers, honest men who hate ill-gotten gain" (Exod. 18:21), but in Deuteronomy Moses describes the men he chose as "wise and experienced" (Deut. 1:15). So we might suppose that the Deuteronomistic History presents Solomon as wise because that was the quality demanded in a ruler.

But it's not so. In fact, Solomon is the *only* king described in this way, and his wisdom is mentioned over and over again. At the beginning of his story, in his last meeting with his father, who is on his deathbed, David tells his son to pay back Shimei son of Gera for the way he treated David when David fled Jerusalem during Absalom's coup: "You are a wise man, and you know what to do to him!" (1 Kgs. 2:9). At the peak of Solomon's fame, the Queen of Sheba comes to Jerusalem "to test him with riddles" (1 Kgs. 10:1):

> **1 KGS. 10:3** Solomon answered all her questions. Not a thing escaped the king; there was nothing he was not able to tell her. **4** When the Queen of Sheba saw all of Solomon's wisdom—and the palace he had built, **5** the food and drink served on his table, how his courtiers were seated, how his uniformed attendants served them, and the offerings he brought to the Temple of YHWH—it completely took the wind out of her sails.

Finally, Solomon's reign is summed up this way: "The other events of Solomon's reign—all he did, and his wisdom—are they not recorded in *The Chronicles of Solomon*?" (1 Kgs. 11:41).

But except for the story of the baby, where do we find any of Solomon's legendary wisdom? The answer, at least as far as tradition is concerned, comes in 1 Kings 5, where we have still another report about Solomon's incredible wisdom:

1 KGS. 5:10* Solomon's wisdom was greater than the wisdom of all the ancients and the wisdom of the Egyptians. **11** He was wiser than any other man, wiser than Ethan the Ezrahite, and Heman, Chalkol, and Darda the sons of Mahol. He was famous in all the nations round about. **12** He uttered 3,000 proverbs, and his songs were 1,005. He spoke about trees—from the cedar in Lebanon to the hyssop that grows out of the wall—and about animals, birds, lizards, and fish.

There is of course a large collection of proverbs elsewhere in the Bible; and the original title of the biblical book that we call Proverbs is in fact "The Proverbs of Solomon." Are the proverbs in that book actually chosen from among the three thousand proverbs uttered by Solomon? To examine this question, and to begin to hear the Bible's "voices of the wise" more clearly, we must take a closer look at just what is in the book of Proverbs.

Proverbial Wisdom

As we saw in chapter 1, the book of Proverbs is divided into separate sections by verses that serve essentially as headings:

> "The proverbs of Solomon, son of David, king of Israel" (Prov. 1:1).
>
> "The proverbs of Solomon" (Prov. 10:1).
>
> "These, too, are attributed to the sages" (Prov. 24:23).
>
> "These, too, are proverbs of Solomon, which were transmitted by the men of King Hezekiah of Judah" (Prov. 25:1).
>
> "The words of Agur son of Jakeh" (Prov. 30:1).
>
> "The words of Lemuel" (Prov. 31:1).

As you remember, we originally looked at these because the Greek translation of Proverbs contains the same sections, but not in the same

---

* These verses are 1 Kgs. 4:30–32 in Christian Bibles.

order. In the Septuagint, the Hezekiah collection of Proverbs 25–29 comes just before the poem about the "Woman of Valor" that begins in our Bibles at Prov. 31:10, separating the poem from the first nine verses of chapter 31 in the Hebrew Bible. Though I have capitalized the words as if they were a title, there is no obvious heading for this poem. Yet the order of the Greek text shows clearly that Proverbs 31 of our Bible is divided into two separate sections. How are readers of the standard Bible, where the second section has no heading, supposed to know this?

The answer is quite simple—if we read the Bible in the original Hebrew. Proverbs 31:10–31, the last twenty-two verses of the book, are an acrostic. Like the "A is for Apple" in a children's book, each verse begins with one of the twenty-two letters of the Hebrew alphabet, starting with *alef* and ending with *tav*. (Some English editions print the Hebrew letters alongside these verses to demonstrate this.) Nothing could be clearer—this poem is a self-contained section, not part of "the words of Lemuel."

Another Missing Title

There is one more place where a heading that "should" be in the book is missing. See whether you can't find it yourself, by reading the following chapter (given here in the NJPS translation*) and noting where one biblical voice changes into another:

> PROV. 22:1 Repute is preferable to great wealth,
> Grace is better than silver and gold.
> ² Rich man and poor man meet;
> YHWH made them both.
> ³ The shrewd man saw trouble and took cover;
> The simple kept going and paid the penalty.
> ⁴ The effect of humility is fear of YHWH,

---

* I have altered the translation so that the Tetragrammaton appears as YHWH—but I have also removed the NJPS formatting to give you the chance to replicate scholarly study of this chapter.

Wealth, honor, and life.
⁵ Thorns and snares are in the path of the crooked;
He who values his life will keep far from them.
⁶ Train a lad in the way he ought to go;
He will not swerve from it even in old age.
⁷ The rich rule the poor,
And the borrower is a slave to the lender.
⁸ He who sows injustice shall reap misfortune;
His rod of wrath shall fail.
⁹ The generous man is blessed,
For he gives of his bread to the poor.
¹⁰ Expel the scoffer and contention departs,
Quarrel and contumely cease.
¹¹ A pure-hearted friend,
His speech is gracious;
He has the king for his companion.
¹² The eyes of YHWH watch the wise man;
He subverts the words of the treacherous.
¹³ The lazy man says, "There's a lion in the street;
I shall be killed if I step outside."
¹⁴ The mouth of a forbidden woman is a deep pit;
He who is doomed by YHWH falls into it.
¹⁵ If folly settles in the heart of a lad,
The rod of discipline will remove it.
¹⁶ To profit by withholding what is due to the poor
Is like making gifts to the rich—pure loss.
¹⁷ Incline your ear and listen to the words of the sages;
Pay attention to my wisdom.
¹⁸ It is good that you store them inside you,
And that all of them be constantly on your lips,
¹⁹ That you may put your trust in YHWH.
I let you know today—yes, you—
²⁰ Indeed, I wrote down for you a threefold lore,
Wise counsel,

²¹ To let you know truly reliable words,
That you may give a faithful reply to him who sent you.
²² Do not rob the wretched because he is wretched;
Do not crush the poor man in the gate;
²³ For YHWH will take up their cause
And despoil those who despoil them of life.
²⁴ Do not associate with an irascible man,
Or go about with one who is hot-tempered,
²⁵ Lest you learn his ways
And find yourself ensnared.
²⁶ Do not be one of those who give their hand,
Who stand surety for debts,
²⁷ Lest your bed be taken from under you
When you have no money to pay.
²⁸ Do not remove the ancient boundary stone
That your ancestors set up.
²⁹ See a man skilled at his work—He shall attend upon kings;
He shall not attend upon obscure men.

If you read carefully, it is not difficult to see that something changes in v. 17. Instead of an impersonal voice, we suddenly hear an "I" talking to a "you." And where the first voice (let's call it Voice One) dispenses one-line nuggets of Poor Richard-style advice, the second voice (Voice Two) is speaking in paragraphs that extend over two or more verses. So a bit of careful reading has enabled us to distinguish two different voices in Proverbs 22, no knowledge of Hebrew required. Is one of these voices the voice of Solomon?

We have heard this second voice, or one like it, before:

PROV. 1:8 Hear, my son, the instruction of your father,
And do not reject the teaching of your mother.
⁹ For they are a graceful wreath for your head
And a necklace for your throat.

We can certainly imagine Solomon telling his son, "hear my instruction," and "do not reject the teaching of your mother" as well—even if he did not necessarily remember just which of his thousand wives was the mother of this particular boy. But if Solomon was famous for his proverbs, we have a problem. It is Voice One of our chapter, not Voice Two, that recites proverbs. Let's take a closer look at these two different kinds of wisdom.

Sentence Proverbs and Instructions

Scholars call the proverbs of Prov. 22:1–16, the first voice of the chapter, "sentence proverbs" or "one-line proverbs." The longer form, which we heard in the voice of Prov. 22:17–29, is called an "instruction." The entire book of Proverbs can be divided into essentially these two forms. The two largest sections of the book, 10:1–22:16 and 25:1–29:27, making up a total of almost eighteen chapters, are two separate collections of "proverbs of Solomon," and these are all sentence proverbs. However, if you read Proverbs 1–9, you will see that (as Prov. 1:8–9 would suggest) these chapters are not made up of one-line proverbs, but of the longer-format instructions. Why then are these chapters, too, headed by a verse calling them "the proverbs of Solomon, son of David, king of Israel" (Prov. 1:1)?

The answer is that they are *not*. Proverbs 1:1 is the heading not of Proverbs 1–9, but of the entire book of Proverbs. Those first nine chapters are not made up of "proverbs" at all. Instead, they serve as an introduction to the book. When, at last, the first major collection of proverbs begins, the title is repeated, but just briefly, to remind us what we are reading: "The proverbs of Solomon" (Prov. 10:1). So it must be the voice of the one-line proverbs—Voice One of Proverbs 22, not Voice Two—that is Solomon's own voice.

Or is it? Let's remember the kind of proverbs and songs Solomon was renowned for. According to 1 Kgs. 5:12 (4:32 in Christian Bibles), he spoke about trees, animals, birds, lizards, and fish. But even Prov. 22:13, "The lazy man says, 'There's a lion in the street; I shall be killed if I step outside,'" hardly qualifies as an animal proverb; the lion is an excuse, not a real character in this saying, which is about people—lazy ones. The three thousand proverbs about plants and animals that Solomon is credited with in the Kings verse sound as if they are more like Aesop's fables than the one-line sayings of Voice One and of the book of Proverbs in general.

You might object that a proverb is not the same as a fable. But that's not true of *mashal*, the Hebrew word that gives its name to the book of Proverbs, a word of much wider application than "proverb" in English. True, it can sometimes simply refer to a saying of the kind we call "proverbial"—for example, "Is Saul too among the prophets?" You remember that in chapter 5 we twice saw Saul having a seizure; each occasion was invoked as the source of this proverbial question. Though in 1 Sam. 19:24 the expression is identified as just something that "people say," in 1 Sam. 10:12 we are told that the saying "became a proverb"—a *mashal*. And this word *mashal* is the same word used in Rabbinic literature for a parable. The nineteenth-century translators who created a Biblical Hebrew version of the New Testament used *mashal* for the Greek word *parabolé* that describes the parables of Jesus.

The essence of a *mashal* is the comparison of two things that we wouldn't ordinarily compare. When Prov. 11:22 compares "a gold ring in a pig's snout" and "a beautiful woman without sense," the image makes us see the incongruity of her behavior in a particularly vivid light. If the comparison is drawn out to a great enough length to make a little story, we have the kind of thing we call a "parable" in English:

> JUDG. 9:8 Once upon a time, the trees decided to anoint a king over themselves. They told the olive tree, "Be our king!" 9 The olive tree replied, "Have I stopped giving my rich oil, which is used to honor God and men, that I should go and hold sway over the trees?"

As you might guess, the only tree willing to take the job ends up being the thorn bush. The parable in that chapter has a particular political application: The illegitimate son of Jerubbaal (an alternate name for Gideon, one of Israel's military leaders during the period of the judges) has slaughtered all but one of his brothers and installed himself as king. (It is the surviving brother who declaims the parable.) Israel's (temporary) new king is not a productive and delightful olive tree, fig tree, or grape vine, but a small, prickly thornbush. We saw another parable in chapter 6, where the wise woman of Tekoa presents King David with his own thinly disguised family situation. There is a similar parable in 2 Samuel 12, when Nathan the prophet tricks David into condemning his own behavior in taking Uriah's wife.

The "Woman of Valor"

The poem about the "Woman of Valor" or (better) the "Woman of Substance" that ends our book of Proverbs, is a *mashal*, a parable, of just this same kind, though presented in poetry instead of prose. We know that it is a parable not from the poem itself, which might just be a description of an extremely competent woman, but from an understanding of how the poem fits into the book of Proverbs as a whole.

Proverbs is, after all, a book of *meshalim* (the plural of *mashal*), of images that we are meant to compare to something else. And Prov. 31:10–31 is not a freestanding poem but the conclusion of the entire book of Proverbs. Unlike *Bartlett's Familiar Quotations* or *The Wit and Wisdom of Mao Tse-tung*, Proverbs is a book that tells us, in its first words, what its purpose is:

> PROV. 1:2 To know wisdom and discipline; to comprehend words of understanding;
> 3 To acquire the discipline for success, righteousness, justice, and equity;
> 4 To give cunning to fools, knowledge and cleverness to youths;
> 5 (Let the wise man hear and take a lesson; let the man of understanding acquire the skill to plan)
> 6 To understand *mashal* and metaphor, the words of the sages and their riddles.
> 7 The fear of YHWH is the beginning of knowledge—wisdom and discipline are scorned by fools.

Unlike most of the biblical books, which may want us to know about the past, to learn the proper rules of behavior, or to adopt a particular point of view, Proverbs aims at something more: it is educational.

Lady Wisdom and Lady Folly

To be a successful reader of Proverbs (from the perspective of the book's introduction that we've just seen), you must develop your intellect. The final exam—so to speak—is the poem at the end of the book. If we simply see the woman of that poem as someone who is particularly competent and God fearing, we have failed "to understand *mashal* and metaphor." For the first nine chapters of Proverbs, the introduction to the book, present wisdom and folly not only as abstractions, but also metaphorically, imagined as women.

The beginning of Proverbs 7 shows us how this works. At first, the teaching voice of this instruction begins in straightforward fashion: "Son, keep fast to my words; store up my commandments" (Prov. 7:1). But by vv. 4–5, the metaphor emerges: "Say to Wisdom, 'You are my sister,' and call Understanding your intimate, to protect you from a strange woman, a slick-talking foreigner." The rest of the chapter describes an encounter between just such a woman and a naïve young man whom she is bent on seducing. (We encountered her briefly in chapter 6, when Benjamin Franklin met two such females on the boat to Philadelphia.) But if we have already begun to learn how "to understand *mashal* and metaphor"—if we have begun "to call Wisdom our sister"—we must realize that this is not a real woman at all, but our "sister's" evil twin, Folly. Indeed, Wisdom and Folly are personified throughout Proverbs 1–9 as women who are competing for our attention. These chapters are not a collection of single-line proverbs, but a set of poetic instructions, preparing us to study the proverbs that begin in Proverbs 10.

If we are attuned to the message of the book, two things have happened by the time we get all the way through it, to Proverbs 31. First, we are reading carefully enough to notice that 31:10–31, though it has no title, is an alphabetic acrostic and so makes a self-contained section of its own. And second, we are prepared to understand this poem on two levels, not just one. True, it describes the admirable behavior of a highly competent woman who has it all: she is a wife and mother, but while supervising her household staff she also buys real estate (v. 16) and runs a business (v. 18). How, we may ask, can she do it? The answer is prompted by what we know from Proverbs 1–9, the introduction to the book: This is not merely a woman but also a *mashal*, an image representing Wisdom. The text works simultaneously on two levels, and the ability to recognize that is the foundation of the wisdom that the book of Proverbs hopes to have trained us to continue acquiring throughout our lives.

Was it Solomon himself who created this book? Despite what tradition says, the answer must be no—and for a quite simple reason. Proverbs 25–29 consists of proverbs that are certainly labeled as "Solomonic," but that were transmitted, according to Prov. 25:1, by "Hezekiah's men." Hezekiah lived (if I am counting correctly) eleven generations after Solomon, certainly more than two hundred years later; so even if Solomon composed all the text of the book, it was not he who assembled Proverbs as we find it today.

But someone did so. We do not hear anything recognizably personal in the book, but it was not simply blown together by the wind. It was assembled by someone. Perhaps we should not call this person the book's "writer," since he did not write all or perhaps even much of it. Nevertheless, Proverbs is not a random assortment of material, but a work that was put together in such a way that we would not correctly understand Proverbs 31 without having studied the first nine chapters of the book. The book's creator is therefore something more than a mere compiler. I would like to call him a composer.

The Wisdom School

Is the "composer" of the book of Proverbs any different from the Deuteronomistic or priestly voices that we have already heard in the Torah? Those voices were distinguished by different conceptions of how

God relates to the world, just as the different historical voices of the (pre-Exilic) Deuteronomistic History and (post-Exilic) Chronicles presented David and Solomon in very different ways. The voices we have heard so far in Proverbs, though, fall into a different category. What distinguishes the sentence proverbs and the longer material of the instructions are not any substantial theological differences, but rather differences in *literary genre*—they are two different ways of teaching the skills a wise person needs. One skill focuses on intense analysis of a small but precise comparison; the other focuses on the ability to categorize such details and integrate them into a much more comprehensive view. Scholars think of these skills, the attitudes they reflect, and therefore the book of Proverbs as a whole, as a product of what is often called "the wisdom school."

Obviously this does not refer to a building in a particular location with a sign out front: "The Wisdom School." Instead, it refers to an imagined group who would have shared a wisdom perspective on life and wanted to present it to a wider public. Can we imagine a real-life setting in which such a group could have existed? The most plausible scenario is that this group would have been centered around the scribes of the royal court and those who trained them. In Egypt and Mesopotamia, there are comparable collections of proverbs and instructions, some of which explicitly mention the training of scribes. Though scribes are mentioned more than four dozen times in the Bible, we have no knowledge of how they were trained. Still, there must have been some system for doing so in an ongoing fashion.

Perhaps this explains why the "wisdom school" is not obviously in conflict or even disagreement with others of the biblical voices. It is focused on proper behavior rather than on a particular ideological point of view. If it really was somehow based in Jerusalem, at the center of the apparatus that governed the nation (to the extent that our contemporary concepts of such things apply to the ancient Near Eastern world), wisdom's don't-rock-the-boat, everybody-pitch-in ethos would fit well with their role in society. Scribes, unlike priests, do not pretend to have direct contact with God; unlike prophets, they do not challenge the powerful: "Do not boast before the king or stand forth boldly where great men gather" (Prov. 25:6). Yet it seems that someone from a group of this kind did eventually stand forth boldly enough to assemble the teachings of his colleagues and himself into a biblical book that, despite how it may look at first glance, is not a grab bag, but a work of literature.

Can We Identify the "Composer" of Proverbs?

The voice of the one-line proverbs is anonymous, as one might expect of a proverbial saying. Even the instructions that purport to address "my son," though they are certainly spoken in the first person, do not seem to be spoken to a real person. When Longfellow began his poem by saying

> Listen, my children, and you shall hear
> Of the midnight ride of Paul Revere

he was not speaking to his own children. He was writing a poem in a particular, imagined voice—that of "the Squire" who owned the Red Horse Inn, who himself was pictured as speaking not to children but to a group of the inn's guests, sitting before the fire. So we need not suppose that the proverbial instructions were literally copied down from something parents were overheard saying to their children. More importantly, we don't learn anything about the character who speaks such words in the book of Proverbs. There is nothing personal in the instructions. They are one-size-fits-all.

The person who I've said "composed" the book of Proverbs as a whole does have an individual voice—but we must listen carefully through the whole book to hear it. Nowhere do we hear a voice proclaiming, "I have Wisdom—hear me roar!" But there is one biblical book where we do hear a voice that sounds like an individual speaking to us. He too may be a literary creation, but he has a distinct voice and he is a character in his own story. The Greek translators called him Ecclesiastes; to distinguish the character from the book he appears in, we will call him by his original, Hebrew, name: Qohelet.*

Another Solomon

The book of Ecclesiastes begins with the following strange words:

ECCL. 1:1 The words of Qohelet son of David, king in Jerusalem.

Who was this man? Tradition says he is Solomon, but if that were true, why wouldn't the Bible tell us so? And why is he not referred to as "king of Israel" rather than "king in Jerusalem"? It is extremely unusual to call someone king "in" a particular city. There is only one other place in the Bible where an expression even remotely like this is used: "The length of time that David was king in Hebron, over the house of Judah, was seven years and six months" (2 Sam. 2:11). But in the context of 2 Samuel there is a reason to say it that way: While David was king "in" Hebron, over the house of Judah, Saul's son Ish-bosheth was king in Gilead, over the rest of Israel. When the real Solomon was king, he was in Jerusalem all right—but why not simply call him by his title: "King Solomon of Israel"? (See 2 Kgs. 23:13 and 24:13, and Neh. 13:26, where he is called just that.)

The biggest mystery, of course, is why he would be identified in Ecclesiastes with an alias—as Qohelet rather than as Solomon. We saw that the eventual composer of the book of Proverbs had no problem collecting Israelite wisdom of many centuries and labeling it with Solomon's name. Why not do the same thing here in Ecclesiastes? It's hard to imagine why a pen name would be necessary, but if that was the case, Solomon had a perfectly good one of his own: Jedidiah. Although

---

* Due to the vagaries of transliteration, you will sometimes see this name spelled "Kohelet." I have chosen to use "Qohelet" because Hebrew has letters that are the ancestors of both our "K" and our "Q," and our man's name is spelled with the "Q" letter. You may encounter either name spelled -*th* rather than -*t* at the end; I use -*t* to match contemporary Hebrew pronunciation.

his mother Bathsheba named him Solomon, God (via Nathan the prophet) suggested naming him Jedidiah, which essentially means "David, Jr." (see 2 Sam. 12:25). Yet the speaking voice of most of the book of Ecclesiastes is called neither Solomon nor Jedidiah but Qohelet.

In fact, this is one of the most distinctive voices in the Hebrew Bible. The Solomon of the book of Kings speaks in Standard Biblical Hebrew, but Qohelet speaks in a language that sounds much closer to the Hebrew of the Mishnah—a thousand years later—than to that of the book of Kings. More significantly, Qohelet is a character like none other in the Bible. It is not merely his accent, but what he says, that sounds so unlike the rest of the Bible.

"Nothing New under the Sun"

Let's start by considering one of his sayings that is still common today, centuries later: "There is nothing new under the sun" (Eccl. 1:9). From the "new king" that arose over Egypt after Joseph's death (Exod. 1:1) through the "new house" that exempts a potential soldier from service (Deut. 20:5) to the "new court" of the Temple where Jehoshaphat speaks to the people in 2 Chr. 20:5—not to mention the new Temple built by Solomon himself in 1 Kings 6–8—the Bible is full of things it calls "new."

The most significant new thing in the Bible is of course our world itself, whose creation is described in Genesis 1. Indeed, it seems that Qohelet's complaint that there is "nothing new under the sun" is in direct opposition to the idea that God can create something new. Contrast what Moses tells the Israelites in Numbers 16 about Korah, Dathan, and Abiram, who have challenged his authority over Israel: "If these men die an ordinary human death, and the fate of all men overtakes them, then it was not YHWH who sent me. But if YHWH creates something new, so that the earth swallows them and all they own, and they go down alive to Hell, then you will know that these men have spurned YHWH!" (Num. 16:29–30). But Qohelet remains unimpressed: "There might be a thing of which someone would say, 'Look, that's new!' It already happened ages ago" (Eccl. 1:10).

The author of Lamentations (traditionally, Jeremiah) writes to encourage himself after the destruction of Jerusalem: "The kindness of YHWH is not completed; His mercy is not finished—they are new every morning. How reliable You are!" (Lam. 3:22–23). But that very reliability does not give Qohelet hope; it bores him to tears. That is precisely what leads him to his conclusion that there is "nothing new":

ECCL. 1:4 One generation goes, another comes,
But the earth remains the same forever.
⁵ The sun rises, and the sun sets—
And glides back to where it rises.
⁶ Southward blowing,
Turning northward,
Ever turning blows the wind;
On its rounds the wind returns.
⁷ All streams flow into the sea,
Yet the sea is never full;
To the place [from] which they flow
The streams flow back again.
⁸ All such things are wearisome:
No man can ever state them;
The eye never has enough of seeing,
Nor the ear enough of hearing.
⁹ Only that shall happen
Which has happened,
Only that occur
Which has occurred;
There is nothing new
Beneath the sun! (NJPS)

For Qohelet, there is only one, grim way to get off the somber merry-go-round of life: "Man goes to his eternal home, while the mourners go round and round in the marketplace" (Eccl. 12:5).

"Follow Your Heart"

There is another place where it seems that Qohelet is actually issuing a direct challenge to an earlier biblical text. The fact that all humanity is destined to die—and to know that they will die—poisons all of life for him. So before he draws to his conclusion, he gives the best advice he can: "Enjoy your childhood, young man, and be happy during your youth. Follow your heart and your eyes" (Eccl. 11:9). The reader who is tuned to the biblical voices is instantly reminded of another passage, from the book of Numbers:

> NUM. 15:37 YHWH said to Moses, 38 "Speak to the Israelites and tell them to make fringes on the corners of their garments throughout the generations and to put a blue tassel on the fringe at each corner. 39 Let that be a fringe that you will look at so as to remember all the commandments of YHWH and perform them. Do not follow your heart and your eyes, which cause you to cheat on Me!"

To put it once more in the terms we used when we asked in chapter 2, "Who killed Goliath?"—what exactly is it that "the Bible says" about the correct way to behave? Should we follow our own minds, our own inclinations, our own judgment, as the verse from Ecclesiastes would have us do, or should we not? To be sure, Qohelet adds a caveat to his suggestion: "Just be aware that God will bring you to judgment for all these" (Eccl. 11:9). But "do it, and be prepared for the consequences" is still very different from "don't do it."

Alter Ego

There is another way in which Qohelet's voice is distinct from any other in the Bible. This is a book written almost entirely in the first person. True, there are prophets who tell us of their own experiences; but these are experiences that are conveying a divine message. Moses—"a very humble man, more so than any other man on the face of the earth" (Num. 12:3)—suddenly makes himself the central character of his farewell speech in the opening chapters of Deuteronomy; but we might argue that here he is trying to leave the Israelites with a large enough "dose" of himself that they will continue to follow God's commandments after his death. Only Nehemiah comes anywhere close to Ecclesiastes in his focus on himself as the hero of his own book, and he is a distant second. Add up "I," "me," "my," and "mine," and you get more than 2 percent of all the words in the King James Version of Ecclesiastes.

The book of Ecclesiastes is focused on Qohelet's own search for wisdom. He cannot have been the only person in the biblical period to have made such a search—but he is the only one who has invited us along. Throughout the book, we are invited to follow as Qohelet turns this way and that, examining life and passing judgment on it. He presents us with his own ruminations on his experience in a way that no other biblical character does.

"Everything is Hevel*"*

Despite Qohelet's meandering path through life, cycling over and over again between his conviction that only wisdom can help one understand how to live and his depression on discovering how limited the benefits of wisdom really are, there is one touchstone to which he always returns. It is found in the first words spoken in his voice and in the last. This is a moment when no translation can give the full flavor of what he says, though, so I must try to explain his conclusion about life by letting him use one word in the original Hebrew. Qohelet's take on the world? "Everything is *hevel*."

This is the word translated "vanity" in the famous phrase "Vanity of vanities . . . all is vanity" (Eccl. 1:2 and 12:8, in the KJV translation)—a phrase I must admit I've never quite understood in English. What Qohelet meant by it is only a little less obscure. We know that it was important to him not only because his book begins and ends with it, but because more than half the occurrences of the word *hevel* in the entire Bible are found in this one tiny book. The single place in the Bible where its meaning (as opposed to its significance) seems easiest to grasp is in Ps. 144:4, "Man resembles *hevel*—his days are like a passing shadow." That is, "man is but a breath," something insubstantial.

The word *hevel*, then, describes a breath, a gas, something so tenuous that its very existence is transitory or perhaps even imaginary. The word is regularly used for empty threats, for idols, and for delusions of all kinds. It is even (as you can only know by reading the Bible in Hebrew) the real name of Cain's brother Abel! What his parents called him, we will never know; the Bible names him for his fate. Now you see him, now you don't; he is brought on stage for just one fleeting moment, and only in order to be killed.

And that, according to Qohelet, is our fate as well.

> ECCL. 3:19 For the fate of human beings and the fate of animals—well, they have the same fate. The death of this one is like the death of that one, and they all have the same spirit. Being human is no better than being an animal, for everything is *hevel*.

What does it mean to say that "everything is vanity"? According to the Oxford English Dictionary (and this is how the King James translators must have meant it) "vanity" means "That which is vain, futile, or worthless; that which is of no value or profit." But what is meant by the expression "vanity of vanities"?

It is similar to, if not quite the same as, our expressions "King of Kings" or (not to mention them in the same breath) "capo di tutti capi." "King of kings" refers to a king so supreme that other kings are subject to him. He is literally a king over other kings. The head of the Mob is a boss who bosses other bosses around. But in Biblical Hebrew this construction is an idiom for the superlative. The "Holy of Holies" is the holiest spot on earth; and, yes, the Song of Songs is so named to call it the greatest poem ever written. "Vanity of vanities," therefore, means "the most futile thing ever."

To this we must add the flavor that is missing when you use "vanity" in place of the Hebrew *hevel*. For *hevel* implies not merely that something is worthless, but also that it is at best transient, at worst an actual delusion—not something real at all. No English phrase can capture perfectly what Qohelet is saying; for me, the best way to convey it in English is this: "Utter illusion! All is illusion." If you add to this Qohelet's obsession with the endlessly repeated cycles of life and of nature, you find a voice with a remarkably Buddhist timbre. (I am not the only one who thinks so; an Internet search for "Ecclesiastes" and "Buddhism" gets over a million hits.)

Qohelet's Editor

Before we leave the book of Ecclesiastes, we must look at the other voice in this tiny book, the voice that told us that its words were "The words of Qohelet son of David, king in Jerusalem" (Eccl. 1:1). We tend to think of whoever wrote headings like "The words of Jeremiah son of Hilkiah" (Jer. 1:1) or "The words of Amos . . . of Tekoa, who prophesied concerning Israel in the reigns of Kings Uzziah of Judah and Jeroboam son of Joash of Israel, two years before the earthquake" (Amos 1:1) as a nameless scribe. Even when we think we can perhaps name him, as in the case of Jeremiah's scribe Baruch (see Jeremiah 36), he does not really take on a personality or seem to have anything of his own to say. But the writer of the heading to Ecclesiastes is different.

There is one slight clue near the beginning of the book that the editor of Ecclesiastes will not vanish quite so thoroughly as do the editors of most biblical books. It comes in the second verse of chapter 1, when we think that the words of Qohelet have already begun:

ECCL. 1:2 "Utter illusion!" said Qohelet. "Utter illusion! All is illusion!"

Those two words—"said Qohelet"—are still being spoken by the voice of v. 1. In an ordinary biblical book, we would expect that voice to have recited the title card at the beginning of the book and then disappeared. It *does* disappear after 1:2, though strangely it reappears once more in the main body of the book:

ECCL. 7:27 "Look, this is what I have found," said Qohelet.

But the biggest surprise is reserved for the end of the book. Qohelet's distinctive voice—the most personal of any biblical writer—cycles around one last time to strike the same note in concluding that he did in beginning:

ECCL. 12:8 "Utter illusion!" said Qohelet. "All is illusion!"

That bland little "said Qohelet" brings the anonymous editor who introduced the book back on stage, and, without skipping a beat, he steps smoothly in front of the microphone and begins to talk:

ECCL. 12:9 And more: Since Qohelet was a sage, he taught further knowledge to the people. He considered and rectified many proverbs. ¹⁰ Qohelet sought to discover useful sayings and wrote truly reliable words. ¹¹ The words of the wise are like goads, those of the compilers are like fixed nails. They were given by one Shepherd. ¹² And more: Beware of them, son! The collecting of books is endless, and too much scrutinizing is a wearying of the flesh. ¹³ The sum of the matter, once everything is heard: Fear God and keep His commandments! That is all there is for humanity. ¹⁴ For God will bring every deed to judgment, even every hidden deed, whether good or evil. The sum of the matter, once everything is heard: Fear God and keep His commandments! That is all there is for humanity.*

As is so often true in the Bible, this translation conceals many difficulties in the Hebrew text. (Are the words of wise really "given by one Shepherd," or is it just the nails in the ox goads that are "put there by a shepherd"?) But suddenly, here at the end of the book, we are listening

---

* Note that v. 13, "The sum of the matter . . ." is repeated after the end of v. 14. As we saw in the introduction to this book—"Whose Bible Is It?"—Jewish tradition is that in the books of Isaiah, Malachi, Ecclesiastes, and Lamentations, which end with words of ill omen, the second-to-last verse of the book is repeated after the last verse.

to a different voice. This voice tells us that Qohelet was a sage and teacher, a scholar and editor, who worked diligently and honestly. Nonetheless, we should not take him too seriously; the main thing is to keep the commandments.

Scholars generally assume that this voice belongs to one of the wholesome sages whose voices we hear in the book of Proverbs, trying to neutralize the seemingly radical notions put forth by Qohelet. He is called "a sage," like those quoted in that book; he edited "proverbs" (from the word *mashal*), like the ones that gave our book of Proverbs its name. Moreover, he "rectified" them, that is (as the Hebrew verb might be more literally translated), he "straightened" them—this from the man who thought that human life was "a twisted thing that cannot be straightened" (Eccl. 1:14) and who later pinned the responsibility for that situation directly on God: "Who can straighten what He has twisted?" (Eccl. 7:13).

Can this little paragraph at the end really turn Qohelet's book of despair into something that "belongs in the Bible"? Even if we agree that obedience to God's commandments is the bottom line, it is hard to forget that, as Qohelet has pointed out in Eccl. 3:19, "the sum of the matter" when we view our lives "under the sun" is that we die like animals. And keeping the commandments because it seems to be the best policy is fundamentally different from keeping them because they express God's will.

And more: Is this voice really so different from Qohelet's own? Remember, it was he who, after telling us to "Follow your heart and your eyes" (in direct contradiction of God's command in Num. 15:39), adds, "Just be aware that God will bring you to judgment for all these" (Eccl. 11:9). Given the way the main part of the book has ended, with a corpse being carried "to his eternal home" (Eccl. 12:5), perhaps the voice of Eccl. 12:9–14 is not that of a different writer at all. Perhaps it is Qohelet himself, whistling past the graveyard, trying to convince himself that the bleak picture he painted in the body of the book is not really as bad as he made it out to be. Or perhaps the pessimism of Qohelet, the "king in Jerusalem" of Eccl. 1:1, was a completely imaginative creation, and the writer of the book is reassuring us that it was simply a thought experiment. All will be well if only we will "fear God and keep His commandments."

The Voices of Job

At the beginning of the chapter, I promised to introduce you to the voices of two anonymous sages. We have met one of them, in the person of the sage who put on the mask of "Qohelet son of David, king in Jerusalem." When we hear the voice of Qohelet, we feel we are listening to a real person. What we do not know is whether that person is anything like the book's actual author, or whether it is a persona, a completely imaginative creation. The author of the book of Job, by contrast, does not show himself at all in his work. The voices of the book are those of his characters. Yet we will make something of an acquaintance with him even if we never hear him directly. I spoke of the person who compiled the book of Proverbs, with an apparently literary intent, as a "composer." When I did so, I had in mind another composer of literature: the author of the book of Job. But he is a composer of a very different kind. The compiler of Proverbs created a unified whole, but it is made almost entirely of texts he himself did not write. Job is not a compilation of earlier material, but a work of intense personal expression.

Having explained how we will hear the "voice" of someone who never speaks directly to us, I must now explain why I consider him a "sage." Remember the three sources of knowledge we saw in Jer. 18:18—the sage, the priest, and the prophet. The latter two get their knowledge from God, the prophet directly and the priest through the passing down of tradition. But the sage's knowledge is no more than what any human being could observe or deduce. The talent to discover this knowledge may have been given to him by God, as artistic and technical "wisdom" was given to Bezalel to enable him to design the Tabernacle (see Exodus 36), but the words themselves have no source other than the sage's own mind.

The voices of the wise also share a concern with wisdom itself. Roughly a quarter of all references to wisdom in the Bible are found in Proverbs, along with one-third of all occurrences of the word "sage" (in Hebrew, the words are etymologically related). Ecclesiastes, despite its shortness, is in second place, and Job is third.

The question asked by Job—"Why do bad things happen to good people?"—is not really so different, after all, from the question that is implicit in what Qohelet points out: "The race may not be won by the fastest, or the battle by the strongest; the wise may have no bread, the understanding no wealth, the knowledgeable no luck" (Eccl. 9:11). Why not? Why does reward not go where it belongs? And if I do get the reward I deserve, what is the point, since at last I must die?

The book of Proverbs insists that righteousness is rewarded and crime is punished, making righteousness the *wise* course to follow. We might imagine a sage of this sort responding to Qohelet: "The stupid do not realize, fools do not understand: When the wicked flourish like grass and transgressors blossom, it is only for eternal destruction" (Ps. 92:7–8; 6–7 in Christian Bibles). The book of Job will present an entirely different perspective on this. But it will not do so in a voice that speaks directly to us, as Ecclesiastes did. Instead, we will hear the question argued through the dramatic interplay of eight different voices. Let's take a look at the *dramatic personae* of the book.

Setting the Stage

The book of Job sets its scenes in two separate locations, heaven and earth, and it is not until the conclusion of the book that characters from the two locations interact. In the earthly realm, where most of the book takes place—"under the sun"—there is only one character who is mentioned elsewhere in the Bible, and that is Job himself. We encounter him in the book of Ezekiel as someone who is legendary for his righteousness:

EZEK. 14:12 The word of YHWH came to me: 13 Son of Adam!*
When a land sins by trespassing against Me, and I send forth My

---

* This expression is characteristic of the voice that addresses YHWH's prophecies to Ezekiel.

hand against it to break its staff of bread, letting famine loose against it, [14] even if these three men were in it—Noah, Danel, and Job—they, in their righteousness, would save only their own lives.

It would be déjà vu for Noah, of course. He, in his righteousness, has once already saved only his own and his families' lives while the rest of the world perished. "Danel" is not a misspelling; this is a pre-Israelite hero whom we will meet again in chapter 8. We must assume that Job too was a legendary and presumably pre-Israelite figure renowned for his righteousness. Of the other characters who interact with Job in the scenes on earth, Bildad and Zophar are known only from this story; the name "Eliphaz" is found in Genesis 36 and 1 Chronicles 1 as the name of one of Esau's sons, but that would make him an Edomite, and our Eliphaz is a Temanite; the "Elihu" of 1 Chronicles is also someone other than our man; and Job's wife is not named.

In the heavenly realm, we meet two beings. One, of course, is God, and he is immediately named as YHWH, the same God whom we know from book after book of the Bible. But the other is much more mysterious. The KJV and the NRSV call him "Satan," but that is not an accurate rendering. "The Adversary" of NJPS is better, but still a bit misleading; he is not *God's* adversary at all—the story depicts him clearly as God's employee. I'm going to call him "the Prosecutor."

It is a single letter that makes all the difference in understanding what we are to call him, the letter that serves as the Hebrew definite article, "the." Satan is a character with a name, who appears several dozen times in the New Testament. But he appears only once in the Hebrew Bible, in 1 Chr. 21:1. (Compare that verse with 2 Sam. 24:1 when you are ready to probe deeper into the different historical voices we began to examine in chapter 2.) The Hebrew word *satan* may simply refer to an enemy of any kind.

We find it, for example, when David (on the run from Saul) has defected to the Philistines. The Philistine officers are suspicious of him and warn King Achish of Gath not to bring David along with them when they march to war, "lest he become our adversary [*satan*] in battle" (1 Sam. 29:4). In Job (and in Zechariah 3) we find neither "Satan" the proper name nor *satan* the ordinary word, but *ha-satan*, "the *satan*." Zechariah 3 does not give us enough information to evaluate this being, but the book of Job depicts him as someone who roams the earth checking up on human beings for YHWH. He's a prosecutor, or maybe a cop—not God's adversary, but someone whose task is to be an adversary to human beings on God's behalf.

If anyone is God's adversary in the book, it is not "the *satan*" but Job, whose Hebrew name, *Iyov*, bears an unmistakable resemblance to the Hebrew word *oyev*, "enemy." Nonetheless, though our story avoids calling the Prosecutor "Satan," we cannot say that the KJV and NRSV are wrong to do so just because the Hebrew word includes the definite article "the." Let's look at a similar example, also taken from the KJV:

> **GEN. 2:18** And the LORD God said, It is not good that the man [*ha-adam*] should be alone; I will make him an help meet for him. **19** And out of the ground the LORD God formed every beast of the field, and every fowl of the air; and brought them unto Adam [*ha-adam*] to see what he would call them: and whatsoever Adam called every living creature, that was the name thereof.

This is the same character who even the Hebrew text will eventually call "Adam" (without "the"), but not until Gen. 4:25.* At this point in the story, he is still *ha-adam*, "the earthling," but the KJV has already switched over to the name he will eventually be known by. In just this same way, the KJV and NRSV have gone ahead and turned *ha-satan* into "Satan," the name of the New Testament character, though the author of Job intended it simply as a job description.

* Of the English translations I checked, only the NRSV refrained from using the name "Adam" before Gen. 4:25. (It is interesting that he is still *ha-adam* in Gen. 4:1, when he fathers Cain, and first becomes "Adam" in Gen. 4:25, when he fathers Seth, who will eventually become the ancestor of humanity.)

Looking at 1 Chr. 21:1, we notice there is one more likeness between "the *satan*" of our book and Satan of 1 Chron. 21:1. In that verse, Satan "incited" David to take a census of the Israelites. (Can it be a coincidence that both "incite" and the Hebrew word *va-yáset* sound so much like "Satan"?) This kind of incitement is exactly what God accuses "the *satan*" of doing in the book of Job:

> JOB 2:3 Have you noticed My servant Job? There is no one else like him on earth—innocent, honest, God-fearing, and avoiding evil. He still holds fast to his integrity. You incited Me [*va-t'siteni*] against him, to engulf him in troubles for no reason!

What actually happened is a little more complicated than God is letting on here:

> JOB 1:6 One day, the gods came to attend on YHWH. The Prosecutor was also among them. ⁷ YHWH said to the Prosecutor, "Where have you come from?" The Prosecutor replied to YHWH, "From roaming back and forth on the earth." ⁸ YHWH said to the Prosecutor, "Have you noticed My servant Job? There is no one else like him on earth—innocent, honest, God-fearing, and avoiding evil." ⁹ The Prosecutor replied to YHWH, "Does Job fear God for no reason? ¹⁰ You have set a protective hedge around him, his household, and all he owns. You have blessed the work of his hands, and his wealth has spread through the land! ¹¹ Just send Your hand against him and strike against what he has and see whether he does not curse You to Your face!" ¹² YHWH said to the Prosecutor, "All right. Everything he has is in your power. Just do not send your hand against him personally." So the Prosecutor went forth from the presence of YHWH.

It's true that *ha-satan* issued the dare—but YHWH essentially dared him to do so.

To finish setting the stage for my further discussion of the book, I must tell you one more thing. The Hebrew of the book of Job is extremely difficult. Unlike the other places in the Bible where we face such difficulties, it seems that here the author created them deliberately. The first two chapters of the book, and most of the last chapter, are in rather simple prose, mimicking that of a folktale: "Once upon a time, there was a man in the land of Uz whose name was Job" (Job 1:1). I say "mimicking" because, although the flavor of these chapters is that of the Patriarchal Era that we read about in the book of Genesis, the language actually shows unmistakable traces of Late Biblical Hebrew. But the middle thirty-nine chapters are written in a poetic style more intense and difficult than we find anywhere else in the Bible. It is *Finnegans Wake*, not *Oliver Twist*. The theological challenge of the book has proven equally difficult, not least because there is no agreement on how to translate the last words that Job speaks in the book. So I am going to try something a bit different with the voices we hear in this book. I would like to present the book of Job to you as a symphony.

The Symphony of Job

Like a standard symphony, the book of Job (viewed musically) has four movements:

- Movement 1, Job 1–27, introduces the main themes of the book and presents them in conflict with one another. It is the main movement of the symphony, almost twice as long as all the others combined.
- Movement 2, Job 28–31, begins with an adagio that gives us some respite from the conflict of the first movement, but eventually returns to the conflict and restates it.
- Movement 3, Job 32–37, an allegro, deflates the tension momentarily with a comic interlude.
- Movement 4, Job 38–42, is a dramatic confrontation in which YHWH, the ultimate hero of the book, overwhelms Job, the character with whom we have identified.

Let's look at each of these movements in more detail.

Movement 1, Job 1–27

Introduction, Job 1–2

The music is simple and easy to follow, preparing our ears for the more complicated section to come. The scene alternates between earth and heaven. We are introduced to Job, who is "blameless and upright" (1:1). His integrity prompts YHWH, "incited" by the Prosecutor, to test him. Under intense stress, will Job curse God? (The Hebrew of 1:11 euphemistically says "bless" God, to avoid even expressing the alternative, but what it means is clear.) In a series of military raids and meteorological disasters, Job loses everything. His response? "Naked I came forth from my mother's womb, and naked I shall return there. YHWH gave and YHWH took. Let the name of YHWH be blessed!" (1:21). (Since the test continues, this confirms that "bless" of 1:11 is a euphemism for "curse," and that Job here intends genuine blessing.)

Now the stakes grow higher. The Prosecutor can do anything he likes to Job but kill him (2:6). Job's wife urges him, "Bless God and die!" (2:9). (Which does she mean, "bless" or "curse"?) Eliphaz, Bildad, and Zophar gather to comfort Job and commiserate with him, and we are ready for the main part of the movement. Job and his three friends, each in turn, will face the new conditions of his life. In three cycles of gradually escalating argument and counterargument, commiseration will crescendo into confrontation.

The First Cycle, Job 3–14

Job 3. *Job* ends seven days of silence by suddenly *cursing*. . . the day he was born! (Whew!)

Job 4–5. *Eliphaz* attempts to be reassuring: "Remember, now. What innocent man ever perished?" (4:7) You, Job, are truly innocent—and, therefore, ultimately safe.

Job 6–7. *Job* is in too much pain to be reassured: "Remember, my life is nothing but wind. I will never see happiness again" (7:7). He turns to address God: "What is Man that You make so much of him, that You even notice him? Must You examine him every morning, test him moment by moment?" (7:17–18; to fully appreciate the music of this line, compare Ps. 8:5).

Job 8. *Bildad*, offended, asks Job, "Would God pervert justice?" (8:3), using the same rare verb used by Qohelet when he asked about God, "Who can straighten what He has twisted?" (Eccl. 7:13).*

Job 9–10. *Job* admits, "Truly, I know it is so. How can a human being win a lawsuit against God?" (10:1).

Job 11. *Zophar* retorts, "If only God would speak, would open converse with you. He would tell you the secrets of wisdom!" (11:5–6).

Job 12–14. *Job* insists: "The hand of YHWH has done this!" (12:9). "He leads counselors stripped of their wisdom, turns rulers into fools" (12:19). "But I want to speak with the Almighty—I intend to argue with God" (13:3).

The Second Cycle, Job 15–21

Job 15. *Eliphaz* rebukes Job: "Does a wise man respond with hot air?" (15:2). "What the wise say is this. . . . The wicked writhe in torment all their days" (15:18, 20).

Job 16–17. *Job* reiterates his spiritual pain. "My face is red with weeping, my eyes are dark with gloom, for no crime of my own. My prayer is pure!" (16:16–17).

Job 18. *Bildad* joins the rebuke. "Must the world go off course and mountains be uprooted, for your sake?" (18:4).

Job 19. *Job* insists, "God has acted perversely in my case" (19:6). "I want to behold God. Let me see Him with my own eyes!" (19:26–27).

Job 20. *Zophar* reminds Job what lies in store for the wicked. "Like his own turd, he perishes forever. The onlookers ask, 'Where is he?' . . . That is the lot of the wicked man from God" (20:7, 29).

Job 21. *Job* retorts bitterly, "How do you expect to comfort me with hot air?" (21:34). If you remember our discussion of Qohelet, you already know what Hebrew word I have translated as "hot air." Job

---

* This verb occurs three times in Job, three times in Ecclesiastes, and just five times in the rest of the Bible.

thinks his friends' belief in the essential justice of life is *hevel*, simply an illusion.

The Third Cycle, Job 22–27

Job 22. *Eliphaz* is provoked to rage. "Is it for your reverence that He rebukes you and brings you to justice? Your evil is immense, is it not? There is no end to your crimes!" (22:4–5).

Job 23–24. *Job* turns to challenge God himself. "Test me! I will come out like gold" (23:10).

Job 25. *Bildad*, in a speech of only five verses, rests the case for the prosecution: "How can a human being win a case against God? How can one born of woman be innocent?" (25:4).

Job 26–27. *Job* presents his own rebuttal: "By God who has taken justice from me, by the Almighty who has embittered my life, . . . to my dying day I will never admit that you are right or take away my own blamelessness" (27:2, 5).

The third cycle is an abortive one, with just the truncated response from Bildad and none at all from Zophar.

Movement 2, Job 28–31

Adagio, Job 28

No heading indicates that Job's response to his three friends is over. But as we read, we realize that we are in a place of quiet and calm. There are no human characters here; the argument has died away. It is a poem of three stanzas, in a voice we do not recognize—not that of Job.

Job 28:1–11. Man is enterprising and bold, finding and retrieving precious stones and metals from the most inaccessible places on earth.

Job 28:12–19. But "where can wisdom be found?" (28:12). Though it is more precious than any jewel, even the depths of the ocean and of the underworld know nothing of it.

Job 28:20–28. Only God knows where wisdom is, and he will reveal no more of it to humanity than this: "It is the fear of the Lord that is wisdom, and avoidance of evil that is understanding" (28:28).

Restatement of the "Job" theme, Job 29–31

"If only I was as in time gone by, as in the days when God protected me" (29:2). Job recalls the life we saw him leading as the story opened. But now "I beseech You and You do not answer me" (30:20). "If only I had someone to hear me! This is my bottom line: Let the Almighty answer me! Let my opponent present the indictment!" (31:35). At last "the words of Job have reached their conclusion" (31:40). The three friends too are silent, realizing that nothing they can say will change his mind. At this point, only two possibilities remain. Either YHWH will accept Job's challenge and appear, or Job's final outburst will indeed be the "bottom line"—literally, the *tav*, the final letter of the Hebrew alphabet, the end of the book. Instead . . .

Movement 3, Job 32–37
Allegro

A new character appears, with a belly so full of words that he is like a skin of wine about to burst (32:19). He is Elihu son of Barach-el the Buzite, of the family of Ram—an Israelite, to judge by the sound of his name. Buzi was the name of Ezekiel's father, and Ram was the great-grandson of Judah and an ancestor of King David. Elihu's own name is the same as that of Samuel's great-grandfather. But can we take his father's name seriously? Barach-el! That makes him "Elihu, the son of Bless-God!"

Job has demanded an answer from God, but Elihu assures him, "I will answer you" (33:12), and commands, "Be silent! And let me instruct you in wisdom" (33:33). Then he expands his audience: "Sages, hear my words! You who have knowledge, give ear to me" (34:2). God "rewards man for his actions" (34:11). After a pause, he assures them, "I have more words to speak in God's favor" (36:2). We mere humans cannot attain the level of the Almighty. His justice is as great as his power— "He would not torment" (37:23). But with this serious-sounding assurance the composer of our symphony has played one last musical joke. The same Hebrew letters also spell, "He will not answer"! And what happens immediately after Elihu finally shuts up?

Movement 4, Job 38–42

YHWH answers Job from the tempest (part one), Job 38–39

The response we anticipated at the end of Job 31, when Job's own speech was finished, bursts in, *fortissimo*. "Who is this that darkens counsel with ignorant words?" (38:2). This is not directed at Elihu, who has disappeared from the book as abruptly as he appeared, but at Job: "Gird your loins like a man! *I* will ask the questions, and *you* will inform *Me*. Where were *you* when *I* laid the foundations of the earth? Tell Me, if you have such great understanding!" (38:3–4). This is what Job wanted—"call me, and I will answer, or let me speak and I will respond to You" (13:22)—but a crucial part of Job's request has *not* been fulfilled: "Keep Your hand far from me, and do not let the dread of You terrify me" (13:21). Instead, YHWH demands, "Gird your loins like a man!" This is the Biblical Hebrew equivalent of "Put up your dukes!" It is a challenge Job cannot possibly meet, and YHWH knows it. He bombards Job with four dozen rhetorical questions. Job cannot get a word in edgewise—not that he would have a proper response even if he could.

YHWH answers Job from the tempest (part two), Job 40:1–42:6

At last YHWH pauses, and now it is he who demands an answer from Job. "But I am too insignificant," Job replies. "How can I answer you? I am putting my hand over my mouth" (40:4). The word Job chooses to express his insignificance is indeed significant: it is a different form of the same verb we saw at the beginning of the first movement, when "Job opened his mouth and *cursed* the day of his birth" (3:1). The test was to see whether he would curse God; implicitly, it is himself, not God, whom Job has now "cursed." But YHWH is not satisfied, and demands once again, "Gird your loins like a man! *I* will ask the questions, and *you* will inform *Me*" (40:7). Again, Job is faced with more unanswerable questions, this time about God's most enormous creatures, Behemoth and Leviathan. Their power is immensely greater than Job's. Yet they are mere creatures of YHWH. Job's answer, at the beginning of Job 42, is as quiet as it could possibly be. He cannot face God's power. His final words are expressed in Job 42:6. Those words are the concluding music of the great central section of the book, the last notes before the "simple" music of the first two chapters returns. Every translator must offer a version of them; here are three:

> Wherefore I abhor myself, and repent in dust and ashes. (KJV)

> Therefore, I recant and relent, being but dust and ashes. (NJPS)

And my own:

> So I refuse. But I will take comfort in dust and ashes.

The truth is that we don't know for certain what the Hebrew words are intended to convey. It is clear that Job is silenced. But has he conceded that he was wrong, or has he simply given up the fight, overwhelmed by God's power? We translators, who must all offer just a single one of these choices, are forced to obscure the uncertainty that we are left in by the original Hebrew music.

Coda, Job 42

We have returned to the music of the introduction; we are back in the imitation folktale of Job 1–2. The dramatic conclusion of the symphony is behind us—or so we think. But the argument is not quite over, for once YHWH is through with Job, he turns to Eliphaz: "I am incensed at you and your two friends, for you did not speak rightly about Me, as did My servant Job" (42:7). Job *was* right all along! And he is rewarded with wealth greater than he had had before, and ten new children, including three daughters who are the most beautiful on earth. At last Job dies, "old and full of days" (42:17).

The Voices of Wisdom: Reprise

In this chapter, we have looked at the three biblical books that scholars refer to as "wisdom literature." These three very different books all share a major concern: How are we to make sense of the world using our own understanding? In their different ways, each is trying to answer a question that is trite, but nonetheless true in the most meaningful sense (since it is vital to each of us)—What is the meaning of life? Proverbs is certain that "Fear of YHWH is the beginning of knowledge" (Prov. 1:7); Ecclesiastes thinks fearing God is "the sum of the matter" (Eccl. 12:13). For Job, "fear of the Lord is wisdom" (Job 28:28), but that still leaves us in the middle of the journey.

Beyond their wisdom concerns, I have suggested that these three books have something else in common. They are also literary creations, and their authors had artistic concerns, just as Bezalel must have had when he used his technical wisdom to create the Tabernacle and its equipment. Even Proverbs, which is clearly an anthology of writings from different eras, seems to have been assembled in its final version with a literary, and not just a religious, vision. In Ecclesiastes and Job we certainly have books that present us not merely with information or instruction, but also with art. Each is the esthetic creation of a single mind. In the person of Qohelet, we are convinced that we have met the author of Ecclesiastes (which may or may not be the case). We know for certain that the author of the book of Job stands at some remove from the character by that name. But—if I have convinced you—he has given us a unique work of art, a Beethoven's Ninth of the Bible.

Proverbs, Ecclesiastes, and Job also have one more thing in common: unlike every other book of the Bible but the Song of Songs, they are not part of the story of Israel. They have nothing to do with Jewish history. To be sure, Proverbs mentions Solomon and Hezekiah, and Qohelet calls himself "king in Jerusalem," but these references merely connect those books to the history we learn in the rest of the Bible. They do not tell us any of that history; the connection is tangential. Although these books are written in Hebrew, and Proverbs and Job both mention the Israelite God YHWH dozens of times (Ecclesiastes refers more neutrally to "God"), what is missing in these books is any significant connection to the *story* of the Jews. In these books, the understood reader is not a Jew, but simply a human being whose native language happens to be Hebrew. By the same token, the writers too might be able to find wisdom applicable to themselves and their readers in books from other ancient cultures. As we will see in the next chapter, that is exactly what they did.

8
Foreign Voices

In chapter 4 I suggested that the fact that the Pentateuch was woven together of multiple strands is part of what gives the book its power, and I quoted a proverb from the book of Ecclesiastes in support of my suggestion: "The three-fold cord is not easily broken" (Eccl. 4:12). Now that we have looked more closely at Ecclesiastes, you may be wondering how someone like Qohelet—always able to see the glass as half-full, even when it is completely full—could have come up with such an optimistic saying. The answer is simple. He read it in a book—a *foreign* book.

As we saw in chapter 7, Ecclesiastes and its companion books of wisdom, Proverbs and Job, discuss issues that are not specifically Israelite, but apply to all of humanity. It's reasonable, therefore, that they might have consulted the works of thinkers from other cultures to see how those cultures approach the same problems. As we'll see shortly, wisdom books from elsewhere in the ancient Near East very definitely left their mark on the Bible.

But that is just the beginning. The Israelites were very aware of the cultures around them, at times even politically dominated by them. Even Israelite law, presented in the Torah as being spoken to Moses by YHWH, falls into ancient Near Eastern categories. And the poets of ancient Israel based many of their own creations on the conventions of Canaanite poetry. As we'll see by the end of this chapter, these poets also understood the perspective of Canaanite myth and used it for their own poetic purposes. So this chapter is going to take us on a long geographical journey. Let's begin it with one small step: a look at Qohelet's library.

Qohelet in the Library

Hamlet, as the old joke has it, is full of quotations, and it turns out that the Bible has some, too. One of them is the phrase about the "three-fold cord." The author of the book of Ecclesiastes read this saying in a book called Gilgamesh and the Land of the Living, sometimes known as Gilgamesh and Hubaba. Gilgamesh was a legendary, but apparently real, king of a Mesopotamian city called Uruk ("Erech" in Gen. 10:10) more than 4,500 years ago. In the story, written in the Sumerian language, Gilgamesh is trying to persuade his friend Enkidu to come along on an expedition to the Cedar Forest, ruled by a mysterious figure called Hubaba. Gilgamesh reassures him that if they stick together, they will be safe. To do so, he uses what seems already to be an ancient proverb: "A towed boat will not sink, for no one can break a three-fold cord."

You may think, as indeed some scholars do, that the author of Ecclesiastes never read this story. By his time, certainly no one spoke Sumerian, and precious few could read or write it. Wouldn't it be much more likely that this saying simply came into Canaan with one of the Israelites' ancient ancestors and remained proverbial for centuries thereafter?

"Eat Your Bread in Gladness"

If this proverb were the only thing Qohelet knew that could be connected with Gilgamesh, that would indeed be much more likely. But a more extensive excerpt taken from another version of the Gilgamesh story also appears in Ecclesiastes. We know this version not from Sumerian, which is not related to any other known language, but from Akkadian, a Semitic relative of Hebrew. And this is not a saying, but a passage of poetry that Qohelet quotes, at one point, almost exactly.

In this version of the epic, Enkidu has died and Gilgamesh is searching in despair for something that will bring his friend back to life or at least prevent his own death. He seeks advice from Siduri, the barmaid at the end of the universe. She warns him that his search for immortality is pointless, and suggests that instead he simply enjoy the pleasures of this world with his family:

> Gilgamesh, whither rovest thou?
> The life thou pursuest thou shalt not find.
> When the gods created mankind.
> Death for mankind they set aside,
> Life in their own hands retaining.
> Thou, Gilgamesh, let full be thy belly,
> Make thou merry by day and by night.
> Of each day make thou a feast of rejoicing,
> Day and night dance thou and play!
> Let thy garments be sparkling fresh,
> Thy head be washed; bathe thou in water.
> Pay heed to the little one that holds on to thy hand,
> Let thy spouse delight in thy bosom!
> For this is the task of [mankind]!*

And here is Qohelet, after a rumination about the inevitability of death:

> ECCL. 9:7 Go eat your bread in gladness and happily drink your wine,
> For God has already approved your deeds.

---

* Translated by E. A. Speiser in James B. Pritchard, ed., *Ancient Near Eastern Texts Relating to the Old Testament*, 3rd ed. with suppl. (Princeton NJ: Princeton University Press, 1969), 90.

⁸ Let your garments always be white,
Let your head not lack oil.
⁹ Enjoy life with the woman you love,
All the days of your life of *hevel* that He has given you under the sun—
All your days of *hevel*!

Let's put these two texts side by side for easy comparison.

Gilgamesh	**Qohelet**
Gilgamesh, whither rovest thou?	[One and the same fate overtakes all humanity . . . "At least the living know that they will die. But the dead know nothing!"]
The life thou pursuest thou shalt not find.	
When the gods created mankind.	
Death for mankind they set aside,	
Life in their own hands retaining.	
Thou, Gilgamesh, let full be thy belly,	Go eat your bread in gladness and happily drink your wine,
Make thou merry by day and by night.	For God has already approved your deeds.
Of each day make thou a feast of rejoicing,	
Day and night dance thou and play!	
Let thy garments be sparkling fresh,	Let your garments always be white,
Thy head be washed; bathe thou in water.	Let your head not lack oil.
Pay heed to the little one that holds on to thy hand,	

Let thy spouse delight in thy bosom!	**Enjoy life with the woman you love,**
	All the days of your life of *hevel* that He has given you under the sun—
	All your days of *hevel*!
For this is the task of [mankind]!	

This comparison shows us a number of things.

Ecclesiastes was *using* the Gilgamesh text (or some version of it), not translating it. He integrates it into his composition because this passage of Gilgamesh, like his book, is about how to face life knowing that death is inevitable.

He followed Gilgamesh particularly closely when writing the lines in bold—but with a critical omission that perfectly demonstrates the different flavor of the two passages. Siduri is comforting Gilgamesh with the reminder that there is pleasure in the humble joys of life, and that his children will live on after him. Qohelet, the loneliest man in the Bible, has no room in his book for the hope and joy of children. Instead, he must add (as always) a reminder that such daily pleasures are *hevel*—illusory, transient, absurd—from the perspective of the larger scheme of things.

Siduri's conclusion that ordinary life "is the task of [mankind]" is truncated, but it seems that this too has its place in Ecclesiastes—though not in Ecclesiastes 9, and not in the voice of Qohelet: "Fear God and keep His commandments! That is all there is for humanity" (Eccl. 12:13).

My point, of course, is not that Ecclesiastes was a plagiarist, but that he had absorbed material from a great work of non-Israelite literature and transformed it for use in the book he himself wrote—a book of the Bible.

Since the sages, unlike the priests and the prophets, were concerned with the nature of human life in general more than with specifically

Israelite history or ritual, it is natural (as I have said) that there should be room for foreign voices in the wisdom books. The Israelite sages drew from the wisdom of sages in other cultures who faced the same questions about the meaning of life or why bad things happen to good people; there is even a text that modern scholars call "The Babylonian Job" (though the name "Job" appears nowhere in it, and it has no connection to Job of the Bible). The author of the biblical book of Job must have taken his character's name, and perhaps other details of his story, from a much older folktale that probably originated outside Israel, but as far as I am aware there are no "foreign voices" in it. It is such a remarkable work of literary art that it is unique of its kind.

But the same cannot be said for Proverbs. All societies, including our own, have books meant to teach people how to behave correctly and how to succeed, using both aphorisms (sentence proverbs) and longer forms (instructions). Was any foreign wisdom of this kind adapted for use in the book of Proverbs? A closer look will show us that it most certainly was.

Foreign Voices in Proverbs

Let's turn once more to the headings in Proverbs marking the separate sections that were assembled to create the finished book. There we will find the first clue to the foreign voices in the book of Proverbs. Let's examine them carefully:

> "The proverbs of Solomon, son of David, king of Israel" (Prov. 1:1).
>
> "The proverbs of Solomon" (Prov. 10:1).
>
> "These, too, are attributed to the sages" (Prov. 24:23).
>
> "These, too, are proverbs of Solomon, which were transmitted by the men of King Hezekiah of Judah" (Prov. 25:1).
>
> "The words of Agur son of Jakeh" (Prov. 30:1).
>
> "The words of Lemuel" (Prov. 31:1).

We know much more about Proverbs, and about the Bible in general, than we did when we first encountered these back in chapter 1. As often happens, the more we know, the more questions we have:

- Why is there no heading for the poem about the "Woman of Valor" that begins at Prov. 31:10?
- Why are some of these sections called "proverbs" and others simply "words"?
- Are "these" that are "attributed to the sages" proverbs or words?
- How can they "too" be "attributed to the sages" if we have not previously attributed anything to "the sages"?
- Who are "the sages"?

Let's examine each of these questions in turn. The answers will lead us to the foreign voices in Proverbs. It turns out that they are hidden in plain sight.

The "Woman of Valor"

The first question, regarding the absence of a heading for the "Woman of Valor,", it seems to me, is no longer hard to answer. We saw in chapter 7 that the famous poem of Proverbs 31 is an alphabetic acrostic, where each line begins with a letter of the alphabet, in order. We also saw that the supercompetent, supersuccessful woman who is the heroine of the poem was not just a woman who was God fearing, but a woman who herself was "fear of God." She is Wisdom herself, as we encounter her in Proverbs 1–9. So identifying these twenty-two lines as a separate section, and then understanding that the woman described in them is both real and symbolic, may be considered the final exam that determines how successful we have been in learning wisdom. (Perhaps the section of sayings involving numbers in the second half of Proverbs 30 was supposed to help prepare us to find a separate section in Proverbs 31 as well.)

Proverbs 22 Shifts Gears

The rest of the questions may still seem somewhat mysterious. But we have learned something else about Proverbs that will give us the key to solving them all. Remember that in Proverbs 22 we discovered a series of single-line proverbs suddenly followed by an instruction. As a refresher, look at the following excerpt, and spot where the proverbs stop and the instruction begins:

> ¹⁵ If folly settles in the heart of a lad,
> The rod of discipline will remove it.
> ¹⁶ To profit by withholding what is due to the poor
> Is like making gifts to the rich—pure loss.
> ¹⁷ Incline your ear and listen to the words of the sages;
> Pay attention to my wisdom.
> ¹⁸ It is good that you store them inside you,
> And that all of them be constantly on your lips,
> ¹⁹ That you may put your trust in YHWH.
> I let you know today—yes, you—
> ²⁰ Indeed, I wrote down for you a threefold lore,
> Wise counsel,
> ²¹ To let you know truly reliable words,
> That you may give a faithful reply to him who sent you.

There is no heading before v. 17, where the "I-you" voice of the instruction begins, but in v. 17 itself we find a phrase that looks very much like the missing heading: "the words of the sages." If this were the title of a new section, then the two difficulties we posed regarding Prov. 24:23, "These, too, are attributed to the sages," vanish at once. The material that begins in Prov. 22:17 consists of "words of the sages," and so "too" is the material that follows Prov. 24:23 "words of the sages."

Was this our midterm exam? Were we supposed to be able, by this point in our wisdom education, to figure out that the phrase "the words of the sages" in the middle of Prov. 22:17 was actually a title? I don't think so. I believe that this is a confusion that was introduced in the text accidentally as it was copied and recopied over the years. What leads me to think so is that the apparent confusion in v. 17 is followed by more confusion in v. 20. Where the NJPS translation we've just seen has "a threefold lore," KJV writes "excellent things." Understanding why the two translations disagree will lead us to a distinctly foreign voice in Proverbs.

It would be bad enough if Prov. 22:20 contained a difficult word, but it actually contains *two* difficult words. This is yet another example of the Ketiv/Qere phenomenon we saw in chapter 1, where the written text has one word (the "Ketiv") but a marginal instruction (the "Qere") tells us to read the word differently. If I put a bracketed space into the middle of the verse in place of the problem word, v. 20 reads:

"I wrote down for you [   ] wise counsel."

The written word that goes into the blank space is the Hebrew word *shilshom*, which literally means "the day before yesterday" but is always used in the Bible to mean "previously, in the past." The marginal word, the word that is supposed to be used when the text is read aloud, is *shalishim*, literally "thirds," a word that grew (apparently from an original usage referring to the third man in a chariot) to mean something like "army officer" and then to refer to officialdom more generally. (See 2 Kings 7, where the king's aide who is trampled to death in the rush of the starving Samarians for grain is a *shalish*.) When the variants given in the text are so different in meaning, and when neither of them makes immediately obvious good sense, it is reasonable to suspect that some misunderstanding has crept into the text. And indeed it has. Knowing that this section consists of "words of the sages" gives us the clue that will tell us what happened.

"Proverbs" versus "Words"

Just what is the difference between a section of "proverbs" and a section of "words"? The two clear headings that refer to "words" instead of "proverbs," in the two chapters at the end of the book, Proverbs 30 and 31, will show us.

In Prov. 31:1 we are introduced to "The words of Lemuel, king of Massa." Massa is known from ancient sources as an Arabian tribe;

note that Massa is identified in Gen. 25:14 as one of the sons of Ishmael. Lemuel appears nowhere else in the Bible but here (his name recurs in v. 4). In any case, he is certainly not an Israelite king; this is *foreign* wisdom. Agur the son of Jakeh, in Prov. 30:1, is not identified as a king, but Massa appears in connection with him too, though not all translations show it: "The words of Agur son of Jakeh, [man of] Massa" (Prov. 30:1, NJPS). "Man of Massa" could mean that he too was king there, but as you can see from the brackets, the Hebrew text does not contain the words "man of." The Hebrew word, *ha-massa*, can also refer to the pronouncement or oracle given by a prophet (see, for example, Isa. 13:1, 15:1, 17:1, 19:1, and more.)

Nonetheless, neither Agur nor Jakeh is known from anywhere else in the Bible. The continuation of the verse provides either more unknown names—"the man spake unto Ithiel, even unto Ithiel and Ucal" (Prov. 30:1, KJV)—or more words that are not exactly Hebrew. It seems likely, then, that Agur's wisdom and that taught to Lemuel by his mother are both identified as "words" rather than "proverbs" because they come from a foreign source.

Wisdom from Egypt

Do "the *words* of the wise" that start in Prov. 22:17 also come originally from a foreign source? Yes! And that foreign source, discovered a century ago, also solves the linguistic puzzle of our mystery word *shilshom/shalishim*. The text that unravels the mystery is an Egyptian wisdom text called the Instruction of Amenemope.

After a prologue identifying Amenemope (a government official called the "overseer of grains") and the son to whom he is offering his wisdom, the instruction proper begins with these words:*

Give your ears, hear the sayings,
Give your heart to understand them;
It profits to put them in your heart,

---

* The translation is taken from Miriam Lichtheim, *Ancient Egyptian Literature*, 3 vols. (Berkeley: University of California Press, 1990), 2:148–62.

Woe to him who neglects them!
Let them rest in the casket of your belly,
May they be bolted to your heart;
When there rises a whirlwind of words,
They'll be a mooring post for your tongue.

And its last section begins with these:

Look to these thirty chapters,
They inform, they educate;
They are the foremost of all books,
They make the ignorant wise.

The beginning of this instruction is extremely close to that of the instruction that begins in Prov. 22:17, "Incline your ear and listen to the words of the sages," too close to be coincidence; and there are other similarities to Amenemope throughout this section of proverbs. As with Qohelet and Gilgamesh, it is not a translation of the Instruction of Amenemope, but an Israelite version of it.

The clincher is the organization of the Instruction of Amenemope into thirty chapters. With that, the answer to our last puzzle falls into place, for that provides the explanation for the difficult word of Prov. 22:20. It is not *shilshom* or *shalishim*, but *sheloshim*, "thirty"; not the "threefold" lore of NJPS, but a *thirty-fold* lore like that of the Instruction of Amenemope.

In the original Hebrew text, written as it was for many centuries without vowels, *sheloshim* would have looked essentially if not exactly like the other two words. The similarities between the Egyptian instruction and the biblical one, especially the fact that they begin with a nearly identical passage, tell us that the biblical instruction was written by a sage who believed that the thirty chapters of Amenemope's Egyptian wisdom had a great deal to teach Israelites as well. Centuries later, a transmitter of the text who was not familiar with the nature of its original composition introduced some confusion into the text by misunderstanding the word that should have been read as "thirty." The discovery and deciphering of Egyptian literature in the last century and a half has solved a textual difficulty in Prov. 22:20; more importantly, it has given us a wider perspective on the intellectual background of the book of Proverbs.

Common Law in the Ancient Near East

People are people everywhere, so it seems reasonable that ideas regarding human values should be able to be shared between nations. And indeed, we've now seen that Ecclesiastes and Proverbs, two biblical books of human wisdom, use or reuse material from similar books in other languages. The human authors of these books, well educated and (it seems) well read, drew on their reading to help convey their ideas in Hebrew to their own readers. But divine revelation falls into a different category. God never went to school, and he is entitled—almost required—to create his pronouncements on his own and not copy them from other sources. So let's look next at some divine pronouncements to the Israelites.

The Goring Ox

You'll remember from our discussion in chapter 4 that the first extended series of laws given to the Israelites occurs in Exodus 21–23, immediately following the Ten Commandments of Exodus 20. The laws given there are the legal framework on which the covenant between Israel and God at Sinai was based, and they are therefore called by scholars the Covenant Code. At the end of Exodus 20 God is speaking once more to Moses, and his voice continues at the beginning of Exodus 21: "These are the rules that you shall set before them." Among those divine rules is the following:

> EXOD. 21:35 If one man's ox strikes another man's ox so that it dies, they shall sell the living ox and divide the money, and shall divide the dead ox as well.

Now look at this:

> If an ox has gored another ox and caused its death, the owners of the oxen shall divide between them the sale value of the living ox and the carcass of the dead ox. (Laws of Eshnunna, 53)*

Eshnunna is an ancient town at a site now called Tall al-Asmar, about twenty miles southwest of Baghdad in today's Iraq. The laws found there date to the nineteenth century BCE, six hundred years before the time of Moses. Yet the book of Exodus presents God as essentially quoting one of those laws when he tells Moses the rules that he wants the Israelites to follow when they create their own independent society in the land of Canaan.

You may wish to object that this is, after all, a "rule"—that is, not a *ḥok*, which is a law decreed with no explanation, but a *mishpat*, something that a human judge (*shofet*) might well decide on his own as a reasonable way to handle a situation. But that, of course, only shows that law (at least in some respects) falls into the same realm as wisdom. Every reasonable society has laws against theft and murder, and we cannot accuse God of plagiarism for stating "You shall not murder" and "You shall not steal" in the Ten Commandments.

The similarities between the Covenant Code and other ancient Near Eastern law codes, though, go well beyond what a reasonable person might come up with by coincidence. This is especially noticeable when the biblical law *disagrees* with an earlier law. For example, if the ox had gored not another ox but a human being . . .

> If an ox was a habitual gorer, the local authorities having so duly notified its owner, yet he did not keep his ox in check and it then gored a man and caused his death, the owner of the ox shall pay two-thirds of a mina of silver (to the survivors of the victim).

---

* Translations from the Laws of Eshnunna and the Code of Hammurabi are taken from J. J. Finkelstein, "The Ox That Gored," *Transactions of the American Philosophical Society*, n.s., 71, no. 2 (1981): 20.

> If it gored a slave and caused his death, he shall pay fifteen shekels of silver. (Laws of Eshnunna, 54–55)

From the Code of Hammurabi, dating about half a century after the Laws of Eshnunna:

> If an ox, while walking along the street, gored a person and caused his death, no claims will be allowed in that case.
> But if someone's ox was a habitual gorer, the local authority having notified him that it was a habitual gorer, yet he did not have its horns screened nor kept his ox under control, and that ox then gored a free-born man to death, he must pay one-half mina of silver.
> If (the victim was) someone's slave, he shall pay one-third mina of silver (to the slave's owner). (Code of Hammurabi, 250–51)

And from the Covenant Code:

> EXOD. 21:28 If an ox gores a man or a woman to death, the ox is to be stoned and its meat must not be eaten; but the owner of the ox is in the clear.
> 29 But if the ox had been a habitual gorer in the past and its owner was put on notice but did not keep it under control, and so it caused the death of a man or a woman, the ox is to be stoned and its owner is also to be put to death. 30 If a ransom is set on him, then he can pay whatever amount is set on him to redeem his life. 31 The same rule is to be followed if the ox gores a boy or a girl.
> 32 If the ox gores a slave, male or female, 30 shekels of silver are to be given to the slave's owner, and the ox is to be stoned.

All sorts of instructive comparisons can be made between these three sets of laws—but I will leave that challenge to you. For present purposes, the point is that Israelite law, like Israelite wisdom, did not arise in a vacuum, but was produced in a world where other legal frameworks already existed that would be known to those in the profession. Not every aspect of Mesopotamian law would be congenial to Israel or to Israel's God, but neither was there any reason to reinvent the wheel. From Abraham's time right through the Persian Empire, the Israelites lived among other cultures with law codes of their own. These could be, and were, adopted—or adapted—for the Israelites themselves. The adaptations, still carrying a bit of their foreign accent for those who were knowledgeable enough to hear it, found their way into the Bible just as the nonlegal wisdom of other cultures did.

The Calendar

What other aspects of life might the Israelites have shared with other cultures? One obvious answer comes to us from Gen. 1:14, "God said, 'Let there be lights in the firmament of the sky to distinguish between day and night. They shall be signs to mark the festivals, the days, and the years.'" These "lights," as v. 16 goes on to tell us, are of course the sun, the moon, and the stars. Months (curiously) are not mentioned specifically in v. 14, but the Israelites had them, of course, and they were indeed marked by the moon; in Biblical Hebrew, as in English, "month" and "moon" are related. But, as the song says, "the moon belongs to everyone." Other cultures also had months, and their months had names—some of which we find, in Hebrew versions, in the Bible.

Back in chapter 2 we noted that Solomon built the Temple "in the 480th year after the exodus of the Israelites from Egypt, in Solomon's 4th year over Israel, in the month of Ziv, that is, the 2nd month" (1 Kgs. 6:1). Our attention was directed elsewhere at the time, but perhaps you noticed that the person who wrote this chronological note thought that some readers might not recognize a month called "Ziv." It's clear that in this writer's time the months were not usually named, but instead were numbered.

You might think that "Ziv" is a neologism, created to mark some new turning point in Israelite history (as the French revolutionaries created Thermidor and so forth), but it's the other possibility that turns out to be correct. "Ziv" was an ancient name that had fallen out of use. In fact, the Bible also uses a third system of month names—the names that are still used in today's Jewish calendar:

System 1	System 2	System 3	Modern Equivalent
Abib	1st	Nisan	March/April
Ziv	2nd		April/May
	3rd	Sivan	May/June
	4th		June/July
	5th		July/August
	6th	Elul	August/September
Ethanim	7th		September/October
Bul	8th		October/November
	9th	Kislev	November/December
	10th	Tevet	December/January
	11th	Shevat	January/February
	12th	Adar	February/March

As you can see, of the three systems used in the Bible to identify the months of the year, the only one for which we have all twelve months is System 2, the one that counts the months in order as they occur during the year, starting in the spring. (Our names September, October, November, and December—months seven through ten—are relics of a similar system that numbered the months.) It seems reasonable to assume this was the standard Israelite way of identifying the months for most of the biblical period.

The Alternative Month Names

But where do the other two systems come from? A couple of the month names from System 1 are known (from inscriptions) as Canaanite names. Are these "foreign" names? The Israelites were certainly not the only ones who used them, but it seems these were the "local" names where the Israelites lived. And "Ethanim," at least, is a perfectly good Hebrew word; Psalm 89 is identified as having been written by "Ethan the Ezrahite." System 3, however, is foreign even geographically—these are the month names that were used in Babylonia—and, sure enough, we find them occurring in the Bible only in books from the post-Exilic period, when the descendants of the Jews who had been taken to Babylon after Jerusalem fell returned to Judea.

With the names of System 1, the situation is just the reverse. Abib occurs as a month name only in the Torah; the other three names occur only in connection with the building of Solomon's Temple. The only complete system is the Israelite system of counting the months by the Hebrew words for the ordinal numbers: 1st, 2nd, and so forth. The other systems, we might guess, added a bit of foreign or historical flavor to the texts in which they were included.

The Influence of Egypt

Up to this point, we've seen that if you listen closely you can hear many voices from the east—the ancient cultures of Mesopotamia—in wisdom, in Israelite law, and even in the names of the months. Are there voices in the Bible from the equally ancient civilization to the west of Israel, that of Egypt, outside the one example that we saw in Proverbs? We know that the Israelites understood themselves to have originated in Mesopotamia, and of course the destruction of the Temple in 586 BCE sent a much later generation back to spend the years of exile in Mesopotamia as well. But Egypt was looked on as foreign, and its language is only distantly related to the Semitic languages; the Egyptians who had enslaved the Israelites were "a people of strange speech" (Ps. 114:1). Is widespread Egyptian influence on the culture of biblical Israel even plausible?

The answer to that question too is a definite "Yes." Both biblical historical books and ancient, newly rediscovered historical records tell us that Egyptian influence would often have been felt in ancient Israel; at times, it would have been pervasive. Geopolitically, Canaan had always been the point of contact between Egypt and Mesopotamia, the two great superpowers of the ancient world, and this did not cease when Israel took up residence there.

Modern biblical scholars, like the ancient Israelites, find it easier to learn Semitic languages than Egyptian, so it is easy to think of Mesopotamia as providing the stronger influence. But Hebrew inscriptions from throughout Israel, from the ninth all the way to the sixth centuries—the duration of the divided kingdoms—show us the other side of the coin. The system of numerals used in these inscriptions is not the cuneiform number signs of Mesopotamia, but the "hieratic" numerals of ancient Egypt. "Hieratic" means "priestly"; eventually, the script from which these numerals were derived was used only to record Egyptian religious texts. It is as Egyptian as apple pie is American. Yet this was the everyday number system of ancient Israel. There must therefore have been some kind of cultural link between Egypt and Israel.

Despite the great difference between the Egyptian language and Hebrew, then, there are some areas in which Egypt influenced the Bible. We have already seen that the Egyptian Instruction of Amenemope directly influenced the biblical book of Proverbs, which implies an Israelite awareness of and interest in Egyptian literature. But an Israelite might have spent a lifetime using hieratic numerals without thinking of them as Egyptian, just as Americans eat hamburgers without thinking about Hamburg. Since people are people the world over, we must also be careful not to identify a foreign source underlying a biblical text unless the relationship is clear. Ecclesiastes has some ideas that strike a contemporary reader as very Buddhist, but no one (so far as I'm aware) has suggested that there is a relationship between the biblical book and actual Buddhist writings of any kind. But the connection between Egypt and ancient Israel is a historical fact, and we can point to a biblical passage (in Proverbs) that was directly influenced by a specific Egyptian text, the Instruction of Amenemope.

Love Poetry

At the other extreme of the spectrum of influence is the realm of love poetry. A great deal of ancient Egyptian love poetry has been found that is comparable to the great Hebrew love poetry in the Song of Songs. This is not a case where we can say that specific lines or images were copied from Egyptian poems into Hebrew ones, though the possibility of future discoveries does not permit us to rule this out entirely. What we can say is that poems from this genre exist in both cultures and share certain features that suggest some continuity between them.

For example, when the poet talks about the beloved one, the person's physical features are described as if a camera were panning up or down the body:

> SONG 5:10 My beloved is clear-skinned and ruddy,
> Preeminent among ten thousand.
> 11 His head is finest gold,
> His locks are curled
> And black as a raven.
> 12 His eyes are like doves
> By watercourses,
> Bathed in milk,
> Set by a brimming pool.
> 13 His cheeks are like beds of spices,
> Banks of perfume
> His lips are like lilies;
> They drip flowing myrrh.
> 14 His hands are rods of gold,
> Studded with beryl;
> His belly a tablet of ivory,
> Adorned with sapphires.
> 15 His legs are like marble pillars
> Set in sockets of fine gold.
> He is majestic as Lebanon,
> Stately as the cedars. (NJPS translation)

(In the biblical Song of Songs, both the male and female lovers are described like this.) The Song of Songs most likely dates to almost a thousand years after the Egyptian love poetry, but the literary chain of transmission of this kind of description continued even longer, for it is also found in pre-Islamic Arabic love poetry dating from the first half of the first millennium CE. Still, here we can see at most a kind of indirect influence. (This is probably also the place to mention that some have seen the influence of ancient Tamil love poetry on the Song of Songs. The connection would have come through Mesopotamia, which we know had contact with India through trade.)

Psalm 104

A closer connection to Egyptian literature—something in between the generic influence of "love poetry" and the creation of an Israelite version of the Instruction of Amenemope—may be found in Psalm 104. The fourteenth-century BCE Pharaoh Akhenaten (father of the famous King Tut) is well known, not just in the history of Egypt but also in the history of religion, for the far-reaching but short-lived religious "reforms" he made during his seventeen-year reign. Akhenaten is the first recorded thinker to suggest that there was only a single god in the universe. He worshiped this god under the name of "Aten," the Egyptian name for the disk of the sun, which he made part of his own name. (Akhenaten was called Amenhotep IV when he first took the throne.) He, or a poet writing under his direction, wrote a "Hymn to the Aten," which is still preserved.

Scholars of Egyptian tell us that Psalm 104, the hymn to God's marvelous creation that describes Leviathan as God's plaything, takes some of its imagery from the Egyptian Hymn to the Aten. Psalm 104 is not an Israelite version of the poem in the way that the Proverbs passage of thirty pieces of wisdom was intended as an Israelite version of Instruction of Amenemope, but it does seem to be a poem that was inspired by the Egyptian hymn.

The Wellspring of Israelite Poetry

As great as the Egyptian influence on biblical Israel must have been, the tremendous difference between Hebrew and the non-Semitic language of ancient Egypt must have limited it—on the one hand, to people like the highly educated writer of "the words of the wise" in Prov. 22:17–24:22 and, on the other hand, to certain practical matters, like the hieratic numerals, resulting from contact with Egyptian soldiers, traders, and travelers who passed through Israel. The other peoples with whom the Israelites had contact, however, spoke Semitic languages that were much closer to Hebrew: Canaanite languages like Moabite, Edomite, and Ammonite; Akkadian; and, later, Aramaic, Arabic and various Ethiopian languages. Remember, too, as we mentioned in chapter 1, that the Hebrew of today's Bible is primarily the Hebrew of Jerusalem.

As one went further and further north, the language spoken by Israelites no doubt got closer and closer to that of their northern, non-Israelite neighbors. We might well expect to hear some of these foreign but Semitic-speaking voices in the Bible, and in fact we do. The voice we hear loudest, a voice with a much greater influence on biblical poetry than Egyptian, is that of a language that was completely unknown until a century ago: Ugaritic.

Most of what we know about the Canaanites comes from the lucky chance that a farmer plowing his field in 1928 uncovered the first remains of a major city of the ancient world. This discovery took place at a village called Ras Shamra (Cape Fennel), a few miles north of the famous tobacco-growing town of Latakia on the Mediterranean coast of modern-day Syria. Buried in the earth under Ras Shamra was what is left of an ancient town called Ugarit, and we call its reconstructed language Ugaritic.

In the ruins of the city archaeologists have found hundreds of cuneiform documents. But this particular kind of cuneiform was not, like Babylonian cuneiform, Egyptian hieroglyphics, or modern Chinese characters, a set of hundreds of different symbols representing various words and syllables. Instead, it was a set of merely thirty symbols that were used to represent letters, like a modern alphabet. (As in Hebrew and Arabic today, only consonants, not vowels, were represented.) Because this language is apparently so close to Hebrew, even without vowels we have been able to decode and read a great amount of this literature.

Coincidentally, the documents found at Ugarit, like the Hymn to the Aten, also date to about the year 1400 BCE. Thus some of the differences between Ugaritic and Biblical Hebrew may simply come from the fact that even the oldest parts of the Bible are several centuries later than the Ugaritic writings. Most of the Bible probably is anywhere from two hundred to as much as twelve hundred years older than these Ugaritic materials. If you think back that far in the history of the English language, you have to go past Shakespeare to Chaucer and beyond to Beowulf. So the language that later developed into Biblical Hebrew (of which we know little) must have been even closer to that of the discoveries at Ras Shamra. And their kinship was not just linguistic, but also cultural.

Ugaritic literature gives us a literary window through which to see the Canaanite milieu in which Israelite culture would develop. Reading through the Ugaritic literary texts (we also have ritual texts, letters, and various kinds of administrative documents), we find lines of poetry written in a style that is instantly familiar to any reader of the psalms. To recognize this familiar aspect in these ancient and unfamiliar works, we must first take a quick look at the most characteristic feature of biblical poetry.

The Poetry of Parallels

What rhyme and rhythm do for English poetry is done in Biblical Hebrew poetry by what scholars call "parallelism." The essence of this phenomenon is the use of matching pairs of words, synonyms or antonyms, in each half of one line of poetry. We have already seen an example of this when we looked (in chapter 6) at Prov. 1:8. A somewhat simplified version of Deut. 32:1 will illustrate it once more:

Give ear, O heavens . . . and listen, O earth.

This simple line has both kinds of word pairs. (The full verse also includes a more complicated kind of pair.) There are two verbs ("give ear" and "listen") that mean essentially the same thing, and two nouns ("heavens" and "earth") that represent opposites—but opposites that make a natural pair. (Think of Gen. 2:4, "This is the story of heaven and earth when they were first created, on the day when YHWH God made earth and heaven.")

Many such pairs recur over and over again in biblical poetry. You can probably think of some yourself: silver and gold, day and night, mountains and hills, and so forth. We now know, from the Ugaritic poetry discovered at Ras Shamra, that the use of such parallel pairs by the biblical writers was a literary inheritance from the linguistically closely related Canaanite culture that surrounded them. Ugaritic literature does not merely use such pairs, it actually contains dozens of the exact same pairs—not just the words, but the pairs—that are found in the Bible. And that's not all. The Bible is largely made up of prose stories, but Ugaritic literature takes the form of epic poetry. Besides using parallel pairs like those of biblical poetry, the Ugaritic epics are full of idiomatic phrases that are also regularly found in Biblical Hebrew prose: "he arose and went on his way," "he lifted up his eyes and saw." One of the most common of them is "he answered and said."

Readers of older, more literal translations of the Bible are sometimes surprised to see a character "answer and say" when he hasn't been asked a question. In fact, this phrase is what is technically called a "hendiadys," a phrase where two words mean a single thing. A familiar example from English is the expression "sick and tired." It doesn't mean that you are sick and that you are tired. It means that you're the one single thing that we call by the double phrase "sick and tired." Similarly, "he answered and said" means something like "he declared." This too is a usage that we now know was not coined by the biblical writers, but adopted by them from pre-Israelite languages. There are many such biblical idioms that, though they have become completely naturalized into Hebrew, are really an inheritance from the Israelites' cultural ancestors.

Ugaritic Myth

The fact that Israelite writers used the same idioms and the same poetic word pairs as the Ugaritic writers implies something more—that they knew the stories told in the Ugaritic poems. We have glanced very briefly (in chapter 7) at one case in which this was so; as I promised you then, we are now ready to look at it a bit more closely. It occurs in God's famous pronouncement to Ezekiel:

> **EZEK. 14:13** When a land sins by trespassing against Me, and I send forth My hand against it to break its staff of bread, letting famine loose against it, **14** even if these three men were in it—Noah, Danel, and Job—they, in their righteousness, would save only their own lives.

(See also vv. 19–20.) Your Bible most likely says "Daniel" here, but my "Danel" is not a misspelling; this is one more example of the Ketiv/Qere phenomenon we saw earlier in the chapter, when we looked at Prov 22:20. Again the written text has one word (the "Ketiv") but a marginal instruction (the "Qere") tells us to read the word differently. I have translated the written version, not the reading version, because Ezekiel is not talking about the biblical Daniel—his younger contemporary, a nice guy but not celebrated for his perfect righteousness—but about Danel, the righteous king whom we now know from the Ugaritic "Epic of Aqhat" (Aqhat was Danel's son). Ezekiel is not speaking of Israelites here—note that he does not even mention Abraham—but of three men who were known worldwide, inside Israel and outside it, for their extraordinary righteousness.

We do not know exactly what version of Danel's story the Israelites knew, but they did know him; Ezekiel was certain that his hearers would get the point of his very pointed remark. So some of the Ugaritic stories, in one form or another, were part of the cultural background possessed by ordinary Israelites just before the Babylonian destruction of Jerusalem—eight centuries after Ugarit flourished and six centuries after Ugarit was destroyed.

A Surprise Visitor to the Garden of Eden

In fact, some of the most well-known stories in the Bible are variants on stories told in Ugarit or elsewhere in the ancient Near East, and one more mention of Danel in Ezekiel will lead us directly to the heart of this topic:

> EZEK. 28:1 The word of YHWH came to me: ² O mortal! Say to the ruler of Tyre: Thus says my Lord YHWH: Because your heart has become so high that you said, "I am a god! In the dwelling place of the gods do I dwell, in the heart of the seas!"—but you are a mortal and no god, though you imagine your mind to be like that of God. ³ Oh, yes—you are wiser than Danel! Nothing concealed is too dark for you. . . .
>
> ¹¹ The word of YHWH came to me: ¹² O mortal! Intone a dirge over the king of Tyre, and say to him: Thus says my Lord YHWH: You were of perfect measure, full of wisdom and flawless in beauty. ¹³ In Eden, the garden of God, were you, covered with precious stones. . . . ¹⁵ You were perfect in your behavior from the day you were created until iniquity was found in you.

Tyre is indeed "in the heart of the seas," on a peninsula (originally an island) jutting out into the Mediterranean from the coast of Lebanon, some 150 miles south of Ugarit. In biblical times, as now, it was the closest non-Israelite town north of Israel itself. Its king pictures himself as the epitome of perfection, another Danel; then he takes it even a step further. He is not merely the wisest and most righteous of men, but the *first* of them, created "in Eden, the garden of God." Yet, as the prophet goes on to say, "Through your widespread commerce, your insides were filled with violence—and you sinned. So I have expelled you from the holy mountain of God and obliterated you . . . from within the stones of fire" (Ezek. 28:16).

Poor king; I'm not trying to pile on. What I want to show you here is a picture of Eden that's different from the one we are used to reading about in Genesis. Yet in this Eden too, as in Genesis 1, creation is followed by sin and expulsion. If we don't know what version of Danel's story the Israelites knew, we certainly can't guess what Ezekiel thought the king of Tyre knew. Nonetheless, the prophet has told us that the people in Tyre had a story about Eden very different from the one our Bible tells. All cultures have their own stories of how the world was created, of course, and ancient Israel's neighbors had them as well. Tantalizing glimpses of these stories appear not only in Ezekiel but in many other places in the Bible. As we will see in the next chapter, there are even reflections of them in Genesis itself, in the familiar story of creation that we all know—or think we know.

9
Voices of Song and Legend

We have seen in earlier chapters several examples of how different biblical voices tell the "same" story in a slightly different way: the diverse and sometimes contrasting historical ideologies of Kings and Chronicles, the Sinaitic law collections revealed by Moses to the Israelites at varying stages of their journey through the wilderness, even the interleaved telling of the flood story by the J and P writers. In this chapter, we will go beyond the narrative prose of most of the biblical stories we have heard so far, and begin to listen to some poetic voices. As we will see, these "voices of song and legend" often refer to events that we remember from the more well-known stories in the Bible. But, like the prose variations we have already seen, they sometimes open a window to a new perspective on these familiar tales.

We should not be surprised that Israel's history was told in poetic as well as prose form. We know the story of the Trojan War, after all, from an epic poem—Homer's *Iliad*—not from a novel or a history book. Our discovery during the past century and a half of a vast trove of literature from the ancient Near East makes clear that many peoples in the wider civilization out of which Israel grew told their basic stories in poetic form. In a world without the capability of mass reproduction of written texts, among a population where literacy was most likely not widespread, it is reasonable to think that the rhythm and repetition of poetry made it preferable to prose for long stories. Perhaps the fact that Israel's basic story is told in prose, though it seems natural to us, is the surprising phenomenon that needs explaining.

Stories in Prose and Poetry

The Bible does have a few examples of poetic storytelling. The two most famous are the "Song of Deborah" (Judges 5) and the "Song at the Sea" (Exodus 15). Judges 5 is a poetic version of the story of Deborah, a ruler of Israel during the period of the "judges"—better translated "magistrates"—who governed Israel before the kingship was established; it tells how she and her army commander, Barak, defeated the army of Jabin, the Canaanite king of Hazor, a story whose prose version appears in Judges 4. Similarly, the poem of Exodus 15 retells the story of the Israelites' crossing the Red Sea while the Egyptian army drowned in it, a story recounted in prose in Exodus 14.

Since both these poems immediately follow the prose accounts of the events they retell, it is easy to compare the two versions. Indeed, when we think of these occurrences as "Bible stories," we sometimes combine elements of the narrative and the poem to imagine a single version of the tale. But there are other biblical stories that are referred to in poems far removed from the familiar prose narratives. The plot elements of these poems rarely enter our thinking about the "original" prose story.

In this chapter, we will look at two stories in particular. Poetic references to the plagues of Egypt will show us that some stories that are familiar to us may have been told in ancient Israel in more than one way, and for varying purposes. When we turn to poetic references to the story of creation, we will see that they reveal to us a version of that story quite different from the one we know from Genesis. Eventually, this poetic version of the creation story will lead us back, via Exodus 15, to Israel's escape from Egypt.

How Many Plagues Were There?

Way back at the beginning of our discussion, in chapter 2, we asked a question that had a surprising answer: Who killed Goliath? We saw that the biblical texts offered two answers to this question and that the "standard" answer offered in the main story line of the Bible ("David") has made most of us forget the second answer ("Elhanan"), offered in what is essentially an appendix to the story (2 Sam. 21:19). A similar process has taken place with some famous details of the story of the exodus from Egypt. We can begin to focus on this by asking a similar question: How many plagues were there?

The obvious answer is "ten." The Ten Plagues are almost as familiar an aspect of the story as the Ten Commandments. But we saw in chapter 4 that Exodus 20, where the Ten Commandments are given to the Israelites, does not call them by that name. It is the "Ritual Decalogue" of Exodus 34 that is first called "the Ten Commandments," not the divine utterances of Exodus 20. So perhaps it will not be quite so surprising that the destructive miracles God inflicted on the Egyptians are not called "the Ten Plagues" either in Exodus or anywhere else in the Bible. (The first place they are actually counted as ten is Jubilees 48:7; we will meet the book of Jubilees in chapter 10.)

But the stories of Israel's history were not told only in the form of historical narratives. They were also told in songs and poems. In this particular case, we have two poems that tell the story of the plagues of Egypt. They are Psalms 78 and 105, two of what I call in this chapter the "voices of song and legend."

These voices of song and legend are too varied to display as distinct a theological agenda as do, for example, the priestly writings and Deuteronomy. Some of them may have been written to be part of the temple service, others for religious gatherings outside the Temple. Some of them, written as expressions of personal creativity, display literary qualities; some, perhaps, were written simply for entertainment. No doubt many more of these poems from ancient times have not survived till our days. So the ones we have may be just a glimpse of the various ways the Israelites once told the stories that have become canonized into our Bible.

Psalm 106

Biblical poems that retell or refer to well-known biblical events often had a different focus than do the versions of the stories that we today consider standard. Psalm 106, for example, tells the story of the exodus from Egypt and the Israelites' wandering through the desert, but it isn't interested in the plagues at all. Not that it denies they happened; the focus is simply elsewhere—on the rebelliousness of the Israelites in the desert despite all the good things God has done for them. So the only reference to a "plague"—this time (in the literal sense of "disease"; the Hebrew word commonly used in Exodus for the plagues is different) comes in vv. 29–30, where an epidemic is sent against the Israelites as punishment for their disobedience:

> PS. 106:29 They angered [God] with their deeds, and a plague broke out amongst them; 30 Then Phinehas stood forth to intervene, and the plague was stayed.

(See Numbers 25 for the narrative version of this story.) The "plagues" against the Egyptians are not an important part of the "plot" of Psalm 106, as we see by the casual reference to them in v. 21: "They forgot God their savior, the doer of great deeds in Egypt." This version of the story simply doesn't consider the plagues worth mentioning in detail, because its focus is on a different aspect of the exodus—the fact that the Israelites for whom God had performed such wonders were not properly appreciative and understanding of their significance, but rebelled against God again and again. How many "great deeds" did God do in Egypt? Psalm 106 does not bother to say.

Psalm 78

Psalm 78, another "historical" psalm, does tell the story of the plagues as part of its recounting of the exodus story. Like Psalm 106, however, it has a particular purpose in telling the story, not merely a journalistic desire to present the facts. The first indication of this is that this long (72-verse) psalm does not tell the story in chronological order. Thus, in vv. 13–16, God splits the sea and leads the Israelites through, just as he "splits" the rock so that water may gush forth for them to drink. All this happened after the escape from Egypt, of course, but it is not until many verses later, vv. 44–51, that this psalm gets around to telling the story of the plagues that forced the Egyptians to release them:

> PS. 78:44 He turned their rivers into *blood*, they could not drink from their streams.
> 45 He sent swarms amongst them that consumed them: *frogs* that destroyed them.
> 46 He gave their yield to the cicada, the fruit of their toil to the *locust*.
> 47 He killed their vines with *hail*, their sycamores with ice.
> 48 He abandoned their cattle to plague and their livestock to *pestilence*.
> 49 He sent against them His ire: anger, wrath, and distress, an embassy of evil messengers.
> 50 He tore open a path for His anger and did not spare them from death; He abandoned their lives to *plague*.
> 51 He struck each *firstborn* in Egypt, the first issue of strength in the tents of Ham.

Count them up: *seven* plagues, not ten! Ten, after all, is a round number. Remember that the "Ten" Commandments are divided into ten in different ways by Jews, Catholics, and Protestants, and remember once more that even in the Bible they are not identified as being "ten" when they are originally given. Ten is indeed an interesting and significant number, but so is seven. Think about the seven days of the week or the seven "planets" known to the ancients (Sun, Moon, Mercury, Venus, Mars, Jupiter, and Saturn). If the psalm had described four plagues, or thirty-four, we might have taken it as a precise number, but seven, like ten, suggests an attempt to organize the confusing facts of a real "situation on the ground" into a pattern that will make sense.

The book of Psalms contains poems dating from various periods throughout most of the thousand-year history of the Bible; we don't know when Psalm 78 was written, or by whom. Its heading ("an Asaphesque *maskil*") doesn't really give us any useful historical information. Asaph has his name attached to twelve psalms—Psalm 50 and the eleven psalms at the beginning of "Book Three" of the Psalms, 73–83—but this does not necessarily mean that the historical Asaph wrote them; the Hebrew word *maskil* implies something insightful—but what would that mean as the name of a category of poetry or a genre of music? By comparison, we know much more about who wrote P and D, and *why* they wrote. But why was Psalm 78 written?

Like Psalm 106, Psalm 78 is concerned with the Israelites' disobedience. We said before that the story is told out of chronological order in this psalm. Here are the lines (vv. 40–43) that introduce the recitation of the plagues and reveal their poetic purpose:

> **PS. 78:40** How many times they rebelled against Him in the wilderness, grieved Him in the desert!
> **41** They tested God over and over again, they distressed the Holy One of Israel.
> **42** They did not remember His power when He redeemed them from the foe,
> **43** How He exerted His signs upon Egypt and his wonders in Zoan.

(Zoan was a place in the Nile delta.) As in the Pentateuch, where the "plagues" are also more often called "signs and wonders," the destructiveness of the plagues is underplayed here in favor of their miraculous nature and especially their value as "signs"—that is, indicators of God's power.

Similarly, at the beginning of Psalm 78, the psalmist announces his intention to proclaim the greatness of God, "praises of YHWH and

His might, and the wonders that He performed" (v. 4). But the Egyptians no longer need to learn this. Their part in the story is over. By the time Psalm 78 was written, it was the Israelites who needed to learn (or relearn) this lesson. The message here is essentially a threatening one. Just as God directed his power against the Egyptians, who were insistent on keeping his people in slavery, so too can he direct that same power against the Israelites if they persist in their disobedience of his commandments.

Psalm 105

Psalm 105 tells the same story yet again, but with an entirely different message. Here, the psalmist tells the exodus story as a continuous narrative, just as the Torah did, not pulling one incident from here and then a chronologically earlier incident from there as did the author of Psalm 78. Here too (in vv. 28–36) there are seven plagues:

> PS. 105:28 He sent *darkness* and it grew dark; had they not defied His word?
> 29 He changed their waters to *blood* and killed their fish.
> 30 He made their land swarm with *frogs*, to the innermost royal rooms.
> 31 He spoke, and the insects came, *lice* throughout their land.
> 32 He turned their rains into *hail*, flaming fire throughout their land,
> 33 And struck their vines and their figs, shattering trees throughout their land.
> 34 He spoke, and the *locust* came, grasshoppers without number,
> 35 To eat all the grass of their land, every fruit of their soil.
> 36 And he struck each *firstborn* in their land, the first of all their strength.

Again (just as in Psalm 78 and in the book of Exodus as well) the last plague is the killing of the firstborn. Once more the purpose is to recall God's mighty power. But the invocation of that power here totally lacks the threatening aspect that Psalm 78 gave to the story. There, God's destruction of the enemy was offered as proof of the power he might also turn against the Israelites themselves if they displeased him. In Psalm 105, the emphasis is on the original use of that power, for the Israelites' protection. God has always protected the Israelites, the psalm emphasizes, and, if they will "keep His laws and follow His instructions" (v. 45), he will continue to do so.

In contrast to the threatening voice of Psalm 78, the voice of Psalm 105 is a very reassuring one. In each case, the (seven) plagues with which God struck the Egyptians, according to these psalms, are an indication of God's power. But the significance of recalling that power is very different in the two poems. In our present state of knowledge, it is impossible to tell whether the two poems come from different historical periods, or whether we are hearing the differences between two contemporaneous poets, expressed in their own individual voices.

Comparing the Lists of Plagues

Let's match up the plagues as told in Exodus and in our two psalms:

Exodus	**Psalm 78**	**Psalm 105**
blood (7:14–24)	blood (v. 44)	blood (v. 29)
frogs (7:25–8:11)	frogs (v. 45)	frogs (v. 30)
lice (8:12–15)		lice (v. 31)
swarms (8:16–28)*		
pestilence (9:1–7)	pestilence (v. 48)	
boils (9:8–12)	plague (vv. 49–50)	
hail (9:13–35)	hail (v. 47)	hail (vv. 32–33)
locusts (10:1–20)	locusts (v. 46)	locusts (vv. 34–35)
darkness (10:21–29)		darkness (v. 28)
killing firstborn (11:1–10, 12:29–36)	killing firstborn (v. 51)	killing firstborn (v. 36)

* The plagues of frogs, lice, and swarms are numbered from 7:25–8:15, 8:16–19, and 8:20–32 in Christian Bibles.

Do these three different versions of the Egyptian plagues have anything in common? Certainly. Five plagues appear in all three: blood, frogs, hail, locusts, and the killing of the firstborn. The other five—assuming that the plague of disease that kills the people in Ps. 78:49–50 is comparable to the boils of Exod. 9:8–12—all appear in two of the three accounts (since the Hebrew word for the "swarms" of Exod. 8:16–28 [20–32 in Christian Bibles] is used in Psalm 78 to refer to the "swarm" of frogs). The plague of blood is followed by the plague of frogs in each of the three versions although their contexts differ slightly: they are the first two plagues in Exodus and Psalm 78, whereas in Psalm 105 the plague of darkness precedes them (although Psalm 105 otherwise follows the same order of plagues as does the Exodus version). In both Exodus and Psalm 105, the hail is miraculously accompanied as well by fire.

So how many plagues were there, really? We will never know, any more than we can know whether what happened to the Egyptians was a perfect storm of scientifically explainable events or a series of obviously supernatural attacks. The psalms are poetry, not history, and even the book of Exodus is not written as reportage, but as literature. You can see this from the pattern in which the plagues are presented there:

"Early in the morning, as Pharaoh is going out to the water" (blood)	"Early in the morning, as Pharaoh is going out to the water" (swarms)	"Early in the morning, as Pharaoh is going out to the water" (hail)
"Go to Pharaoh" (frogs)	"Go to Pharaoh" (pestilence)	"Go to Pharaoh" (locusts)
no warning (lice)	no warning (boils) (killing of the firstborn)	no warning (darkness)

There is *no* authoritative version of the plagues of Egypt; even the prose narratives of the Bible are not journalistic reports. What we can know from these different versions is what was important to the Israelites about the story and what was not. It's impossible for us to imagine the story of Goldilocks with only two bears (you would never have anything that was "just right"), but it was perfectly possible for not one but two different Israelite poets to tell the story of the plagues by listing seven of them rather than the ten that we would insist on today.

The Story of Micah

In the case of the Egyptian plagues, we have the advantage of being aware of them not just from these psalms but from the much fuller narrative accounting in the book of Exodus. But other stories alluded to in the Bible may be just hinted at elsewhere, or not told at all. In these cases, the allusions are all we have, and we must tease out from them stories that were certainly much more widely known in the biblical period itself.

One fairly clear example comes in the dispute in Jeremiah 26 about whether Jeremiah should be executed, which we have already seen in chapter 5. As we pointed out there, this is one of the rare places in the Bible where we actually hear the voices of both sides of an argument, presented dramatically. (Jeremiah 44, where the survivors of the Babylonian conquest who had fled to Egypt blamed all Judah's troubles on the failure to sacrifice to the Queen of Heaven, is another. It may be that the author of the book of Jeremiah was particularly fond of this dramatic technique.) In Jer. 26:18–19, Jeremiah is saved from those who wish to execute him for his prophecy against Jerusalem and the Temple by another group, which argues:

> **JER. 26:18** Micah of Moreshet was prophesying in the days of King Hezekiah of Judah, and he said to the entire people of Judah,
> "Thus said YHWH of Hosts:
> Zion shall be plowed like a field,
> Jerusalem shall be a heap of rubble and the Temple Mount like a forest shrine."

¹⁹ Did King Hezekiah—and all of Judah—put him to death? Did he not fear YHWH and implore YHWH for mercy? Then YHWH changed His mind about the evil He had intended to do to them.

The quotation in this passage also appears among the prophecies in the book of Micah that is in today's Bibles; you will find it in Mic. 3:12. The point of this example for our present discussion is that the incident in Jeremiah 26 serves as a tiny window onto the story of Micah. In the book of Micah we have seven chapters of his prophecies, but (except for the name of his hometown) essentially nothing from which to put together a picture of his life. Though our friends in Jeremiah 26 do not explicitly say so, it seems likely that Micah's bold prophecy endangered his life just as Jeremiah's did his. Certainly in Jeremiah 26 we are given a glimpse of the tremendous drama that must have attended Micah's prophecy. Yet if this incidental remark had not been included in the story of Jeremiah, we would not have known about it, for the book of Micah gives only his prophecies, not the story of why he proclaimed them and what happened when he did so. The book of Jeremiah is not merely the words of a different prophet; it is a different kind of book. For in it we *do* have both the prophecies of Jeremiah 7 and (in Jeremiah 26) the story of what happened when he proclaimed them.

It is clear from the way the story of Micah is presented in Jeremiah 26 that, though his story is not told in the Bible, it was a story that was generally known in ancient Israel a century after he lived. There must have been many such stories, known quite widely in biblical times, that have not come down to us. The plague stories that Psalms 78 and 105 hint at have likewise not come down to us, at least not in narrative form. Yet, although they differ—at least in certain details—from the Exodus version, they do not contradict the familiar story; the "plot" of the plagues is essentially the same in all three places. For the rest of this chapter, however, we will focus on a story whose alternative versions, hinted at in various places in the Bible, are quite different from the familiar version of the book of Genesis. This is the story of creation.

Two Kinds of Creation

Even when told in full, the story of creation is presented in two different voices: first in a carefully structured version that lays out the order of creation beginning with the creation of light (that is, energy) in Gen. 1:1–2:3, and then in the story—simultaneously more dramatic and more down-to-earth—that describes the details of the creation of humanity and its consequences. In the prophet of the return from Babylonian exile whom we call "Second Isaiah," from around the year 538 (whose prophecies are found in Isaiah chapters 40 and following), there is some lovely poetic description of the same thing that the first chapters of Genesis describe much more straightforwardly. Here are Isa. 45:12 and 18:

> ISA. 45:12 It was I who made the earth, and created humanity upon it.
> It was I! My hands stretched out heaven, I gave its host their orders. . . .
> 18 For thus said YHWH:
> The creator of heaven—He is God;
> The shaper and maker of the earth, He set it firm.
> Not a wasteland did He create it—He formed it to be settled.

(The "host" of heaven, of course, is the stars.)
And in Isa. 40:12–14 we read:

> ISA. 40:12 Who measured the waters in the hollow of His hand,
> And gauged the heavens with His fingers,
> And scooped out dust for the earth by the cupful?
> Who weighed the mountains in a scale and the hills in a balance?
> 13 Who could gauge the spirit of YHWH, tell Him what plan He should follow?

¹⁴ Whom did He consult with, to make Him understand and
teach Him the path of justice,
To teach Him knowledge and make known to Him the way of
understanding?

Answer: Not you. No one. God did all these things by himself. And of course this is our standard assumption today about the biblical view of creation: it was God's unchallenged and unmatched power alone that created the heavens and the earth and all that is in them. Yet as it is presented in Isaiah—not complete, but a line here and two lines there—the prose of the first chapters of Genesis is not merely transformed into poetry; it is blended together. Two versions of the story become one.

In this new version, God achieves his creation of the world not only in Genesis 1 fashion, by speaking his commands (as when he "gave the stars their orders" in Isa. 45:12), but also by (so to speak) getting his hands dirty, mixing and measuring on a cosmic scale to match his forming man out of clay in Genesis 2. Moreover, though Genesis is silent about the implications of such a creation, Second Isaiah is using this depiction of creation to make a deliberate theological argument: YHWH is the *only* God. No one shared in the creation of the world with him, or possibly could have. No other god was "present at the creation." Genesis says this only by implication, but Second Isaiah states it boldly: "The creator of heaven—He is God!"

We find a similar argument, used for a somewhat different purpose, at the end of the book of Job. (I mentioned in an aside in chapter 6 that there are some close resemblances between Second Isaiah and the book of Job, and this is one of them.) Job has challenged God's justice—that is, the way he runs his universe—and God responds by demanding, "Where were *you* when *I* laid the foundations of the earth? Tell Me, if you have such great understanding!" (38:4). Here, it is not the possibility of other gods sharing in creation that is being denied. Such a possibility has never crossed Job's mind. It is the sheer complexity of creation that is at issue. There *are* no other gods, but there is something on earth that was created in God's image: humanity. Yet creation is far beyond humanity's feeble grasp.

A Partner in Creation

The book of Proverbs also includes a discussion of creation, yet in this telling God is not by himself. In fact, this version provides one answer to a long-standing exegetical puzzle: When God says, "Let us make Man in our image, according to our likeness" (Gen. 1:26), whom is he talking to? Proverbs 8:22–28 gives a surprising answer to that question: It was Wisdom, personified throughout Proverbs as a woman (as we saw in chapter 7), to whom God was speaking. Let's listen while she tells us how she served as God's creative Muse:

> PROV. 8:22 YHWH created me at the beginning of His way, before his works of yore.
> 23 Before eternity was I woven, at the first beginnings of the earth.
> 24 I was birthed when there were no Deeps, no flowing springs of water.
> 25 Ere the bases of the mountains were sunk, before the hills was I born.
> 26 Back before He made the open fields of earth, the world's first dirt.
> 27 When He prepared the heavens, there was I; when He etched a circle on the surface of Deep,
> 28 When He installed the sky above, and connected the springs Deep below.

Just as the psalmists used the story of the plagues for their own literary and theological teachings, just as Second Isaiah turned the creation story into poetry, so has the author of Proverbs 8. The poet is careful to make sure we understand that Wisdom is one of God's creations as well and hence is no rival to him as creator of the universe. Yet it is clear that, for this writer and for the book of Proverbs, personified

Wisdom somehow rounds out the picture created by Genesis 1. The world is not simply a magical illusion, as God's abracadabra "Let there be light" of Gen. 1:3 might make us think. No, the ease with which God brings heaven and earth into being merely reveals the incomparability of his power. But for the one who understands more deeply, everything about creation reveals the subtle complexity and deep interconnectedness of all creation. For the author of Proverbs 8, the straightforwardness of Genesis 1's account of creation belies the incomprehensible sophistication of the world that God made. It is only with the aid of Wisdom that human beings can hope to get some hint of the true nature of the universe.

Yet, as in Genesis, there is more to creation than science; it is about relationships as well. For Wisdom does not describe herself simply as a tool used by God, but as his companion: "I was with Him as an *amon*, a plaything day by day, gamboling before Him all the while" (Prov. 8:30). *Amon* is a word of famous difficulty among Bible scholars. Its etymology provides three possible suggestions for its meaning: (1) an artisan, (2) a nursling, (3) a faithful companion. Since Proverbs 8:30 is poetry, I would suggest that the writer wanted some flavor of each meaning of *amon* to come through. Just as when God created humanity "in His image," in Proverbs 8 as well God is not just making an object but a kindred (if lesser) spirit.

Proverbs 8 and Isaiah 40, then, add a poetic dimension to the Genesis story of creation, and this poetic dimension has not just a literary but also a theological aspect. But the story they tell—the "plot" of creation, as it were—is still basically the same as that in Genesis. The Bible, however, also hints at a second, very different version of creation that was also known in ancient Israel. Unlike the version of Genesis 1, to which Proverbs and Second Isaiah refer, this second version of creation is not explicitly narrated. Yet from the various biblical references to it, and from the literature of the other nations of the ancient Near East which the discoveries of the last century and a half have given us, we know the outlines of this alternative version of creation. In it, creation was not the result of careful and loving design, but the culmination of a theomachy (to use the technical term for it)—a battle royal between rival gods.

Creation and Contest

The first biblical hint at this story of creation as the aftermath of a contest between rival gods actually comes from the more familiar story of Genesis 1 (v. 2):

> The earth was formless and void, with darkness on the face of Deep.

We know from the literature of ancient Mesopotamia, and in particular from the epic poem called (from its first words) the Enuma Elish ("When, on high . . ."), that the Mesopotamians had a creation myth in which the world was created out of the body of the goddess of salt water, who was beaten in a battle by the great god Marduk. (It is from this god that Mordecai of the book of Esther got his name.) This goddess was split into two pieces, one forming the heavens and one the earth.

Her name was Tiamat—a name that provides the most likely derivation of the Hebrew word *tehom*, which I have translated "Deep" in Gen. 1:2 above, and in Proverbs 8 as well. The usual English translations (check yours) translate it as "the deep," but the word "the" is never used with this word anywhere in the Hebrew text of the Bible; it is a proper noun. This suggests that the teller of the story in Genesis 1 wanted to contradict the battle story—but silently. Those who did not know the "battle" version of creation (like most readers nowadays) would see nothing amiss; those who knew it would understand that the Genesis 1 story completely precluded any such notion. Creation, as presented here, is totally under God's control.

We saw some similar "counterpropaganda" in the priestly version of the flood story, in chapter 3. Remember that in the J version of that story, the flood was caused by forty days and nights of rain, but in the P version, it was caused by God opening the windows of the firmament and the floodgates of the earth and allowing the waters above and the waters below to return to the dry land from which he had separated them in Genesis 1. Again, we have material from the ancient Near East—in this case, literature from the civilization of Ugarit, on the Mediterranean coast of today's Syria, which we met in chapter 8—that presents the primordial waters not as a simple substance but as a personified god, Sea, who battles with the creator god for control of the earth.

In Gen. 7:11, God opens the floodgates briskly, almost as if he were turning on a faucet. But to the knowledgeable reader this was another reminder that "Sea" was the enemy of life on earth. Nonetheless, even this version of the flood story emphasizes that creating forty days and nights of rain was not a turn in the fortunes of battle between two gods, but a deliberate reversal of God's own actions in creating the world.

In both these cases, the creation story of Genesis 1 and the flood story of Genesis 6–9, there is not enough detail to actually tell the battle version of the creation story to those who don't know it. But it is very likely that most Israelites did know this other story in some form and only an allusion was necessary. Ancient Israel did not live in a vacuum, but was well acquainted with the wider civilization in which her own culture had developed. As we saw in chapter 8, the Bible is full of foreign voices. Ugaritic, in which the story of creation as a battle with the waters of the personified Sea is told, is linguistically very close to biblical Hebrew; and Akkadian, in which the Mesopotamian myths are recounted, is if not a sibling language at least a cousin. The fact that the P writer found it necessary to include these veiled references to the battle myth suggests that he felt a need to contradict it, but without calling attention to the alternative story if the reader was not aware of it.

More Hints of Battle

Now I must confess that I have done something similar. Did you notice that I left out a line in our discussion of Proverbs 8? I quoted vv.

22–28 and then v. 30 as well. But here is v. 29, where Wisdom claims to have been present at the creation, when God "established His perimeter for the Sea, so the waters would never transgress His command, and etched in the foundations of the earth." Why would it even occur to anyone that the waters might "transgress God's command," as if they had a mind of their own? Because, in the alternative creation story of battle between gods, this is exactly what happened. The P versions of the creation and the flood story, in which the waters are under God's complete control, are an implicit denial that the "battle of the gods" story is the true version of creation. By contrast, Proverbs 8—relaxed enough to provide YHWH with Wisdom as his companion when he created the world—is a bit more forthcoming about the ancient myth. Those who were familiar with it would understand that the primordial waters might indeed wish to "transgress YHWH's command." In Second Isaiah the idea that anyone might challenge God as creator is laughable; there is no possible challenger. But Proverbs 8 and Genesis as well, though more subtly, acknowledge this much truth to the ancient myth: it was God's might, not merely his creative power, through which he established heaven and earth.

Here is another biblical excerpt from the "battle" version of creation:

PS. 104:5 He established the earth on its foundations, that it never ever shake.

(Now the psalm turns to address YHWH directly.)

> 6 You covered it with Deep like a cloak, waters stood over the mountains.
> 7 They fled from Your rebuke, bolted at the sound of Your thunder.
> 8 The mountains rose, the valleys sank to the place You established for them.
> 9 You set a boundary they could not cross, never returning to cover the earth.

The truth is that the battle version of the story is no secret to a Bible reader who is paying attention. In fact, when YHWH is bullying Job, he brags about his victory over the sea:

> JOB 38:8 Who blocked the Sea with double doors when it gushed forth from the womb?—
> 9 When I dressed it with cloud, made fog its swaddling clothes,
> 10 When I made it break at the limit I decreed, slamming the doors with a bolt,
> 11 And said, "Come this far and no further! Your presumptuous waves will stop here!"

It is like listening to King Canute, who, according to legend, ordered the tide not to come in—with one major difference: YHWH did indeed have the power to issue that order, and to enforce it.

Here There Be Dragons

One more clue in Genesis 1, in the nature of "a word to the wise," allows us to see another aspect of the "battle" version of creation:

> GEN. 1:20 God said, "Let the waters swarm with swarming creatures, and let birds fly above the earth, across the firmament of heaven." 21 God created the great dragons and every living thing that creeps (with which the waters swarmed) according to their kinds, and every winged bird, according to its kind, and God saw that it was good.

That is, God created everything that flies in the air, and everything that swims in the sea . . . *and* he created the great dragons. (It is clear from the context that these are not land dragons, but marine ones, like the Loch Ness monster or Cecil the Seasick Sea-Serpent.) Why single out this particular sea creature for special mention? Why not just say God created everything in the sea and saw that it was good? You have undoubtedly already guessed the answer: The great sea monster (in the singular) was another character in one version of the battle myth of creation. This sea monster even had a name, one that you will recognize—Leviathan. In the Ugaritic version of the myth, he is called "Lotan":

> When you smite Lotan, the fleeing serpent, finish off the twisting serpent, the close-coiling one with seven heads,
> The heavens wither and go slack like the folds of your tunic.*

We know that the Israelite reader would have been familiar with this story because we have a mention of Leviathan in the book of Psalms:

> **PS. 104:25** There is the great, broad-reaching sea, swarming with creatures beyond counting, the small alongside the great;
> **26** There go the ships back and forth, and Leviathan, whom You formed to sport with.

Yes, there is a Leviathan, the incredible sea monster of legend; YHWH created him—as a pet!—because he wanted someone his own size to play with. Leviathan appears again in the book of Job, in the famous scene when YHWH appears to Job from the storm to demand, "Who are you to tell me how to run the universe?":

> **JOB 40:25** Could you yank out Leviathan with a hook, muzzle his tongue with a rope?
> **26** Could you put a line through his nose, pierce his jaw with a barb?
> **27** Would he beg you over and over again, speak gentle words to you?
> **28** Would he make a covenant with you, let you take him as slave forever?
> **29** Could you play with him like a bird, leash him for your girls?

---

* Dennis Pardee, "The Ba'alu Myth," in *The Context of Scripture*, ed. William W. Hallo (Leiden: Brill, 2003), 1:265.

> 30 Shall a company trade him, split him up among the peddlers?
> 31 Could you fill his hide with harpoons, his head with spears?
> 32 Just lay a hand on him! You will never think of battle again!*

The answer to all these questions, which Job did not need explained to him, was: Could you? No, you couldn't. But I can. I, YHWH, can do all these things because I operate at a level so far above yours. The unspoken "back story" behind this passage, which Job the character and the ancient Israelite readers all knew, was that Leviathan was not mild by nature, but had been beaten and tamed at the time of creation—domesticated, if you will—by YHWH's superior power. Psalm 74 says so in plain Hebrew:

> PS. 74:12 O God, my king since ancient days, winner of great victories in the midst of the earth,
> 13 You split the Sea with Your power, shattered the heads of the dragons in the waters.
> 14 You smashed the heads of Leviathan, left him food for desert creatures.
> 15 You split spring and stream, You dried up the mighty rivers.
> 16 Day is Yours, Yours too is night; You established moon and sun.
> 17 You set up all the bounds of earth—summer and winter, You fashioned them.

In this psalm of praise, the echoes of the creation story are quite clear. The establishment of day and night following upon the creation of light is the first step of creation (Gen. 1:3–5). Summer and winter, though not explicitly mentioned yet, are part of the "seasons" of Gen. 1:14; with day and night, they become part of God's promise after the flood that creation is no longer in danger:

> GEN. 8:22 As long as the earth shall last,
> Seedtime and harvest, cold and heat,

---

* This is Job 41:1–8 in Christian Bibles.

> Summer and winter, day and night
> Shall never cease.

All these elements are in the creation story with which our Bible begins. But, for Psalm 74, the taming of Leviathan and the establishment of control over the waters is just as much a part of the creation story as the establishment of day and night. This element, however, is not told in Genesis 1—at least, not until you have sharpened your ears enough to be able to hear the few notes of it that echo in the casual phrase, "God created the great dragons."* We see too that there is more to God's creating the world by acts of speech than we might have suspected. Speaking—"Let there be light!"—is not merely an invocation. It is also a command. God's power is to be measured not merely by the magnitude of his creativity, but also by the magnitude of his competition, the forces against which he had to contend in the course of creation.

Even Second Isaiah, the prophet of the return from Babylonian exile, who denied that anyone other than YHWH alone was involved in the creation of the world, knew this story. He invokes the story to reassure the people—less theologically sophisticated than he is—that God's power to rescue them from their Babylonian captivity is unchallengeable. Notice, however, that all these epithets are addressed not to YHWH himself but to his mighty "Arm":

> ISA. 51:9 Awake! Awake! Put on your strength, O Arm of YHWH!
> Awake as in days of old and generations of yore!
> Are not you the Hewer of Rahab, Piercer of Dragon?

---

* It is "God" in Genesis 1, not YHWH, because the priestly voice recounting this story does not want the name YHWH revealed until the time of Moses. Psalm 78 is part of the Elohistic psalter (Psalms 42–83), which prefers the generic "God" to the name YHWH, which most likely originally appeared here. (Compare Psalm 14 and Psalm 53 to see that such changes were indeed made.)

¹⁰ Are not you the Scorcher of Sea and the waters of great Deep,
Who puts a path in the depths of Sea for the redeemed to cross,
¹¹ So that YHWH's redeemed may return and come back to Zion in joy?

This time, the elements of the creation battle story—slaying the sea monsters and forcing the sea back so that the dry land might appear—have another element added to them that is familiar to us from a totally different story in the Bible. In Genesis, the dry land vacated by the sea is simply the continents and islands of the earth on which human beings can live. But in the lines we have just seen, the dry land from which the sea has been pushed back by God's might is not a place for settlement, but a path by which the people can travel back to Zion—that is, the Land of Israel. This aspect of the image comes not from creation, but from the story of the exodus and the Israelite slaves' crossing the Red Sea ahead of the pursuing Egyptian army.

Creation and the Exodus

Clearing a path through the desert for the return from Babylonia, then, was a comparable feat to pushing back the waters of the Red Sea so the Israelites could escape from Egypt—and even that was a rematch, another episode in the same fight that had begun as long ago as creation. Second Isaiah was not the first to come up with this idea. It is intrinsic to the exodus story itself. Exodus 15, the famous "Song at the Sea," describes the parting of the Red Sea not just as a formative event in the life of the People of Israel, but (when one's ear is tuned to the subtle nuances of the text) as the actual culmination of creation:

> EXOD. 15:4 Pharaoh's chariots and his army He cast into the sea; the pick of his cavalry were drowned in the Sea of Reeds.
> ⁵ Deeps covered them, they sank in the depths like a stone.
> ⁶ Your right hand, O majestically mighty YHWH, Your right hand shatters the foe.

> ⁷ With Your stature so awesome You destroy those who rise against You—You let loose a blaze of anger that consumes them like straw!
> ⁸ At a blast from Your nostrils, the waters pile up; the flow stands still as a dam: Deeps freeze in the heart of the sea.

"The foe" here, of course, is not the sea but the Egyptians. God splits the sea to let the Israelites through and then restores it to its natural place to drown the pursuing army. Yet this is poetry, not reportage. When we read that "Your right hand shatters the foe," we cannot help recalling that God's primordial foe was not the Egyptians but "Sea" itself. Once we remember that, we notice what God is doing in this story. In Exod. 15:8, as in Genesis, he is shoving the sea out of the way to make room for people.

This implies that, as late as the exodus, creation was not yet completely finished. And indeed the poem of Exodus 15 will, at last, bring creation to its long-awaited culmination. This is the subtle but unmistakable point of the song's triumphant conclusion:

> EXOD. 15:15 The movers of Edom and the shakers of Moab are stunned.
> Trembling seizes them, all the inhabitants of Canaan are shaken.
> ¹⁶ Fear and terror fall upon them—at the might of Your arm they become still as a stone,
> Till Your people crosses, YHWH, till Your people crosses whom You created.
> ¹⁷ You bring them and plant them in the mountain of Your possession, the site You made for Your dwelling place, O YHWH,
> The Sanctuary, O Lord, which Your hands established.
> ¹⁸ YHWH shall reign forever and ever!

Listen to it closely. The song that celebrates the Israelites' hairbreadth escape from their Egyptian slavemasters—an escape dependent upon YHWH's power to command the sea to withdraw and return at his word—ends with an event that, from a purely historical perspective, is still far in the future. The Israelites are still forty years away from entering their land, and (according to 1 Kgs. 6:1, which we saw in chapter 2) another 440 years have yet to pass after that before Solomon will build YHWH's Temple in Jerusalem. Yet according to Exodus 15, the planting of the people in "the mountain of Your possession," "the Sanctuary . . . which Your hands established," is the inevitable culmination of this second round of the cosmic battle with the Sea.

Here too the Mesopotamian creation legends in the Enuma Elish give us a clearer perspective on the background to a biblical text. In Genesis, the story of creation is like a prologue. It describes the preparation of the stage set, as it were, for the history of humanity, and specifically for the relationship between God and Israel that begins with the friendship between God and Israel's first ancestor, Abraham. But in the Enuma Elish, the epic of creation is a story unto itself. It begins with a mighty battle between the gods, and it culminates with the triumph of one of the gods and the capstone of that triumph, the building of the god's temple on earth.

Thus the plot of the Enuma Elish concludes majestically with the building of the Esagila Temple in Babylon, where the Babylonian god Marduk can rule forever and be worshiped as the great creator of all things. Exodus 15 translates this idea into Israelite terms. A song that begins with God's control of the sea ends with the establishment of his Temple on his holy mountain (presumably Mount Zion in Jerusalem) and his installation as eternal king. This undoubtedly also explains why so much of the book of Exodus is devoted to the construction of the Tabernacle. In the prose story, *it* is the culmination of creation. (I will leave to you the opportunity to trace connections between creation and the Tabernacle; you can start by comparing the beginning of Gen. 2:2 with the end of Exod. 40:33.)

The great biblical innovation in this idea, the invention of some unknown genius of literature and religious thought, was to integrate the earthly history of a people into what otherwise would be an essentially mythological story of a god's struggle for supremacy. The exodus, the event that marked the entrance of the People of Israel onto the world stage, was in this reading not just a historical event. It was a cosmological one. The forging of this mass of escaped slaves into a nation was not just another page in history, but a chapter in the process of turning the world into a civilized place. It was an intrinsic part of the unfinished work of creation. Looked at from another angle, an Israel out of its place—whether in Egypt or across the earth in Mesopotamia—meant that the work of creation was still unfinished.

Exodus and Creation in Psalm 114

Let us look at one final example of this theme, one whose resonance is clear now that we have become attuned to the implications of God's power over the sea. This is Psalm 114, from the section of the book of Psalms that is considered the "Praise" of God par excellence and is still used in Jewish prayer services on the holidays when special praise of God is called for:

> **PS. 114:1** When Israel went out of Egypt, the house of Jacob from a barbarian folk,
> **2** Judah became His holy place and Israel His dominion.
> **3** The Sea saw and fled, the Jordan turned backward.
> **4** The mountains danced like rams, the hills like lambs.
> **5** What's with you, O Sea, that you flee? O Jordan, that you turn backward?
> **6** O mountains, that you dance like rams? O hills, like lambs?
> **7** Quake before the Lord, O Earth, before the God of Jacob!—
> **8** Who turns rock into a pool, flint into a spring of water.

No need for battle here; the issue had been decided at the dawn of time. The Sea saw that God's people were approaching and fled from the confrontation with him. Forty years later—the whole process of the exodus is compressed here into a single moment of cosmological time—the Jordan too flees to permit Israel to cross into their land dry shod. (For the prose description of this event, see Joshua 3.) The mountains too quake at God's approach, showing his complete domination over the processes that created the primordial earth. Dry land and sea are opposites, the two great poles in the physics of geological creation seen in biblical terms. But as easily as God can lift up a dry mountain where once there was sea, so he can turn that mountain's very bedrock back into water.

Yet this control over the great elemental processes of geology does more than demonstrate God's power. It is also an essential moment, not merely in world history, as Israel crosses the uninhabited desert to take possession of its homeland, but in individual human lives. God's mighty power to mobilize and (when necessary) reverse the process of creation is exerted to let his people drink when they are thirsty. Physics becomes metaphysics, and history with a small "h" becomes History with a capital H, in this unique event that shaped the People of Israel. To understand it, you must first be able to hear, as the ancient Israelites could, the echoes of God's battle with the Sea at the beginning of creation.

In this chapter, we've taken a long journey to arrive at the same place we started—with the exodus (and its "ten" plagues)—but on higher ground. We've seen that the stories of the Bible were told not only in prose, but also in poetry, and that the poetic versions can flesh out the stories with details that may dramatically change our view of them. In particular, we've seen that the Bible clearly presents the creation of the world as the culmination of a battle between the God of the Bible and a god who was the personification of the Sea. I say "clearly" because we've encountered verses in biblical poems that make no secret of this. But the standard version of creation, at the beginning of Genesis, reflects this ancient myth in a much more subtle way.

Perhaps more surprisingly, we've seen that, from some biblical perspectives, the creation story does not end with Genesis 3. The entire story of the exodus from Egypt, in this view, is not primarily about freeing the Israelites from slavery, but about creating a Tabernacle/Temple in which YHWH could be worshiped on earth, thus establishing once and for all his divine supremacy over the rival Sea that had obstructed, first, the creation, and subsequently, the exodus. This message is there for all to see, but it is biblical poetry, not the simple stories we learned as children, that conveys it—poetry that assumes a familiarity with ancient Canaanite myths about a battle with the god of Sea.

It was not sea, of course, but desert that separated Babylonia from the Land of Israel. Yet the brilliant insight of Second Isaiah was that the return from exile was a new exodus. The ancient Near Eastern world, throughout the biblical period, had two great centers of power: Egypt and Mesopotamia. The exodus from Egypt had marked Israel's birth as a people. Now, according to Second Isaiah's conception, a renewed exodus—this time from the other end of the earth, from Babylonia—would turn the tribulations of the intervening centuries into a symmetrical, *planned* pattern that would culminate in the end of political history, leaving only a peaceful world where, in the words of Micah, "Everyone will sit under his vine and his fig tree, with none to disturb him" (Mic. 4:4). Only then—at last!—the work of creation would finally be over, and God's mighty Arm could be still.

10
Echoes and Reverberations

As we've seen, the biblical voices carried on a lively exchange for a thousand years. So the obvious question arises: Why did this exchange stop? That is, why didn't the voices continue? Why aren't there more books in the Bible than we have today?

The first answer, of course, is that there *are* more "books of the Bible." The most obvious example is the Christian New Testament. The books in it are not part of the Jewish Bible, but they are part of a different Bible, one that was not willing to shut off the conversation quite so soon. Admittedly, the books of the New Testament are separated from those of the Jewish Bible (the same ones, in a different order, that make up the Christian Old Testament) by a gap both in time and in language. This gap is filled by the books of the Apocrypha, which are part of the Catholic Bible, but not of the Protestant Bible. (For a refresher on this topic, return to "Whose Bible Is It?") As the earliest of the books that are biblical for some but not for others, these will begin to open a window for us on how the books that are in everyone's Bible have echoed down the centuries.

The Wisdom of Ben Sira

The kind of timeless wisdom that we encounter in the book of Proverbs did not cease to be written when that book was completed. We find much more of it in one of the Apocryphal books, the Wisdom of Ben Sira. To pick just one example, compare "He that loveth his son causeth him oft to feel the rod, that he may have joy of him in the end" (Sir. 30:1) with "He that spareth his rod hateth his son: but he that loveth him chasteneth him betimes" (Prov. 13:24; both in the King James translation). But Ben Sira and Proverbs have one significant difference: Ben Sira is concerned with Jewish history.

As we learned in chapter 7, the wisdom books of Proverbs, Ecclesiastes, and Job are unique in the Jewish Bible because the story of the Israelites is completely missing from them. They speak to their readers not as Jews, but simply as human beings whose native language happens to be Hebrew. Much of Ben Sira is the same—but in chapter 44 of the book, this changes dramatically, with the following invocation: "Let us now praise famous men." From here on, the book is a kind of travelogue, moving through the Jewish story in a hymn of praise to the great heroes of that story: Enoch, Noah, Abraham, Isaac, Jacob, Moses, Aaron, Phinehas, Joshua, Caleb, Samuel, David, Solomon, Elijah, Elisha, Hezekiah, Isaiah, Josiah, Jeremiah, Ezekiel, Zerubbabel and his priestly counterpart Jeshua son of Jozadak, Nehemiah, and the High Priest of Ben Sira's own time, Simon (or Simeon) son of Onias.

Yet Ben Sira was not merely continuing the wisdom tradition. He clearly had an eye on Proverbs itself as his model. Remember that in Proverbs Wisdom declares, "YHWH created me at the beginning of his way, before his works of yore. . . . I was birthed when there were no Deeps, no flowing springs of water. Ere the bases of the mountains were sunk, before the hills was I born" (Prov. 8:22, 24–25). Ben Sira too has this image of Wisdom as a living, female character:

> SIR. 24:1 Wisdom shall praise herself, and shall glory in the midst of her people. ² In the congregation of the most High shall she open her mouth, and triumph before his power. ³ "I came out of the mouth of the most High, and covered the earth as a cloud. ⁴ I dwelt in high places, and my throne is in a cloudy pillar. ⁵ I

alone compassed the circuit of heaven, and walked in the bottom of the deep."

And after his long sweep through Israelite history, just before a final hymn of praise to God, we find these lines: "There be two manner of nations which my heart abhorreth, and the third is no nation: They that sit upon the mountain of Samaria, and they that dwell among the Philistines, and that foolish people that dwell in Sichem" (Sir. 50:25–26). These verses recall the numerical sayings found in the second half of Proverbs 30. For example:

> PROV. 30:18 There be three things too wonderful for me,
> Four that I do not understand:
> ¹⁹ The way of an eagle in the sky,
> The way of a serpent on a rock,
> The way of a ship in the heart of the sea,
> The way of a man with a maiden.

You will also find this n, $n + 1$ pattern—"two things, yea, three"; "three things, even four"—at the beginning of the book of Amos: "Thus said YHWH: For three transgressions of Damascus, yes, for four, I will not reverse the punishment" (Amos 1:3). The pattern is repeated seven more times in the first two chapters of Amos. In fact, this pattern is far more ancient than the Bible. Here is an example from the Ugaritic myth of Baal, a millennium before Ben Sira:

> Now there are two (kinds of) feasts (that) Ba'alu hates,
> three (that) Cloud-Rider (hates):
> An improper feast,
> a low-quality feast,
> and a feast where the female servants misbehave.*

---

* The translation is taken from Florentino García Martínez and Eibert J. C. Tigchelaar, eds., *The Dead Sea Scrolls Study Edition* (Leiden: Brill, 1997–1998), 1:41.

This chapter is about the voices that echo after the Bible. But as we learn from this example, and as we saw over and over in chapters 8 and 9, the Bible itself echoes voices from texts still more ancient.

Since Ben Sira is part of the Catholic and (Christian) Orthodox Bibles but not of the Jewish one, it was preserved not in Hebrew but in a Greek translation by Ben Sira's grandson, sometime after he moved to Egypt in 132 BCE. It was not until the late 19th century that the first, partial manuscripts of Ben Sira in the original Hebrew were found again. Yet a few verses of the book did survive through the ages in Hebrew, and indeed were treated in Rabbinic literature as if they were biblical verses after all.

To see how this was possible, let's look first at one of the most important things we learn from the preface that Ben Sira's grandson affixed to his translation. He tells us that his grandfather was especially devoted "to the reading of the law, and the prophets, and other books of our fathers." This is the earliest indication that we have of the three parts of the Jewish version of the Bible: the Torah or "law," the Nevi'im or "prophets," and the Ketuvim or "writings." (These three sections give the Jewish Bible its modern name, "Tanakh," an acronym of their Hebrew names.) The New Testament has a similar, somewhat later reference to three categories of biblical writings, when Jesus refers to the things he says were written about him "in the law of Moses, and in the prophets, and in the psalms" (Luke 24:44).

Nowadays the books that fall into category three, "the Writings," are specifically defined. But we can see from these two references that, in the centuries when the Bible was just coming together as a unified collection of books, the third category was somewhat undefined: "the psalms" (in the verse from Luke) and "the other writings" in the words of Ben Sira's grandson two centuries before. This looser definition must have continued to be the case for some centuries afterward, for the Babylonian Talmud (ca. 600 CE) cites Ben Sira a number of times as if it were a biblical book. It was, of course, the open-ended nature of the Bible as an anthology that gave rise to the four different collections in use as "Bible" today by Jews, Catholics, Orthodox Christians, and Protestants. Ben Sira, though it is an entirely Jewish book, was ultimately excluded from the Jewish Bible, yet found its way into two of the Christian Bibles.

The Dead Sea Scrolls

But there are other books whose authors equally intended them to be part of the Bible that are not accepted by anyone. Indeed, the ones we know about at all have only barely managed to survive. The most famous of these are well known to everyone, by name if not by contents—they are among the Dead Sea Scrolls. One of them, called the Temple Scroll, was clearly written to be part of the Pentateuch, or perhaps even to replace it. More interesting for the long-term history of the Bible is another, lesser-known kind of book, of a kind that scholars call "rewritten Bible." Such books take biblical texts as their starting point and rewrite those earlier texts, changing and expanding them as they go. It is not that different from what we saw in chapter 2, when the Chronicler came along, two hundred years later, and rewrote the Deuteronomistic History.

Here, for example, is a passage from a text called the Genesis Apocryphon:

> "How lovely are her eyes; how pleasant her nose and all the blossom of her face. . . . How graceful is her breast and how lovely all her whiteness! How beautiful are her arms! And her hands, how perfect! How alluring is the whole appearance of her hands! How pretty are the palms of her hands and how long and supple all the fingers of her hands! Her feet, how lovely! How perfect her thighs! No virgin or wife who enters the bridal chamber is more beautiful than her. Above all women her beauty stands out; her loveliness is far above them all. And with all this beauty there is in her great wisdom. And everything she does with her hands is perfect."

When the king heard the words of Hirqanos and the words of his two companions, which the three of them spoke in unison, he desired her greatly and sent immediately for her to be fetched. He saw her and was amazed at all her beauty, and took her for himself as a wife. He wanted to kill me, but Sarai said to the king, "He is my brother," so that I could profit at her expense. I, Abram, was spared on her account and I was not killed. But I wept bitterly that night, I, Abram, and my nephew Lot with me, because Sarai had been taken away from me by force.*

The first paragraph of this excerpt sounds as if it came from the Song of Songs. But the second paragraph makes clear that this is an expanded version of a story we know from Genesis. Let's look at how the story was told in the original book of Genesis, the one that's in our Bibles today:

> GEN. 12:10 It happened that there was a famine in the land. So Abram went down to live in Egypt—for the famine in the land was very severe. 11 When he got near Egypt, he said to Sarai, his wife, "Look—I know that you are a good-looking woman. 12 When the Egyptians see you, they will think, 'She is his wife,' and they will kill me and let you live. 13 Tell them you are my sister, so that they will treat me well on your account. Then, thanks to you, my life will be safe."
> 14 When Abram reached Egypt, the Egyptians saw that the woman was very beautiful. 15 Pharaoh's officials saw her and praised her to Pharaoh, with the result that the woman was taken into Pharaoh's palace. 16 Meanwhile, Abram was treated very well on her account—he acquired sheep, cattle, donkeys, slaves, asses, and camels.

The Genesis Apocryphon (a name given to the "rewritten Bible" text we just quoted by the twentieth-century scholars who first pub-

---

* Translated by Dennis Pardee in *The Context of Scripture* (Leiden: Brill, 2003), 1:258.

lished it) has expanded the biblical phrase "Pharaoh's officials saw her and praised her to Pharaoh" by providing the panoramic description of Sarai that we read above. We no longer have to take Abram's word for how beautiful Sarai is; we can see her beauty for ourselves. But the second paragraph in the Genesis Apocryphon version does not merely tell us more than the original story does; it changes how we understand the story. In Genesis, Abram seems rather cold-blooded about the whole affair. In the revised version told by the Genesis Apocryphon, he weeps bitterly at the idea that his wife is with another man. Sarai too weeps (in a passage I did not quote) when Abram originally proposes the plan to her. Even Lot weeps!

The surprising thing about Lot's tears for his aunt is that Lot is not in the Genesis version of the story at all. So his weeping must play a more significant role in the story than merely changing the neutral tone of the original narrative to a more emotional one. Why has the author of the Genesis Apocryphon added Lot to the story? The answer is simple. In Genesis, Lot travels with Abram and Sarai to Canaan at the beginning of chapter 12 and then vanishes. When Abram and Sarai return from Egypt, in Genesis 13, Lot is accompanying them. It would seem, then, that Lot must have gone down to Egypt with them. After all, the famine would have affected him as much as it did them. If Lot was indeed on the scene, he would naturally have been almost as distraught as Abram that Sarai had been seized by Pharaoh.

Even this brief excerpt from the Genesis Apocryphon is enough to show us some of the ways in which the "facts" of the biblical stories could be clarified or augmented in a "rewritten Bible" text:

> Lot is with Abram and Sarai in Egypt. This *makes explicit* something that seemed to the author of the Genesis Apocryphon to be implicit in the original version of the story.
>
> Abram weeps when his wife is taken from him. This *adds* to the original story an aspect that the author of the Apocryphon felt was missing from it. Genesis tells the story in an

emotionally neutral way; the Genesis Apocryphon describes Abram's feelings when his wife is taken away.

Sarai's beauty is described. This magnificent burst of *poetry* gives the author an opportunity to entertain his audience; to frame the story as part of a Bible that also includes the Song of Songs; and, perhaps most of all, to express his own creative impulses in a way that could make an ancient, sacred story fresh and new.

The story of Abram and Sarai in Egypt is perfectly recognizable in the new, later version told in the Genesis Apocryphon. But it is given an overall flavor that is somewhat different from that in the Bible. Sarai does not tell "the king" that Abram is her brother until the threat to kill him—merely anticipated in the original version—is made explicit. Abram is not stolid (or stoic), but emotional. Sarai is described as being wise as well as beautiful. Some of these differences in how the story is told may have been prompted by cultural differences between two societies separated by many centuries; others are due to the authors' differing individual perspectives.

The New Testament

The Genesis Apocryphon vanished for close to two thousand years. Even Ben Sira is somewhat obscure nowadays (though San Franciscans will find a verse from it inscribed under the clock face of Old St. Mary's Cathedral at the corner of California and Grant). But there is one book that is still very contemporary in which the Hebrew texts of the Bible (albeit in English translation) continue to reverberate in our own society. I refer, of course, to the Greek part of the Bible, the books that are not biblical for Jews but are biblical for all three different Christian groupings: the New Testament.

As with the Apocrypha and the Dead Sea Scrolls, we will be able to look at just the smallest sampling of how earlier biblical texts echo in the New Testament. The examples we'll look at—all originating in the book of Isaiah—will give us a variety of perspectives on the afterlife of biblical texts.

A Prophecy Fulfilled

Let's begin with a story from Matthew 13. Jesus has just preached to a crowd on the shore of the Sea of Galilee (today's Lake Kinneret), speaking to them "in parables," that is, stories that are not factual but metaphorical. (Remember that the Hebrew word for such parables in Rabbinic literature, *mashal*, is the same word used for a "proverb" in the Bible.) Jesus tells the following story: A man is sowing a field. Some of the seeds are eaten by birds, some fall on stony ground, some fall among thorns, and some on good ground; only the last of these bring forth fruit. Jesus concludes, "Who hath ears to hear, let him hear." But his disciples are puzzled:

> MATT. 13:10 Then the disciples came and asked him, "Why do you speak to them in parables?" 11 He answered, "To you it has been given to know the secrets of the kingdom of heaven, but to them it has not been given. 12 For to those who have, more will be given, and they will have an abundance; but from those who have nothing, even what they have will be taken away. 13 The reason I speak to them in parables is that 'seeing they do not perceive, and hearing they do not listen, nor do they understand.' 14 With them indeed is fulfilled the prophecy of Isaiah that says:
>
> "'You will indeed listen, but never understand,
> and you will indeed look, but never perceive.
> 15 "'For this people's heart has grown dull,
> and their ears are hard of hearing,
> and they have shut their eyes;
> so that they might not look with their eyes,
> and listen with their ears,
> and understand with their heart and turn—
> and I would heal them.'
>
> 16 "But blessed are your eyes, for they see, and your ears, for they hear. 17 Truly I tell you, many prophets and righteous people

longed to see what you see, but did not see it, and to hear what you hear, but did not hear it." (NRSV)

Jesus is referring to Isaiah 6. In this chapter, Isaiah sees a vision of God on his throne, being praised by the angels. (It is v. 3 of this chapter that contains the famous trisagion ["three holies"] when the angels call out to each other, "Holy, holy, holy is YHWH of Hosts!") After the angels' praise dies away, Isaiah hears God call out, "Whom shall I send? Who will go for us?" He replies, "Here I am—send me!" (Isa. 6:8). And here are the instructions he is given:

ISA. 6:9 Tell this people:
"Listen, indeed, but do not understand;
look, indeed, but do not perceive."
10 Make this people's heart dull,
and their ears hard of hearing,
and shut their eyes;
so that they might not look with their eyes,
and listen with their ears,
and understand with their heart and turn—
and I would heal them.

Isaiah, like the people to whom he was sent, has been dead for 750 years by the time Jesus speaks, but he reuses the prophet's words to explain to his disciples why he spoke in riddles and not plainly. His message, he implies, is only for "those who have ears to hear." The ancient prophet's words apply once again, just as they had in 734 BCE, "the year of King Uzziah's death" (Isa. 6:1).

Jesus' saying that, with his foolish hearers, "the prophecy of Isaiah is fulfilled" is of special interest. We have already seen (in chapter 5) a case where the unnamed prophet of Isa. 40:2 declared that a prophecy in Jer. 16:18 had been fulfilled. Here too an earlier prophecy reverberates in a later text that declares it fulfilled. In Matthew alone there are half a dozen mentions of Isaiah, three of Jeremiah, one of Jonah, one of Daniel, and still more that simply refer to the words of "the prophet" without mentioning the prophet's name. There are many more such references in the other books of the New Testament. And of course in our own time we still hear people declare that a biblical prophecy has been fulfilled.

A Voice Crying in the Wilderness

One of the most interesting references to an earlier biblical text is the phrase from the gospel of Mark identifying John the Baptist:

> MARK 1:3 The voice of one crying in the wilderness, Prepare ye the way of the Lord, make his paths straight.

This is in fact a quotation from "the prophets," which (as we might expect) the parallel text in Matthew makes clear:

> MATT. 3:3 For this is he that was spoken of by the prophet Esaias [Isaiah], saying, The voice of one crying in the wilderness, Prepare ye the way of the Lord, make his paths straight.

Luke gives us even more of the original:

> LUKE 3:4 As it is written in the book of the words of Esaias the prophet, saying, The voice of one crying in the wilderness, Prepare ye the way of the Lord, make his paths straight. ⁵Every valley shall be filled, and every mountain and hill shall be brought low; and the crooked shall be made straight, and the rough ways shall be made smooth; ⁶And all flesh shall see the salvation of God.

The original source of these citations, however, is just a bit different from the way Luke (originally in Greek) has cited it:

> ISA. 40:3 The voice of him that crieth in the wilderness, Prepare ye the way of the LORD, make straight in the desert a highway for our God. ⁴ Every valley shall be exalted, and every mountain and

hill shall be made low: and the crooked shall be made straight, and the rough places plain: ⁵ And the glory of the LORD shall be revealed, and all flesh shall see it together: for the mouth of the LORD hath spoken it. (KJV)

Luke concludes "the cry in the wilderness" by saying that "all flesh shall see the salvation of God," while the original cry ended by saying that "the glory of the LORD shall be revealed, and all flesh shall see it together: for the mouth of the LORD hath spoken it." The prophet was saying that God's Presence would be revealed in the world; the gospel writer drew the implication that this revelation was to bring salvation.

I've chosen this example because the "voice crying in the wilderness" (thanks to King James) is a common phrase in English now, though we use it differently than the New Testament examples do. When John the Baptist identified himself as the "voice crying in the wilderness" of Isa. 40:3, he was calling himself a harbinger of God's imminent appearance on earth, and "in the wilderness" applied to him literally (Mark 1:4, Matt. 3:1, Luke 3:2). Nowadays, the phrase denotes someone with something important to say who is not listened to. His message is not heard on Main Street—let alone on AM radio, where he might really have an influence—but in the wilderness, that is, in an uninhabited region where there is no one to listen.

A Voice Crying, "In the Wilderness . . ."

Most Bible readers have probably never wondered exactly why the prophet was invoking the image of "a voice crying in the wilderness." The New Testament explains it: it was indeed a prediction about John the Baptist, who did preach "in the wilderness," so the phrase makes perfect sense. There is only one problem. The King James translation is not what the original Hebrew says.

It is not that the King James translators misunderstood the words. Rather—as in the story about the panda who eats, shoots, and leaves—they ignored the punctuation. Here is how the NJPS translators, following the Hebrew punctuation, translated the Isaiah text:

ISA. 40:3 A voice rings out:
"Clear in the desert
A road for the LORD!
Level in the wilderness
A highway for our God!
⁴ Let every valley be raised,
Every hill and mount made low.
Let the rugged ground become level
And the ridges become a plain.
⁵ The Presence of the LORD shall appear,
And all flesh, as one, shall behold—
For the LORD Himself has spoken."

Don't let the slightly different English word choices distract you. The difference between the two translations boils down to this:

> KJV: A voice cries in the wilderness . . .

> NJPS: A voice cries, "In the wilderness . . ."

In the original text, it is not the person crying out who (like John the Baptist) is in the wilderness. Rather, he is crying out the *words* "in the wilderness"! To carry the quotation a bit further: he is not crying out in the wilderness "Prepare a way for the LORD"; he is crying out, "In the wilderness, prepare a way for the LORD."

The historical context of the original passage makes clear what it is about. These are not the words of the eighth-century prophet Isaiah of Jerusalem, but those of the prophet scholars call "Second Isaiah," the sixth-century prophet during the era of the Judean return from exile on the heels of the Persian conquest of Babylonia. The vision of this prophet, as we saw in chapter 9, is that the return from exile is a bookend to the ancient Israelites' return to their land from slavery in Egypt. Just as YHWH opened a path through the sea (and later through the Jordan) so the escaped slaves could get to their land easily, now again he would create a smooth highway through the wilderness—the rugged, inhospitable, uninhabited desert between Mesopotamia and Israel—so that this second (and in the prophet's eyes, final) return could take place with a minimum of difficulty.

The Poetry of Parallels (Reprise)

I said that the KJV translators ignored the punctuation, but that is a bit of a stretch. What they ignored was the *implicit* punctuation of the verse. The system of Hebrew punctuation was devised, along with the vowel markings, not much more than a thousand years or so ago. That means that the punctuation itself is a kind of commentary on the much older text, which consisted only of consonants. How can I be so sure that the punctuators, and not Mark, Matthew, and Luke, correctly understood what the prophet was trying to say?

The answer is that this text is not written in prose, but in poetry. It will take an entire book—the sequel to this one—to demonstrate how the great poems of the Bible work, but the essential secret to biblical poetry is in a single word: parallelism. We encountered this in chapter 8 when we looked briefly at Deut. 32:1, which uses one of the word pairs known to us from Ugaritic poetry. Let's look now in more detail at Isa. 40:4, in the King James Version's own language but arranged in four lines, to see how the parallelism there works:

1	Every valley	shall be	exalted,
2	and every mountain and hill	shall be made	low:
3	and the crooked	shall be made	straight,
4	and the rough places		plain

Without going into too much detail, you can see that the first two phrases (lines 1 and 2) and the last two phrases (lines 3 and 4) of this verse are matching pairs. As scholars would say, they are "parallel" to each other. "The rough places" is just another way of referring to "the crooked" ground over which the returnees would have to travel; "plain" is another way of saying "straight." (Notice that we implicitly read "shall be made" in *both* phrases, not just the phrase in which it appears.)

The first two phrases work in a similar but slightly different fashion. "Low" is not the same as "exalted"; rather, it is the polar opposite, just as "mountains and hills" are the opposite of "valleys." These two pairs are antonyms instead of synonyms, but they are nonetheless clearly parallel to each other. Most importantly, these two opposite phrases share a meaning. When valleys are raised, just as when mountains are lowered, difficult terrain becomes flat and easy to cross.

Now let's examine the parallelism of v. 3, this time in my translation:

> A voice calls out:
> "Clear a road in the wilderness for YHWH;
> Straighten in the steppe a highway for our God."

These lines are also parallel to each other, though the pairs are not lined up in the same order (even in the Hebrew) the way they are in v. 4. This simply means that the poetry is more intricate. Here is how it looks when we rearrange the words to show how everything matches:

| In the wilderness | clear a road | for YHWH |
| In the steppe | straighten a highway | for our God |

"In the wilderness" matches "in the steppe." It is not *where* the voice is speaking, but part of what it is saying. That is why Luke's quotation from Isaiah omits "in the desert" of the KJV (= "in the steppe" of my translation). Because its parallel phrase, "in the wilderness," has been moved *outside* of the quotation, so "in the desert" had to be removed as well. There was no longer anything for it to be parallel to.

Making the Bible Cohere

Were the King James translators misreading Isa. 40:3 out of ignorance? Certainly not. They would most likely say that they were not misreading it at all—merely reading it as it was intended to be read in later ages instead of the way it was meant to be read when it was written. Once John the Baptist used the biblical words to describe his own preaching, he transformed how they would be read in all future time. The King James translators—for whom, as Christians, the New Testament was also part of the Bible—translated the original Hebrew phrase to make it cohere with the other occurrences of the phrase in their own Bible. This is the same reason that the King James Bible translated the first word of Genesis as "In the beginning"—to match the first words of the gospel of John—even though (as we saw in chapter 1) that is not its original meaning.

The sages who created the classic postbiblical literature of the Jews were masters of rereading the Bible in this way. This activity of seeking answers from the biblical text that were not explicitly written in it, pursued by later generations of Jews, is called "midrash," from the Biblical Hebrew verb *darash*, meaning "to seek an answer" or "to investigate." The assumption was that even if the Bible does not say something in plain Hebrew you can often find it out if you read between the lines. This, for example, is how the creators of Jewish tradition "discovered" the names of the many biblical characters whose names are not recorded in the text. As an example, let's look at this question: What was the name of Job's wife?

What Was the Name of Job's Wife?

As we saw in chapter 7, the name of Job's wife is not given in the biblical book itself. Her only appearance in the story is in Job 2, after the Prosecutor has afflicted Job with a terrible skin disease:

> JOB 2:9 Then his wife said to him, "Do you still cling to your propriety? Bless God and die!" 10 He replied to her, "What you are saying is outrageous! Should we accept good from God and not willingly accept evil also?"

The Aramaic translation makes one slight addition to the text:

> Then his wife Dinah said to him . . .

How did the translator come up with this name?

Though we cannot know for sure, he was probably following the same logic that we find in a midrashic text called *Bereshit Rabbah* ("Genesis Plus"). There is, after all, a quite obvious connection between Genesis and Job: Job comes from "the land of Uz" (Job 1:1), and Uz happens to be the name of one of Abraham's nephews:

> GEN. 22:20 After these things, Abraham was told, "Milcah has borne children to your brother Nahor: 21 His firstborn, Uz; his brother Buz; and Kemuel, the father of Aram; 22 Chesed, Hazo, Pildash, Jidlaph, and Bethuel."

On recognizing this name, *Bereshit Rabbah* is prompted to ask, "When did Job live?" One sage takes the obvious cue: he lived in the time of Abraham. But another responds with a different analysis:

> R. Abba son of Kahana said he lived in the time of Jacob. For R. Abba son of Kahana said: Dinah was Job's wife. It is written of Job's wife, "What you are saying is *outrageous*" (Job 2:10), and it is written of Dinah, "He had committed an *outrage* against Israel by sleeping with Jacob's daughter" (Gen. 34:7).

According to this kind of thinking, the Bible reveals its secrets to us by using unusual words. A woman who has been outraged says something outrageous. It "clicks," and we now know who the second woman was even though her name is not written in the text. (Other sages argue that Job lived as late as the time of King Ahasuerus, the husband of Queen Esther, but R. Abba is the only one who identified Job's wife—and his identification stuck.)

There is more to this kind of biblical "investigation" than just identifying unnamed characters; it can also create thought-provoking connections between named characters. If you look again at the Genesis passage where Uz is mentioned, you will notice that it comes from the end of Genesis 22, and (more importantly) that it begins with the same phrase as the chapter does: "After these things." What happened "after these things" at the beginning of the chapter was that God tested Abraham—just as he would test Job. A talmudic source explains that what prompted God to test Abraham was a challenge by the Prosecutor of exactly the same kind that prompted the testing of Job. Indeed, our understanding of both stories can be much more profound when we compare them—as perhaps the author of Job deliberately intended for us to do.

Creative Midrash

Discovering this kind of connection between verses that are far apart from each other in the actual Bible was not always a strictly intellectual endeavor. It also provided an opportunity for literary creativity. The same impulse that leads writers of our own day to create stories and novels, poems and plays, led careful readers of the Bible in earlier centuries to create their own imagined background to the biblical stories. Just as two of Hamlet's supporting actors become stars in their own right in Tom Stoppard's *Rosencrantz and Guildenstern Are Dead*, so characters who play a small role in the Bible as we have it may step up to the footlights in later texts, as the Bible echoes down the centuries. An example will demonstrate not only how creative such later readings can be, but also how carefully such creativity was combined with an extremely precise reading of the text of the Bible.

We start with a biblical verse: "May the Glory of YHWH endure forever—let YHWH rejoice in His works!" (Ps. 104:31). When we saw Job's wife mentioned, it was natural to wonder what her name was; she must have had one. It is a more creative question to wonder just who is saying these words at the end of Psalm 104, and what would prompt such an exclamation. But R. Hanina son of Pappa, in Tractate *Hullin* of the Babylonian Talmud, has done some "investigation" that answers this question. He knew, as we too have seen in chapters 8 and 9, that Psalm 104 is a poem describing the marvels of God's creation. The obvious place to turn to discover the story behind these words at the end of the psalm is, therefore, the story of creation in Genesis 1. The passage that caught R. Hanina's attention was the description of the third day of creation:

GEN. 1:9 God said, "Let the waters be collected under heaven into a single place so that the dry land can appear." And it was so. **10** God called the dry land "earth," and the collection of waters He called "seas." And God saw that it was good. **11** Then God said, "Let the earth bring forth green plants bearing seed, and fruit trees producing fruit with a seed in it of the same kind." And it was so. **12** The earth brought forth green plants bearing seed of the same kind and trees producing fruit with a seed in it of the same kind. And God saw that it was good. **13** There was evening and morning: a third day.

What R. Hanina noticed is the difference between what God commanded and what actually happened. In God's command, the earth is to bring forth:

green plants bearing seed

fruit trees producing fruit with a seed in it of the same kind

What actually came forth was this:

green plants bearing seed *of the same kind*

trees producing fruit with a seed in it of the same kind

The command to produce seeds "of the same kind" (that is, as we would say nowadays, that the various species should reproduce themselves genetically, an apple tree producing another apple tree and not a seed that would grow into a pine or an oak) applies only to the trees, not to the "green plants." Yet they too end up producing seed "of the same kind." How did this happen?

R. Hanina explains:

When the Holy One said "of the same kind" in His command about the trees, the green plants applied an *a fortiori* argument to themselves: "If the Holy One wanted reproduction to be chaotic, why would He say "of the same kind" about the trees? Moreover, if He found it necessary to say this of trees, which do not grow in chaotic profusion, how much more so must He want it to apply to us, who do." Immediately each and every plant produced seed "of the same kind." The Angel of the World opened his mouth and said, "May the Glory of YHWH endure forever—let YHWH rejoice in His works!" (b. Hul. 60a)

What would make God rejoice in his creation? Obviously—a creation (the green plants) that was clever enough to deduce on its own what God wanted, and then to carry out his wishes. The angel supervising creation (himself an interpretation of Wisdom in Proverbs 8) could only marvel at a creation that was smart enough to pitch in and help with the job.

Biblical Voices of Our Own Day

The green plants were not the only creatures who were eager to think along the same lines as the Creator and join him in his work. We human beings have always wanted to do the same. And that—according to what "the Bible says"—is how we were originally made:

> GEN. 1:26 God said, "Let us make an earthling in our image, according to our likeness." . . . 27 And God created the earthling in His image. He created him in the image of God; He created them male and female.

Even before the various works that make up the Bible coalesced into the single book (in all its various forms) that we call by that name, they had seized the human imagination. The biblical voices continue to sound, in the phrases that still pepper our speech, in customs and attitudes, and in some of the most profound creations of the human mind. The few samples we've seen in this chapter of biblical texts living on after the Bible was finished are just "a drop in the bucket" (Isa.

40:15). Tuesday is an especially lucky day in the Jewish imagination, so much so that even nowadays some couples will get married on Tuesday to ensure good fortune. Why? Because according to Genesis 1 that is the day (did you notice?) when "God saw that it was good" *twice*.

Thinking of Tuesday as a lucky day, though it is ultimately derived by interpretation of a biblical passage, is no more than a custom. But sometimes the biblical text reverberates in ways that are almost as profound as the Bible itself. Second Isaiah said:

> ISA. 40:6 All flesh is grass, and all its warmth is like flowers in the field.
> 7 Grass dries up and flowers wither when the spirit of YHWH blows on them. . . .
> 8 Grass dries up and flowers wither—but the word of our God endures forever.

The prophet's own flesh has withered long ago, but his words have not. They occur again in a text from six hundred years later, 1 Peter 1:24–25, where Brahms found them and made them blossom again in the music of his *German Requiem*. Biblical stories live on too, and contemporary writers still discuss the things that matter most to us by creating new works with characters and imagery drawn originally from the Bible. Here, in a twentieth-century poem, God speaks once more to Job:

> I've had you on my mind a thousand years
> To thank you someday for the way you helped me
> Establish once for all the principle
> There's no connection man can reason out
> Between his just deserts and what he gets.
> —Robert Frost, *A Masque of Reason*

Many scholars would agree that this is in fact the message of the book of Job. But it is one thing to say so in a biblical commentary, quite another to say it in a new poem that echoes the biblical poem.

Our world still has many people who proclaim, "The Bible said it, I believe it, and that settles it." But if you have followed me this far on the journey, you know that what "the Bible says" doesn't settle anything. "The Bible says" that David killed Goliath (1 Sam. 17:50) and also that Elhanan killed him (2 Sam. 21:19). Should you answer a fool according to his folly? "The Bible says" that you should (Prov. 26:5) and also that you shouldn't (Prov. 26:4). "The Bible says" that King Solomon told the people he had built a magnificent Temple for God to dwell in forever (1 Kgs. 8:13) and then denied that God's dwelling in it was even possible (1 Kgs. 8:27).

I made a number of promises at the beginning of this book, and I have tried my best to keep them. I said that I would help you tune your ear to the biblical voices, but I also promised that the biblical voices repay careful listening. I said that I would leave you wanting to argue with some of the voices we would hear and to make friends with others. Finally, I said that this book would be no more than an introduction, but not to worry, because "the Bible isn't going anywhere." I know for sure that last statement is true. The Bible has long been, and remains, the most influential book of all time.

On one level, the music of the Bible is simple enough for children to enjoy. The closer you listen to the biblical voices, though, the more you realize that underlying the simple melody of the Bible stories is a complex harmony. If the Bible is the word of God, then (as you might expect) this harmony is not merely intricate, but infinitely intricate. If it is "merely" our human attempt to understand our place in the universe, the music is not infinite but still sufficiently complex to be beyond anyone's ability to grasp fully. Nonetheless, if you have followed me this far, I'm confident you are willing to do what I promised my professor I would do, and that is to keep learning. I have only scratched the surface of biblical poetry in this book, so I have one more promise to make: I intend to write another book that will give you an inside look at the great poems of the Bible. So perhaps we will able to keep learning together.

Jewish and Christian Biblical Order

Jewish	Christian
Genesis	Genesis
Exodus	Exodus
Leviticus	Leviticus
Numbers	Numbers
Deuteronomy	Deuteronomy
Joshua	Joshua
Judges	Judges
1 Samuel	Ruth
2 Samuel	1 Samuel
1 Kings	2 Samuel
2 Kings	1 Kings
Isaiah	2 Kings
Jeremiah	1 Chronicles
Ezekiel	2 Chronicles
Hosea	Ezra
Joel	Nehemiah
Amos	Esther
Obadiah	Job
Jonah	Psalms
Micah	Proverbs

Nahum	Ecclesiastes
Habakkuk	Song of Songs
Zephaniah	Isaiah
Haggai	Jeremiah
Zechariah	Lamentations
Malachi	Ezekiel
Psalms	Daniel
Proverbs	Hosea
Job	Joel
Song of Songs	Amos
Ruth	Obadiah
Lamentations	Jonah
Ecclesiastes	Micah
Esther	Nahum
Daniel	Habakkuk
Ezra	Zephaniah
Nehemiah	Haggai
1 Chronicles	Zechariah
2 Chronicles	Malachi

Index

Books are listed according to the order in the Jewish Bible. When a chapter or verse number differs between the Jewish and Christian Bibles, the Christian numbers are included in a footnote.

Genesis		2:3	143
1	38, 39, 106, 108, 144, 300, 313, 315, 317, 319, 322, 346, 349	2:4	103, 297
		2:5	105
		2:18–19	264
		3	327
1:1	2, 23, 24, 25, 26, 28, 29	3:16	230
		4:1	264n
1:1–2:3	103, 312	4:4	109n
1:1–3	30	4:7	230
1:2	24, 25, 28, 50, 106, 316	4:8	33
		4:25	264, 264n
1:3	315	4:26	116
1:3–5	321	5	102
1:9–13	347	5:1	102
1:14	289, 321	6:9–7:5	104
1:16	289	6–9	317
1:20–21	319	7:1	108
1:26	29, 314, 348	7:4	105, 106
1:29–30	108	7:11	317
2	313	7:11–12	106
2:2	325	8	214

8:15–21	107	4:10	176
8:16	214	4:16	177
8:22	321	6:2–3	36, 115
9	108, 109	7:1	118, 177
9:1–4	109	7:14–24	308
10:10	276	[b]7:25–8:11	308
12	335	[c]8:12–15	308
12:1	116	[d]8:16–28	308, 309
12:5	218	9:1–7	308
12:8	116	9:8–12	308, 309
12:10–16	334	9:13–35	308
13	335	10:1–20	308
20:7	177	10:21–29	308
22	345	11:1–10	308
22:2	82	12:29–36	308
22:20–22	345	14	302
24	209	15	219, 221, 302, 323, 324, 325
24:3	209	15:1	221
24:28	229n	15:4–8	323
24:37	210	15:8	324
24:55	229n	15:15–18	324
25:14	284	15:20	177
32	117	15:20–21	220
[a]32:27–30	117	16	140
34:7	345	16:22–30	140
36	263	17:14	103
36:5	40, 43	18:21	162, 165, 240
36:14	40	18:21–22	162
36:18	40	19	149, 222
38	169, 225	19:10–11	223
38:8–9	168	19:15	223
38:11	169	20	125, 141, 144, 145, 147, 148, 149, 152, 160, 286, 303
44:8	24	20:1	13
Exodus		[e]20:1–14	148
1:1	253	20:8–11	141
1:5	34		
3:15	116		
3:28	146	b. 7:25–8:15	
4	176	c. 8:16–19	
		d. 8:20–32	
a. 32:26–29		e. 20:1–17	

20:10	214	40	114, 121, 122, 150
20:13	135	40:33	325
20:19–23	153	40:33–38	114
ª20:21	125		

Leviticus

20:21–24	130	1:1	150
20:22–26	153	1–7	150, 151, 163
21	125, 286	1–16	165
21:1	149	2:1	217
21:1–23:19	149	4:1	15
21:2	158	8–9	149
21:2–6	153, 156	11:46–47	163
21:4	158	11–16	150, 151, 163
21:28–32	288	13:29	218
21:33–34	154	17–24	165
21:35	286	17–26	151
21–23	11, 152, 163, 286	19:2	161
22:4	154	19:9	227
22:5	154n	19:9–10	170
23:19	154	23:22	170, 227
23:20–33	155	25:1	151, 165
24:4	11	25:39–46	160
24:16	119	25:55	162
24:16–17	112	25–26	165
25:1–31:18	149	26	131, 151
25:8	149	26:46	151, 166
26:3	213	27	151
28	181	27:34	151
28:30	182		

Numbers

32:19	102, 145	6	216, 217
34	102, 145, 148, 303	6:2	217
34:1	102, 103	12:3	255
34:17–26	150	15:32–36	136
34:17–28	146	15:37–39	255
34:27	103	15:39	260
34:27–35	112	16	253
34:28	11, 103, 145	16:29–30	253
35–40	149	19	152
36	261	19:20	215
38:8	212	21:14–15	101
		21:27–30	102
a. 20:24		22:6	185

22:21–35	184	12:5	119, 125
22–24	184	12:11	125
23:12	185	12:32	164n
23:16	184	12–26	119, 152
24:2	184	13:1	164
25	304	15:12	173
26	139	15:12–18	155, 156
27	139	16:13–14	214
27:1–11	137	16:14	214
28–29	152	17:14–20	88
[a]30	215, 229, 237	17:18	103
[b]30:3	215, 216	18:15	177
30:4	215, 216	19:1–13	135
30:4–6	216	19:4–5	135
[c]30:4–16	229n	19:20–23	49
30:7–16	216	20:5	253
30:10	216	24:16	38
30:15	216	24:19–22	170, 227
33	11	25	169, 171, 172
33:2	103	25:5–6	168
35	135	25:5–10	168, 225
36	139	25:7–10	170
		28:58	103
		28:61	103

Deuteronomy

1:5	152	[e]29:20	103
1:15	165, 240	30:10	103
2:8–13	47	30:12	131
2:16–25	48	30:13	131
5	11, 141, 144, 148, 152, 155, 160	30:14	131
		31	102
[d]5:6–18	152	31:12–13	166
5:12–15	141	31:22	102
5:14	214	32	11
6:5	128, 129	32:1	24, 232, 296, 342
12	121	32:1–43	102
12:4–5	119		

Joshua

1:8	7
3	327
8:30–32	164

a. begins at 29:40
b. 30:2
c. 30:3–15
d. 5:6–21
e. 29:21

INDEX

Judges
2:11–23	94
3	93
3:12–30	94
3:15	94
4	302
4:4	177
5	219, 220, 221, 302
5:1	220
9:8–9	266
11:30–31	236
11:34–35	236
11:36–40	237
12:5–6	45
13	117, 226
13:17–18	117
13–16	217
17–18	181
18:14	181

1 Samuel
1:24	201
2:22	212
3:1	180
9	180
9:6	180
9:9	47, 180, 184
9:11	180
9:12–13	46
10:9–13	178
10:12	246
11	35
14	182
14:37	182
14:41	182
15	17
15:11	16, 17, 99, 100
15:24–31	99
15:29	16, 17, 99, 100
15:35	99, 100
16:14	180
16:23	180
17	63
17:4	63, 66
17:7	65, 66
17:23	63
17:48–51	63
17:50	350
18:6–9	220
19:18–24	179
19:24	246
21	65
21:9–10	64
[a]21:12	220
25:29	65
28:6	181, 182
29:4	264
29:5	220
30:7–8	181, 183
30:8	182

2 Samuel
1:19–27	219
2:11	252
7	80, 121, 127, 183, 184
7:4	183
7:6	121
7:7	121
7:13	121
11	70
11:11	70
11:15	70
12	75, 235, 247
12:15	41
12:24	41
12:25	253
13	234
14	233, 235
14:3	234
14:5–7	234
14:13	234
16:16–19	50

a. 21:11

16:18	50	8:46–49	129
19:24	76	8:48	95, 124
20:16–22	234	9:10–11	73
21:19	66, 67, 303, 350	10:1	240
23	70, 71	10:3–5	240
23:8–39	70	10:23	82
23:39	71	10:23–25	83
24	81	10:24–25	82
24:1	263	10:26–29	82, 83, 88
		10–11	89
		11	87, 89, 92

1 Kings

1:1–4	75	11:1–8	82
1:13–14	75	11:3	83
1:31	76	11:4–8	83
1–2	77	11:26–28	87
2	76, 78	11:26–40	84
2:6	76	11:29–39	87
2:9	76, 240	11:31	86
3:4–9	239	11:33	87
3:25	238	11:35	86
5	78, 89, 120, 240	11:40	87
5:3–5	78	11:41	84, 240
5:6	88	12	87
ᵃ5:10–12	241	12:26–29	93
ᵇ5:12	245	13:2	128, 189
5:17–19	78	15:1–3	126, 213
ᶜ5:19	120	18:3–4	177
ᵈ5–8	80	21:17–19	190
6:1	81, 289, 325	22	183, 186, 191, 197n
6–8	253	22:5	183
7:5–8	94	22:6	183
8	95	22:8	187
8:10–12	121	22:10–12	187
8:13	350	22:17	187
8:27	350	22:19–23	188
8:27–30	122	22:24	187
8:44–49	123	22:25	187
		22:26–28	188
		22:34–38	190

a. 4:30–32

b. 4:32

c. 5:5

d. begins at 4:21

2 Kings

2	177
4:3	42

4:8–17	210	6:1	338
5	131	6:3	338
7	283	6:8	338
ᵃ12:5–17	93	6:9–10	338
ᵇ12:21	93	7:8	175
13:15–17	185	13:1	284
13:18–19	186	15:1	284
17:4–6	56	17:1	284
17:7–8	56	19:1	284
17:13–19	57	20:2–3	180
17:23	20	22:4–5	269
18:26	44	29:12	210
18:27	42	30:20	167
19:6–7	12	40	312, 315
19:18–19	12	40:1	194
22:15–20	192	40:1–2	205
22–23	91, 127	40:2	206, 338
23:4–7	92	40:3	340, 343
23:8	92	40:3–5	339, 341
23:10–14	92	40:4	342, 343
23:13	252	40:6–8	349
23:15	93	40:12–14	312
23:16	189	40:15	349
23:21	91	45:1–4	59, 193
23:22–23	90	45:12	312, 313
23:25	128, 189	45:18	312
23:29	192	51:9–11	322
24	36	52:7	194
24:13	204n, 252		
24:20–25:9	55	Jeremiah	
25	36, 55	1:1	14, 258
25:8–9	36	1:4	13
25:17	37	4:6	197
25:27	37	7	311
25:27–30	95	7:9–10	13
		7:17	58
Isaiah		11:6	58
5:1–7	195	13:15	185
6	113, 338	16:18	206, 338
		18:18	231, 233, 238, 261
		19	198
a. 12:4–16		20:4	198
b. 12:20		25	198

25:1	60, 199	52:12–13	37
25:3–5	200	52:22	37
25:8–9	199	52:31	37
26	200, 203, 310, 311		

Ezekiel

26:4–6	200	1:3	111
26:8–9	201	1:26	110
26:10–11	202	1:27–28	111
26:11	52	8–11	58
26:16	52, 202	11:19–20	55
26:17–19	202	14:12–14	262
26:18–19	310	14:13–14	298
26:19	52	14:19–20	298
26:20–23	52, 202	18:20	38
26:24	53, 202	26:7–14	195
26:30	204	28:1–15	299
27:9–11	204	28:16	299
28:2–4	204	44:6	58
28:5	204	48	132
28:9	204	48:35	132
28:10	205		

Amos

28:10–11	205	1:1	12, 258
28:13	205	1:3	331
28:16	205		

Jonah

31:31	6	3:3	29
31:33–34	54	3:4	175
33:10	58	3:5–10	175
34	172, 173	4	176
34:13–14	172		

Micah

36	258	3:12	203, 311
44	310	4:4	328
44:2–6	57	6:8	174
44:15	224		

Zechariah

44:15–19	223	3	264
44:16–18	58, 223		

Malachi

44:20	224	3:18	9
44:21–22	58	3:22–24	8
45:1	14	4:4–6	7
47	197	4:5	8
47:1	197		
47:2–3	198		
47:4–5	198		
51:59–64	185		
51:64	14, 185		

INDEX

Psalms
- 1:2   7
- 4   211
- [a]8:4–5   53
- 8:5   268
- 14   35, 36, 322n
- 14:1   210
- 42–83   36, 322n
- 50   306
- 53   36, 322n
- [b]57:8–12   35
- 60   35
- [c]60:7–14   35
- 60:10   35
- 60:12   35
- 73–83   306
- 74   321, 322
- 74:12–17   321
- 78   303, 304, 306, 307, 308, 309, 311, 322n
- 78:4   307
- 78:13–16   305
- 78:40–43   306
- 78:44   308
- 78:44–51   305
- 78:45   308
- 78:46   308
- 78:47   308
- 78:48   308
- 78:49–50   308, 309
- 78:51   308
- 78:60   201
- 89   291
- [d]92:7–8   262
- 100:3   40
- 104   294, 346
- 104:25–26   320
- 104:31   346
- 105   303, 307, 308, 309, 311
- 105:28   308
- 105:28–36   307
- 105:29   308
- 105:30   308
- 105:31   308
- 105:32–33   308
- 105:34–35   308
- 105:36   308
- 105:45   308
- 106   304, 306
- 106:21   304
- 106:29–30   304
- 108   35
- 108:11   35
- 108:12   35
- 114   326
- 114:1   291
- 114:1–8   326
- 144:4   257
- 148   38, 39

Proverbs
- 1:1   31, 241, 245, 280
- 1:2–7   247
- 1:7   273
- 1:8   232, 296
- 1:8–9   231, 244, 245
- 1–9   245, 248, 249, 281
- 5:13   167
- 6:9   209
- 6:20   232
- 7   233, 248
- 7:1   248
- 7:4–5   248
- 8   314, 315, 316, 317, 318, 348
- 8:22   330
- 8:22–28   314, 318
- 8:24–25   330
- 8:29   318
- 8:30   315, 318

a. 8:3–4
b. 57:7–12
c. 60:5–12
d. 92:6–7

10	248	1:11	267
10:1	31, 241, 245, 280	1:21	267
10:1–22:16	245	1–2	267, 272
11:22	246	1–27	266
13:24	330	2	344
22	244, 245, 281, 282	2:3	265
22:1–16	245	2:6	267
22:1–29	242	2:9	267
22:13	210, 245	2:9–10	344
22:15–21	282	2:10	345
22:17	244, 282, 284, 285	3	267
22:17–24:22	295	3:1	271
22:17–29	245	3–14	267
22:20	282, 283, 285, 286, 298	4:7	267
23:22	232	4–5	267
23:26	41	6–7	267
24:23	31, 241, 280, 282	7:7	267
24–30:15	32	7:17–18	268
25:1	31, 241, 249, 280	8	268
25:1–29:27	245	8:3	268
25:6	251	9–10	268
25–29	32, 242, 249	10:1	268
26	51	11	268
26:4	350	11:5–6	268
26:4–5	52	12:9	268
26:5	350	12:19	268
30	32, 238, 281, 283, 331	12–14	268
30:1	31, 241, 280, 284	13:3	268
30:18–19	331	13:15	42
31	242, 248, 249, 281, 283	13:21	271
31:1	31, 213, 231, 241, 280, 283	13:22	271
31:2–9	213	15	268
31:4	284	15:2	268
31:9	213	15:18	268
31:10	32, 242, 281	15:20	268
31:10–31	242, 247, 248	15–21	268
31:16	249	16:16–17	268
31:18	249	16–17	268
104:5–9	318	18	268
		18:4	268
Job		19	268
1:1	266, 267, 345	19:6	268
1:6–12	265	19:26–27	268

INDEX

20	268	40:4	271
20:7	268	40:7	271
20:29	268	[a]40:25–32	320
21	268	42	272
21:34	268	42:6	272
22	269	42:7	272
22–27	269	42:17	272
23:10	269		
23–24	269	Song of Songs	
25	269	2:8–13	229
25:4	269	3:4	229, 232
26–27	269	4	228
27:2	269	5:2–5	228
27:5	269	5:10–15	293
28	269	6	228
28:1–11	269	[b]7:2	194
28:12	269	[c]7:11	230
28:12–19	269	8:2	229
28:20–28	269		
28:28	269, 273	Ruth	
28–31	266	1	224
29:2	270	1:11	225
29–31	270	1:19	224
30:20	270	2	226
31	271	2:8–9	227
31:35	270	2:15–16	228
31:40	270	3	226
32:19	270	4	171, 172
32–37	266, 270	4:1	226
33:12	270	4:7–10	171
33:33	270	4:13–17	225
34:2	270		
34:11	270	Lamentations	
36:2	270	3:22–23	254
37:23	270		
38:2	271	Ecclesiastes	
38:3–4	271	1:1	252, 258, 260
38:4	313	1:2	256, 258
38:8–11	319	1:4–9	254
38:28	232		
38–39	271	a. 41:1–8	
38–42	266, 271	b. 7:1	
40:1–42:6	271	c. 7:10	

1:9	253
1:10	253
1:14	260
3:19	257, 260
3:19–20	53
4:12	166, 275
7:13	260, 268
7:27	258
9	279
9:7–9	277
9:11	262
11:9	255, 260
12:5	254, 260
12:8	256, 259
12:9–14	259, 260
12:13	259n, 273, 279
12:14	259n

Esther

4	32
4:13–5:1	32
5	32

Ezra

1:1–3	10
5:11–13	59

Nehemiah

6:14	231
8:8	167
13:26	252

1 Chronicles

1	263
1:1–4	96
1:35	40
7:20–24	96
7:20–29	81
11	70
11:11–25	69
11:25	71
11:26	69
11:41	69
11:47	69
17	80
20:5	68, 70
21	81
21:1	263, 265
22	94
22:7–10	79
22–29	80
29	77
29:23–24	77

2 Chronicles

1:14	88
[a]2–7	80
3:1–2	81
7	94
8:1–2	74
9	82
9:22–24	83
9:25–28	83, 88
9:29	84
20:5	253
20:10	96
29–32	89
30:1	89
30:21–26	89
35:25	222
36	60
36:20	81
36:20–21	96
36:21	60
36:22–23	9
36:23	10

New Testament

Matthew

1:1	8
3:1	340
3:3	339
13	337
13:10–17	337

a. begins at 2:2

Mark
    1:3   339
    1:4   340

Luke
    3:2   340
    3:4–6   339
    24:44   332

Hebrews
    8:6   6
    8:13   6

James
    21:19   68

1 Peter
    1:24–25   349

Revelation
    22:13   24

Apocrypha

Ben Sira
    24:1–4   330
    30:1   330
    44   330
    50:25   331

Jubilees
    48:7   303

OTHER WORKS BY MICHAEL CARASIK

The Commentators' Bible: Exodus,
The Rubin JPS Miqra'ot Gedolot

The Commentators' Bible: Leviticus,
The Rubin JPS Miqra'ot Gedolot

The Commentators' Bible: Numbers,
The Rubin JPS Miqra'ot Gedolot

Theologies of the Mind in Biblical Israel

www.ingramcontent.com/pod-product-compliance
Lightning Source LLC
Chambersburg PA
CBHW030421100426
42812CB00028B/3054/J